CONTENTS VOLUME III.

A

B

CONTENTS

CONTENTS

C

CONTENTS

CONTENTS

CONTENTS

CONTENTS

G

H

CONTENTS

CONTENTS

M

N

CONTENTS

CONTENTS

CONTENTS

LIST OF ILLUSTRATIONS

IRISH BIOGRAPHY

NATIVES OF IRELAND

James Napper Tandy

James Napper Tandy, patriot, was born in
Dublin, in 1740, of which city he was a popular
and prosperous merchant. One of the chief
leaders of the patriotic interests, his influence
more than once turned the scale in favor of the
popular candidate, both at municipal and parliamentary elections. In the restrictive laws
against Irish trade he urged upon every Irishman
to refrain from purchasing goods of English
manufacture until the obnoxious restrictions
were removed. In the affairs of the Irish volunteers, Tandy was a conspicuous figure and threw
himself heart and soul into the movement, seeing
through their powerful influence splendid chances
for asserting the rights of his country. He was
one of the first to join the regiment of which the
Duke of Leinster was commander, and subsequently was appointed to the command of a
corps of artillery.

Tandy was the first secretary of the Society
of United Irishmen at Dublin and was incessant
in his efforts to promote parliamentary reform
by uniting both Catholics and Protestants for
the overthrow of alien legislation. Early in 1792
he challenged the solicitor-general, Toler, to fight
a duel, for abusive language, but instead of being
accepted, Tandy was ordered to prison, until the
close of the session of the House of Commons,

for breach of privilege. Tandy raised a formal
action for illegality against the solicitor-general
and his privy-councillors, which, brought forward
by a man of such republican principles, was naturally dismissed at the final hearing, November
26, 1792. That same year he started a movement for reviving the volunteers, and, with the
assistance of A. H. Rowan, raised two battalions
of National Guards, each 1,000 strong. They
were equipped with green uniforms, harp but-
tons, and in the emblems they had in place of the
crown a cap of liberty. The National Guards
were, however, soon dispersed by the government.

For distributing a pamphlet in County Louth
(entitled Common Sense) against the corruption
of the powerful Beresford family, proceedings
were instituted against him. When the government learned of his meeting with the "Defend-
ers" in the same county for the purpose of effecting a coalition between them and the United
Irishmen, orders were issued for his arrest.
Tandy evaded capture, however, and managed
to escape to this country, lived for some time in
Wilmington, Delaware, and, on learning the success of Wolfe Tone's mission at Paris, crossed
to France in the spring of 1798. On his arrival
Napoleon made him general of brigade in the
French army, and subsequently with a small vessel, the Anacreon, and a few men, Tandy sailed
to Ireland as an auxiliary to the expedition under
General Humbert.

September 16, 1798, he landed on an island off
the coast of Donegal, but hearing of the defeat
of Humbert eight days previous, there was nothing left for Tandy but a desperate chance of escape. The expedition finally managed to reach

Norway; and while on his way back to France, he was arrested at Hamburg and handed over to the British authorities. After being held in prison for about a year he was taken to Ireland, placed on trial at Dublin, February 12, 1800, and acquitted, but detained in custody. He was again placed on trial, April 7, 1801, at Lifford, County Donegal, this time for landing on the island near by, and sentenced to death. Napoleon, however, made Tandy's case a matter of international concern, demanded his release, and forced Hamburg to pay a fine of half a million francs. Also, as a result, Tandy was given his liberty and allowed to depart for France. On landing at Bordeaux, March 14, 1802, he received a public ovation, a banquet was given in his honor, and he was raised to the rank of general of a division in the French army.

The high principles that characterized his whole career close only with death. He died of camp dysentery at Bordeaux, France, August 24, 1803. His funeral was attended by the whole military of the district and an immense concourse of citizens, and every respect was paid to the dead soldier and patriot. The name of Napper Tandy will always be regarded with the highest esteem by his countrymen and his memory has been rendered memorable in the lines of Dion Boucicault's patriotic song, "The Wearing of the Green."

Daniel O'Connell

Daniel O'Connell, Count, was born at Derrynane, County Kerry, in August, 1743; of twenty-two children by one marriage he was the youngest. Having studied mathematics and modern languages, he entered the French army at the age of fourteen, as lieutenant in Lord Clare's regiment of the Irish brigade. He served with honor in the Seven Years' war in Germany; and at its conclusion, having gained much experience and studied military engineering, he was attached to the Corps du Genie, and became one of the best engineers in France.

He distinguished himself at the siege and capture of Port Mahon from the British in 1779, and at the unsuccessful siege of Gibraltar, in September, 1782. From the plans of assault on the latter place submitted to him, he felt satisfied that the attack could not succeed; yet he led a body of troops in the attack, which was made against his opinion, and was wounded in nine places. Soon after this he was appointed inspector-general of the French Infantry, with the rank of a general officer. In this capacity he was intrusted with the organization of the general code of military discipline. His suggestions and regulations were adopted into the French armies after the revolution, and ultimately by other nations, the advantages of which are still felt in warfare.

At the revolution he declined a military command pressed upon him by Carnot, feeling it his duty to remain near Louis XVI., and share the fortunes of the royal family. Eventually he joined the French Princes at Coblentz, and took part in the disastrous campaign of 1792. He then returned to Ireland, and was appointed to the command of an Irish regiment in the British service. During the peace of 1802 he visited France to look after a large property to which his wife was entitled. He was one of the British subjects seized by Napoleon, and remained a prisoner until 1814.

The advent of the Bourbons restored him to his military rank in France; and he enjoyed in the decline of life full pay as general in the French army, and as colonel in the British service. Refusing to take the oath of fidelity to Louis Philippe in 1830, he was deprived of his French emoluments. He died at the country seat of his son-in-law, Madon, near Blois, July 9, 1833. He was uncle of the great Daniel O'Connell.

Patrick Darcy.

Patrick Darcy, Count, mathematician and military officer, was born in Galway, September 27, 1725. He was sent to Paris by an uncle, studied under Clairaut with such success that at the age of seventeen he gave a solution of the problem of the curve of equal pressure, and soon became eminent in mechanics and other sciences. He served with the French army in two campaigns in Germany, and in 1746 was appointed aid-de-camp to Count FitzJames; was made prisoner in Scotland, but obtained his release the following year. In 1749 Darcy was made a captain in the regiment of Conde, and the same year became a member of the French Academy of Science, to which he contributed two able essays on mechanics. Subsequently he served with distinction in the Seven Years' war and fought at the battle of Rosbach (with the rank of colonel) in the Irish brigade.

In 1760 he published an "Essay on Artillery," and in 1765 an essay on the "Duration of the Sensation of Sight." Besides these works he wrote an article on hydraulic machines and communicated numerous papers to the academy. In 1770 he was appointed marechal-de-camp in the French army. In religion Darcy was a Catholic. He died of cholera at Paris, October 18, 1779. Condorcet composed his eulogy in the Academy of Science.

Charles O'Brien

Charles O'Brien, fifth Viscount Clare, was born probably in Ireland the latter half of the seventeenth century. His great grandfather, Daniel O'Brien (brother of the fourth earl of Thomond), was created Viscount Clare for his services in the Irish wars. The grandson of the latter, Daniel O'Brien, third viscount, father of Charles, espoused the cause of James II., raised two regiments of foot and one of dragoons for his service, fought at the Boyne and retired to France. His regiments ultimately formed part of the Irish brigade, in which his dragoons especially distinguished themselves, and his estates, comprising about 60,000 acres in Clare, were forfeited.

Charles commanded a regiment of foot in the army of King James II. in 1689-90; served at the second siege of Limerick in 1691, and the following year retired to France. On arriving in the latter country he was made captain, and at the battle of Marsaglia, October 4, 1693, was promoted colonel. His elder brother Daniel died from wounds received in this battle and Charles succeeded to the title as fifth Viscount Clare. He was made colonel of the Clare regiment, April 8, 1696 (named in honor of his family), served at Valenza and on the Meuse in the campaigns of 1696-97. When the war of the Spanish Succession broke out, he was promoted brigadier-general, April 2, 1703, and took a leading part in the rout of the Imperialists at Hochstadt, September 20, 1703. In 1704 he was promoted major-general, and at the battle of Blenheim, in command of three Irish regiments, he cut his way out of the village of Oberklau, and escaped with his men to the Rhine in excellent order. Created marechal-de-camp, October 26, 1704, he joined the army of Flanders under Marshal de Villars, and fell at the battle of Ramillies, May 23, 1706. A monument was erected to his memory in the Church of the Holy Cross at Louvain. His widow remarried General Daniel O'Mahony at St. Germains in 1712.

Charles O'Brien's only son, sixth Viscount Clare, was born in 1699. King George I. of England offered to procure him the revision of the title and estates of his relative, the Earl of Thomond, if he would enter the British service and change his religion. This he refused to do. O'Brien took a distinguished part in the French victories at Fontenoy, where the Irish brigade turned the fortune of the day, and at Roucoux and Laffeldt. On the death of the eighth Earl of Thomond, in 1741, he assumed the title of Comte de Thomond. He was created Marshal of France, February 24, 1757, and in November of the same year was made commander-in-chief of the Province of Languedoc. He died at Montpellier, September 9, 1761. He left a son, Charles, colonel of the Clare regiment, and on his death at Paris in 1774 this branch of the O'Briens became extinct.

Daniel O'Donnell

Daniel O'Donnell, soldier in the service of France, was born in Ireland in 1666. He was a

descendant of Hugh the Dark ("The Achilles of
the Gaels of Erin"), and elder brother of Manus
O'Donnell, lord of Tirconnell. In 1688 Daniel
was appointed captain of foot in the army of
King James II., and in 1689 acting colonel. After
the treaty of Limerick he went to France, and
was made captain in the Marine regiment of the
Irish brigade, commanded by James FitzJames.
O'Donnell's commission was dated February 4,
1692; he served on the coast of Normandy, and
afterwards in the campaigns of 1693-95 in
Germany.

In 1698 his regiment was reformed; again
served in Germany in 1701, subsequently in five
campaigns in Italy, and held the rank of lieutenant-colonel at the siege and battle of Turin.
In 1707 he was transferred to Flanders; fought
against the Duke of Marlborough at Oudenarde
in 1708; was made colonel, August 7, 1708, and
commanded the regiment of O'Donnell in the
campaigns of 1709-12, including the great battles
of Malplaquet and Quesnoy. He then served
under Marshal de Villars in Germany, which led
to the peace of Rastadt between the latter country and France in March, 1714. He was made
brigadier-general, February 1, 1719, and retired
to St. Germain-en-Laye, where he died without
issue, July 7, 1735.

General O'Donnell possessed a jeweled cas-
ket containing a Latin psalter (said to have been
written by the hand of St. Columba), which was
regarded by him as a talisman of victory if carried into battle by the clan O'Donnell. He deposited it in a Belgian monastery and left instructions by will that it was to be given to the
one that could prove himself chief of the O'Donnells. Through an Irish abbot it was restored

to Sir Neale O'Donnell of County Mayo, in the last century. The latter's son, Sir Richard A. O'Donnell, entrusted the relic to the Royal Irish Academy, in whose custody it still remains.

William O'Shaughnessy

William O'Shaughnessy, soldier in the French army, was born in Ireland in 1674. When a boy of fifteen he was made a captain of foot and afterwards acting colonel in the army of King James II. Early in 1690 he went to France with the regiment of the Irish brigade commanded by Daniel O'Brien (afterwards Viscount Clare), in which he was appointed captain by Louis XIV., July 10, 1691. He served in Italy in 1692, and at the siege of Valenza, in 1696, he was made commandant of a battalion and appointed to the army of the Meuse. In 1698 he was made captain of grenadiers, and with his regiment, one of the most famous in the Irish brigade, served in Germany in the campaigns of 1701-2, and at the memorable battle of Blenheim, August 13, 1704, against the British and Imperialists under the Duke of Marlborough and Prince Eugene.

In 1705 he served with the army of the Moselle, fought at Ramillies in 1706; became major on the death of John O'Carrol, and on September 12th of the latter year, lieutenant-colonel. He was with his regiment in Flanders in 1707; at Oudenarde in 1708, Malplaquet in 1709, at the defense of the lines of Arleux, Denain, Douai, Bouchain and Quesnoy in 1710-12. He subsequently served in the campaigns in Germany, including the sieges of Landau and Freiberg, and April 3, 1721, was made brigadier-general.

He was with the army of the Rhine in 1733

and served in the campaigns of 1734-35, attaining the rank of major-general (marechal-de-camp), August 1, 1734. He again served with the army in Flanders in 1742, commanded at Cambray in 1743, and the same year was appointed to the command at Gravelines, where he died, without issue, January 2, 1744. At the time of his death he was the oldest Irish major-general in the service of France. (See O'Callaghan's "Irish Brigades in the Service of France," Glasgow, 1870.)

Lavall Nugent

Lavall Nugent, Count, field marshal in the Austrian army, prince of the Holy Roman Empire, descendant of the first Earl of West Meath, was born at Ballinacor, County Wicklow, in November, 1777. At an early age he became the heir of his uncle, Oliver Count Nugent. He went to Austria in 1789, and in 1794 entered the Imperial army, where his abilities soon attracted notice. After the battle of Varaggio, in 1799, he was elected a Knight of the Military Order of Maria Theresa, and after the battle of Marengo received his commission as major. In 1805 he became lieutenant-colonel, in 1809 major-general, and in the latter year was plenipotentiary to the congress which preceded Napoleon's marriage to Maria Louisa.

Refusing to sign the conditions forced upon the exhausted Austrians by Napoleon, he retired to England and was made a lieutenant-general in the British army. In 1811 he was sent on a diplomatic mission to Austria, and returned with important communications relative to the coalition against Napoleon. In the winter of 1812-13 he was sent to Spain by the British government, and in 1813 he resumed the sword for Austria, drove the French out of Illyria, and the next year bore a leading part in the successful campaign in Italy. He was gazetted a British K. C. B.

In 1815 he led the forces in Tuscany that defeated Murat, and in the summer of the same year commanded in the South of France. He next became captain-general of the Neapolitan army, but in 1820 again returned to the Austrian service. Although commanding in Italy and Hungary in 1848, he took no very active part in the field. In 1849 he was presented with the baton of a field marshal and honors of all kinds were showered upon him.

He was present with his old companion, Radetsky, in Italy during the war with Sardinia, and accompanied the Emperor of Austria in his unfortunate campaign against the French and Italians in 1859. Field Marshal Nugent married the Duchess of Riario Sforza, a descendant of Augustus III., King of Poland. He died on his estate in Croatia, August 21, 1862. He had among other children Prince Albert, who became a distinguished Austrian staff officer.

Francis MacDonnell

Francis MacDonnell, major, an officer in the Austrian service, was born in Connaught in 1656. At the surprise of Cremona, February 1, 1702, he particularly signalized himself. On that occasion he took Marshal Villeroy prisoner, and refused brilliant offers of rank and money to connive at his escape. On the other hand, he was dispatched by Prince Eugene to attempt

to bring over the Irish regiments under Daniel
O'Mahony, whose troops formed the nucleus of
an effective resistance to the Austrians. Mac-
Donnell's mission proved fruitless and he was
made prisoner, but was soon exchanged. He
fell at the battle of Luzzara, in August, 1702.

John Joseph Coppinger

John Joseph Coppinger, soldier, was born
in Queenstown, County Cork, October 11, 1834.
He received his education at a private school in
his native country. In early life he went to
Italy and received a commission in the papal
army, serving in the campaign of 1860 against
Victor Emmanuel. He rose to the rank of captain, and was made a Knight of St. Gregory
for bravery at the defense of La Rocca gate,
where he was made prisoner.

In 1861 he came to the United States, and
on the recommendation of Archbishop Hughes
was commissioned captain of the 14th infantry
in the regular army, and served throughout the
civil war. Coppinger was severely wounded at
the second battle of Bull Run; was brevetted
major, June 12, 1864, and lieutenant-colonel, October 19, 1864, for gallant and meritorious service
at the battles of Trevillian Station and Cedar
Creek, Va. He was made colonel of the 15th
New York cavalry, January 27, 1865.

After the war he served principally on the
frontier in a number of Indian campaigns. He
was brevetted colonel December 1, 1868; appointed major of the 10th infantry, March 20,
1879, lieutenant-colonel of the 18th infantry,
October 31, 1883, and colonel of the 23rd infantry January 15, 1891. April 25, 1895, Coppinger

was commissioned brigadier-general in command of the Platte.

When the Spanish-American war broke out he was made major-general of volunteers, May 4, 1898, and commanded the 4th army corps. Coppinger was retired by operation of the age law, October 11, 1898. He died at Washington, D. C., November 4, 1909, and was buried in Arlington cemetery. He married Alice, daughter of James G. Blaine, the great American statesman. He was survived by two sons, Blaine and Conor Coppinger.

Denis Francis Burke

Denis Francis Burke, soldier, was born at Cork, April 19, 1841. At the age of fourteen he emigrated to the United States, and was engaged in business in New York City until the beginning of the civil war. He joined the Union army in 1861, served under General Thomas Francis Meagher, fought in all the battles of the famous Irish brigade, and was wounded several times. Early in the war he was made first lieutenant for gallantry at the battle of Malvern Hill, and captain for bravery at Antietam.

He was personally commended by General Hancock at the battle of Gettysburg; and Burke was subsequently made brigadier-general by brevet. While on a visit to Ireland, at the close of the war, he was imprisoned by the British government for several months as a Fenian suspect. After his release he returned to the United States and received an appointment in the Custom House at New York City. Burke edited the Emerald and the Irish People. He died at New York City, October 19, 1893.

Andrew Thomas McReynolds

Andrew Thomas McReynolds, soldier and lawyer, was born in Dungannon, County Tyrone, December 25, 1808. He came to the United States in 1830, lived at Pittsburg until 1833, when he removed to Detroit, Mich. In 1834 he was appointed on the staff of General Williams, with the rank of major, and was one of the organizers of the Brady Guards. In 1838 he was an alderman of Detroit. In 1839 he represented his district in the State Legislature, and was a delegate to the Harrisburg convention that nominated General Harrison as the Whig candidate for the presidency. In 1840 he was admitted to the bar, and the same year helped to organize the Montgomery Guards, of which he was made the first captain. He was also colonel of the First Regiment of Michigan militia, 1840-51; Indian agent for Michigan, 1842-45, and in 1846 was elected state senator from Detroit. In 1847 McReynolds was commissioned captain of dragoons in the United States army and served under General Scott in the war with Mexico. He was made major for bravery in this campaign, and in the charge of the dragoons, under McReynolds and Philip Kearney, on the gates of the City of Mexico, both officers received wounds they bore through life. At the close of the war he returned to Detroit and resumed the practice of law. In 1851 he was elected prosecuting attorney of Wayne County, and in 1852 the first president of the Board of Education of Detroit under its charter.

At the opening of the civil war he was commissioned colonel and organized and led the Lincoln cavalry to the field. This, the first regiment of cavalry enlisted for the Union army, he commanded in 1861, subsequently a brigade for two years, a division for six months, and was honorably discharged in August, 1864. Returning to Michigan he resumed the practice of law at Grand Rapids, and was appointed United States District Attorney for western Michigan by President Johnson. In 1874 he was elected prosecuting attorney for Muskegon County and served until 1876. McReynolds was for many years president of the State Association of Mexican Veterans. He died at Muskegon, Mich., November 25, 1898.

Michael Kelly Lawler

Michael Kelly Lawler, soldier, was born in County Kildare, November 16, 1814. He came with his parents to the United States in 1816 and settled near Shawneetown, Ill. He served in the Black Hawk war and afterwards organized a company of infantry for service in the war with Mexico, which was taken into the United States army June 29, 1846. He served as captain until the end of the war and was mustered out of service, October 26, 1848.

When the civil war broke out he organized and was made colonel of the 18th regiment of Illinois Infantry and took the field in the spring of 1861. His regiment led the advance on Fort Henry and also at Fort Donelson. November 29, 1862, he was commissioned brigadier-general of volunteers for gallant and meritorious service. His command, afterwards known as the "Iron Clad Brigade," covered itself with glory at the siege of Vicksburg, especially in successfully storming the enemy's works on the Big Black river. Charles A. Dana, assistant secretary of war, said of this charge: "It was one of the most splendid exploits of the war, and it was astonishing in going over the field to see how few of Lawler's brave followers had fallen in so audacious an onset."

After the fall of Vicksburg, General Lawler joined General Sherman, and later fought under General Banks. He also served some months in Texas and in Louisiana. March 13, 1865, he was made a major-general by brevet. He was mustered out of service January 15, 1866, having served over four and one-half years, during which time he engaged in many battles, sieges and skirmishes.

In 1837 he married Elizabeth Crenshaw, by whom he had a numerous family. He was a Catholic in religion and a Democrat in politics. General Lawler died July 26, 1882.

Eyre Massey

Eyre Massey, Baron Clarina, was born in County Limerick, May 24, 1719. He entered the British army at an early age, and was wounded at Culloden in 1745. In 1757 he went to North America as a major of the 46th Foot, of which he became lieutenant-colonel in 1758, and the year after commanded the regiment in the expedition to Niagara. He was commandant in the action at La Belle Famille, where he defeated the French, leaving the whole region of the Upper Ohio in possession of the English. He fought under Wolfe at Quebec, and captured Fort Oswegachie in August 1760. He commanded a battalion of grenadiers at the capture of Martinique in 1761, and at the head of the storming party that took Morro castle, Havana, in 1762, he was again wounded. During the revolutionary war he was a major-general in command at Halifax. He was subsequently made a full general, Governor of Limerick and of Kilmainham Hospital, and created an Irish peer, December 27, 1800.

He died at Bath, May 17, 1804, being one of the last survivors who served under Wolfe in Canada. He married Catherine, sister of Robert Clements, first Earl of Leitrim, by whom he had four children. Two of his successors in the title —his son, Nathaniel William, a major-general on the staff in the West Indies, died in 1810; his great-grandson, the fourth baron, served in the Crimea and in the Indian mutiny. Lionel E. Massey, fifth baron, born in 1837, is the present representative of the family.

Humphrey Hunter

Humphrey Hunter, patriot and soldier, was born near Londonderry, May 14, 1755. His father died when he was four years old and his widowed mother emigrated with her family to America, reaching Charleston, S. C., August 27, 1759. A few days after her arrival she removed to Mecklenburg County, N. C. (now Cabarrus), where she purchased a small farm, and remained the rest of her life. In this neighborhood young Humphrey grew up, acquiring the principles and spirit of freedom.

He attended the convention held at Charlotte, N. C., May 20, 1775, that adopted the first public declaration of independence in America, known as the Mecklenburg Declaration of Independence. He later joined an expedition against the Cherokee Indians, who were committing depredations among the inhabitants near the source of the Catawba river. After his return he resumed his studies at Liberty Hall Academy, but upon the approach of Lord Cornwallis, after the surrender of Charleston, the young men of the academy left to take up arms in defense of their country. Hunter was made lieutenant of a company and at the battle of Camden, August 6, 1780, he witnessed the brave Baron De Kalb fall mortally wounded. At this battle Hunter was made prisoner of war and confined seven days in a prison yard at Camden, being then sent to Orangeburg, S. C., where he remained several months without coat or hat. November 15, 1780, he made his escape, with several others, and set out for Mecklenburg, traveling only by night, and supporting himself on raw corn. After remaining with his mother a few days he again joined the army, acting as lieutenant of cavalry under Colonel Henry Lee. At the battle of Eutaw Springs he fought with distinguished gallantry and was slightly wounded. This being the last important battle in the South, he saw no further military service, and in the summer of 1785 entered Mt. Zion College at Winnsborough, S. C., where he graduated in July, 1787.

He next commenced the study of theology and obtained a license to preach in October, 1789. In December of that year he married Jane Ross of Laurens District, S. C. In 1796 he removed with his family to Lincoln County (now Gaston), purchased a home, and resided there the remainder of his life. From 1805 until his death Hunter was pastor of the Presbyterian church at Steele Creek, N. C., where he died, August 21, 1827. He had ten children.

Henry Pottinger

Sir Henry Pottinger, soldier and diplomat, was born at Mount Pottinger, County Leitrim, October 3, 1789. He went to India as a cadet in 1804, where he studied the native languages, and in 1810 volunteered with Captain Christie for the difficult task of exploring the countries between the Indus and Persia. They traveled disguised as Mohammedan merchants—a disguise that required all their tact and linguistic abilities to maintain. After exploring districts which had not been visited by Europeans since the time of Alexander the Great, they returned to Bombay in 1811. A few years afterwards he gave their experiences to the world in an interesting work, entitled "Travels in Beloochistan and Sinde."

Pottinger was then employed for seven years as judge and collector at Ahmednuggar in the Deccan, and then for fifteen years as political resident at Cutch and Sinde. His services in these situations were rewarded with a baronetcy after the Afghanistan campaign in 1839. In the following year he returned to England, but had scarcely landed when war broke out between Great Britain and China owing to the disputes connected with the opium trade. In this emergency Pottinger was sent to China as envoy extraordinary, and minister plenipotentiary, for the purpose of adjusting the matters in dispute. On his arrival at Macao, August 12, 1841, he issued a proclamation, declaring that it was his intention to direct his undivided energies to the primary object of securing a speedy and satisfactory termination of the war. In concert with Admiral Parker he devised measures which soon led to the capture of Amoy, and brought hostilities to a successful issue. A treaty was concluded with the Chinese in 1842, which opened the ports of the Celestial Empire and forced that country to pay an indemnity of $21,000,000.

For these services Pottinger was rewarded with the Grand Cross of the Order of the Bath, and was subsequently appointed governor and commander-in-chief of the island of Hong Kong. On his return to England in 1844 he was made a member of the privy council, and a pension of £1,500 a year was conferred upon him. In September, 1846, he was appointed governor of the Cape of Good Hope, an office which he held until September of the following year, when he was again sent to India, as governor of Madras.

The highest military rank he attained appears to have been that of major-general in the service of the East India Company. He married, in 1820, Susanna M. Cook, of Dublin, by whom he had three sons and one daughter. Pottinger died at Malta, March 18, 1856. Major Eldred Pottinger, nephew of Sir Henry and a soldier in India, died in 1843. Sir Henry Pottinger, third baronet, second son of the first baronet, born in 1834, is the present representative of the family.

John Nicholson

John Nicholson, brigadier-general, son of an Irish physician, Dr. Alexander Nicholson, was born in Dublin, December 11, 1821. He lost his father when eight years old, whereupon his mother moved to Lisburn, and he received most of his education at Dungannon School. In 1837 he obtained an appointment as ensign in the Indian army and joined the 41st Native Infantry at Benares. He took part in the Afghan war of 1842, saw some severe fighting and endured a miserable captivity of some months. On the 6th of November of the same year his brother Alexander was killed in action in India. In 1846 he was appointed one of two military instructors to Gholab Singh's army in Cashmere, and the next year assistant to Sir Henry Lawrence, resident at Lahore. There his great executive ability became apparent, and he was intrusted by his chief with several important missions.

In the Sikh war of 1848 he specially distinguished himself at Attock and the Margulla Pass. His services were fully acknowledged in Lord Gough's dispatches. In 1849, when the Punjaub became a British province, Captain Nicholson, then but twenty-eight, was appointed a deputy commissioner under the Lahore Board, of which Sir Henry Lawrence was president. In 1850 he left for home on furlough, on his way engaging in an unsuccessful plot to liberate Kossuth from captivity in a Turkish fortress.

On his return to India in 1851 he was reappointed to his old post in the Punjaub and for several years did good service as an administrator and governor. The breaking out of the mutiny in May, 1857, found him Colonel Nicholson, at Peshawur. Here he acted with great promptitude, removing a large treasure to a place of safety, dismissing some native regiments under circumstances that required consummate tact and decision, and at Murdan, on the 25th of May, helped to put to rout a force of the mutineers. On this occasion he was fully twenty hours in the saddle, traversed not less than seventy miles, and cut down many fugitives with his own hand.

On the 22nd of June he took command of a
movable column for the relief of Delhi, annihilated a large force of the enemy at Trimmoo, and
on the 14th of August effected a junction with
the small band of British at Delhi. Ten days
afterwards he fought the battle of Nujufgurh, in
which between 3,000 and 4,000 mutineers were
slain. Already he had been created brigadier-
general. On the 14th of September, while leading an attack on a Sepoy position, he was mortally wounded, and died September 23, 1857.

Sir John Lawrence, writing a few weeks
later to his brother, Lieutenant Charles Nicholson, who lost a foot in the same engagement,
said: "His loss is a national misfortune," and
he remarked in a dispatch: "He was an officer
equal to any emergency. . . . His services since
the mutiny broke out have not been surpassed by
those of any other officer in this part of India."
His friend and fellow-countryman, Sir Henry
Lawrence, fell shortly before him.

Nicholson was never married. A pension of
£ 500 a year was granted by the East India Company to his mother, and it was officially announced that, had he survived, he would have
been created a Knight Commander of the Bath.

Charles William Vane Stewart

Charles William Vane Stewart, third Marquis of Londonderry (half-brother of Robert
Stewart, Viscount Castlereagh, second Marquis
of Londonderry) was born in Dublin, May 18,
1778. At the age of fifteen, as ensign of an infantry regiment, he accompanied Lord Moira
to the Netherlands and took part in the campaign
of 1794. Subsequently, while attached to the

British mission at Vienna, he was severely wounded at the battle of Donauwerth. In 1797 he was made lieutenant-colonel of the 5th Dragoons and served in Holland under Sir Ralph Abercrombie, and in 1803 was made under-secretary in Ireland.

He next commanded a hussar brigade under Sir John Moore in the Peninsular war, and covered the retreat of the British army at Corunna with great skill and valor. After a few months' absence in England he returned to the Peninsula, as adjutant-general under Sir Arthur Wellesley (afterwards the Duke of Wellington), and distinguished himself at Fuentes d'Orono, Talavera, and other battles. In 1813 Stewart was appointed British minister to Prussia, and during the campaign of 1814 he acted as military commissioner to the armies of the allied sovereigns, and induced Bernadotte to co-operate with the allies at Leipsic. In June, 1814, he was raised to the peerage as Lord Stewart, and in July of the same year was appointed British ambassador to Austria.

At the congress of Chatillon he was actively engaged in many of the operations, both civil and military, that led to the Peace of Paris, and, after the battle of Waterloo, to the second Treaty of Paris, in November, 1815. In 1819 he married his second wife, Frances Anne, only daughter and heiress of Sir Harry Vane Tempest, and assumed the name and arms of Vane. By this marriage he became the owner of vast estates in County Durham. In 1822, on the death of his brother, he succeeded to the title of Marquis of Londonderry. The same year he acted, with the Duke of Wellington, as plenipotentiary at the Congress of Verona.

In politics Stewart was an uncompromising Tory. He supported Catholic Emancipation, but offered a steady opposition to the Reform bill. In 1835 Sir Robert Peel appointed him ambassador to Russia, but Stewart withdrew the same year owing to parliamentary opposition. In 1837 he attained the rank of general. In 1839 he fought a duel with Henry Grattan, Jr., over political differences. He was a warm friend of Louis Napoleon Bonaparte, who was a frequent visitor at Stewart's residence in Wynyard Park.

He represented Thomastown in Parliament from 1798 to 1800 and County Derry from 1800 to 1814. In 1828 he published the "Story of the Peninsular War"; in 1841, "The War in Germany and France in 1813-14," and in 1848-53, "Memoirs and Correspondence of Viscount Castlereagh." He died at London, March 6, 1854.

His son, William Robert, who inherited the title, died November 25, 1872; and George, the 5th marquis, born April 26, 1821, died November 6, 1884. The latter's son, the 6th marquis, born in London, July 16, 1852, was member of Parliament for County Down, 1878-84, viceroy of Ireland, 1886-89, and chairman of the London School Board, 1895-97.

Robert Rollo Gillespie

Sir Robert Rollo Gillespie, soldier, was born in Comber, County Down, January 21, 1766. He entered the Carabineers, as a cornet, in April, 1783, served in St. Domingo against Toussaint L'Ouverture, became a major in 1796, and a lieutenant-colonel in 1799. Before his return to England with his regiment, in 1802, he received a vote of thanks from the House of Assembly in

ROBERT ROLLO GILLESPIE

ROBERT ROLLO GILLESPIE.

Jamaica. Shortly afterwards he was acquitted of charges brought against him at a court-martial, for his management of the 20th Light Dragoons, with which regiment he had been connected.

In 1805 he proceeded across the continent of Europe to India (at Hamburg being saved from falling into the hands of the French by the interposition of his countryman, Napper Tandy), and was instrumental in suppressing the mutiny at Vellore in 1806. He saw much active service in Java, rose to be a colonel, and on the surrender of the island to the British was appointed military governor.

In 1812 he led an expedition against Sumatra, deposed one sultan and installed another favorable to the British. He received the special thanks of the governor-general in Council of India, and was promoted to the rank of major-general, April 1, 1812. In 1814 he was engaged in the invasion of Nepal, and fell heading his troops in the unsuccessful effort to take the fort of Kalunga, October 31, 1814. He was after his death gazetted Knight Commander of the Bath. A monument has been erected to his memory at Comber. As a commanding officer Gillespie was well liked by his men and admired for his splendid courage.

King Leary

Leary, or Laegaire, monarch of Ireland from 427 to 457. His reign was rendered memorable by the advent of St. Patrick, and by the arrangement of Irish laws and customs in the Senchus Mor. The collection and compilation of the Senchus Mor was brought about by Leary calling a general convention in which the kings, clergy and sages of Ireland were assembled together for the purpose of purifying the national records. The convention selected nine of its members for the duty—three kings, three bishops and three sages. By these nine the traditions were arranged and classified. Professor O'Curry considered "the recorded account of this great revision of the body of the laws of Erin is as fully entitled to confidence as any other well-authenticated fact in ancient history." The work, we are told, was composed at "Tara in the summer and in the autumn, on account of its cleanness and pleasantness during these seasons; and Lisanawer, near Nobber, was the place during the winter and the spring, on account of the nearness of its firewood and water, and on account of its warmth in the time of winter's cold."

Although his wife was a convert to Christianity, Leary continued in his old faith—nevertheless giving every facility for the spread of Christianity. Leary was killed by lightning in 457, and was buried upright in the ramparts of Tara, "as if in the midst of warriors standing up in battle." The republication of the Senchus Mor, with a translation and notes, was commenced by order of the British government in 1865, from MSS. in Trinity College and the British Museum, the oldest dating from the early part of the 14th century.

King Malachy I.

Malachy I., monarch of Ireland, reigned, according to the "Four Masters," from 843 to 860. Before his accession he brought about the assassination of Turgesius, the Danish king, and the expulsion of the Northmen from Ireland; but

they returned in force before long, and his reign
was marked by constant descents and depredations of the Danes and Norwegians. His reign
was also notable for a regal convention, which
he called at Rathhugh, in the present County of
West Meath.

King Malachy II.

Malachy II., monarch of Ireland, flourished
from 980 to 1022, the rival, and afterwards the
tributary of Brian Boru. He succeeded to the
nominal sovereignty of Ireland in 980, soon after
Brian became King of Munster. He married a
sister of Sitric, the Danish King of Dublin; and
after the death of his father, his mother married
Olaf, a renowned warrior of the same nation.
The early part of Malachy's reign was spent in
constant contentions with Brian and other Irish
chiefs, and with his connections, the Northmen.
Upon more than one occasion he inflicted severe
defeats on the latter, carrying away 2,000 hostages, jewels, and other valuables, and "freed the
country from tribute and taxation from the Shannon to the Sea"; and referred to by Moore in his
"Irish Melodies" as one who "wore the collar of
gold, which we won from her proud invader."
    In 982 he invaded Thomond and rooted up
and cut to pieces the great tree in County Clare,
under which Brian and his ancestors of the Dal-
cassian line had been crowned, and where for
generations they had received the first homage
of their subjects. Eventually Brian and Malachy
had to lay aside their feuds and unite against the
common enemy, and in the year 1000 they defeated the Northmen at Glenmama, near Dun-
lavin, in County Wicklow. In 1002 Brian, whose
power had been gradually increasing, marched

to Tara, deposed Malachy, and assumed the supreme sovereignty. Malachy not only submitted, but appears to have entered into Brian's plans for the government of the country, and helped him in his operations against the Northmen.

After the battle of Clontarf and Brian's death, April 23, 1014, Malachy again assumed the supreme authority in Ireland. His energy in following up the struggle refuted the calumny that he secretly favored the Northmen in the fight. He reigned eight years after the death of Brian, and is mentioned as the founder of churches and schools; but the annals of the time show that the latter years of his life were passed chiefly in plundering expeditions in various parts of the island and sanguinary contentions with the chiefs who owed him a nominal allegiance. Malachy died at Cormorant Island, in Lough Ennel, near Mullingar, in 1023. A month before he had defeated the Northmen of Dublin at Athboy.

Turlough O'Conor

Turlough O'Conor, monarch of Ireland and King of Connaught, was born in 1088. He was son of Roderic O'Conor, who died in the monastery of Clonmacnois, where he resided after being blinded by the O'Flahertys. Turlough conquered the princes of Ireland in the south and west, and according to Keating held the nominal sovereignty of Ireland from 1126 to 1156; but the Irish princes were engaged in continual hostilities among themselves and with the Northmen during his reign.

In 1153 he subdued Dermot MacMurrough, King of Leinster, and compelled him to return Devorgilla to her husband (O'Rourke, Prince of

Brefny), with whom he had eloped a short time
previously. We are told that he established a
mint at Clonmacnois, built bridges across the
Shannon at Athlone, also near Shannon harbor,
and across the Suck at Ballinasloe, and that he
was a munificent friend of the Church. He died
in 1156, and was interred in the church of St.
Ciaran at Clonmacnois.

Cathal Crovderg O'Conor

Cathal Crovderg O'Conor, Prince of Connaught, succeeded as head of the O'Conors on
his brother Roderic's death in 1198. The early
part of his reign was passed in contests with the
Anglo-Normans and with his nephew, Cathal
Carrach, who at one time succeeded in expelling
him from his territories. In 1201, however,
Cathal Crovderg, with the assistance of the De-
Burgos, defeated and slew his nephew in battle
near Boyle.

On King John's arrival in Ireland Cathal
paid him homage, and by the surrender of a portion of his territories secured to himself a tolerably peaceful old age. He died in the abbey of
Knockmoy (having assumed the habit of a Grey
Friar), in 1224. The principal abode of the heads
of the O'Conor family at this period was at Rathcroghan, near Tulsk, in County Roscommon.
His son Felim was confirmed in his estates by
the king, while another Felim, a descendant,
joined Edward Bruce, and fell in battle at Athlone, August 16, 1316.

Dermot MacMurrough

Dermot MacMurrough, historically connected with the Anglo-Norman invasion of Ire-

land, was King of Leinster, and a man of cruel, treacherous, and violent nature. He was born in 1090. The abduction of Devorgilla—the wife of his enemy O'Rourke, Prince of Brefny—in 1153 led to an inextinguishable feud between these chiefs. Upon the accession of Roderic O'Conor as King of Ireland in 1166, a large force under O'Rourke was mustered against Dermot, who, in despair, set fire to his capital of Ferns; fled to Bristol and then to France, where King Henry then was, and offered to hold his kingdom under the English monarch on the condition of his assisting him to recover it. This offer fell in with the previous designs of Henry, and he dismissed Dermot with letters authorizing his British subjects to aid him.

Dermot returned to England, and engaged Strongbow of South Wales to invade Ireland, offering him his daughter Eva in marriage. Proceeding secretly to Ireland in 1169, he concealed himself during the winter in the monastery of Ferns. In the following spring he was joined by FitzGerald and FitzStephen from Wales, and a series of contests of various fortune ensued, ending in the subjugation of a part of Ireland. Dermot finally led his troops into the territory of O'Rourke, but was twice signally defeated, and died at Ferns in May, 1171.

John MacHale

John MacHale, R. C. archbishop, known as "The Lion of the Fold of Judah," was born at Tobbernavine, County Mayo, March 6, 1791, the son of a small tenant farmer. The only language spoken by his parents and the people of the district at that time was Gaelic, but by the wishes of his father young MacHale was instructed in English at the neighboring hedge-school. In 1804 he was sent to the school of Patrick Stanton at Castlebar, where he received the rudiments of a classical education. In September, 1807, he entered St. Patrick's College, Maynooth, as an ecclesiastical student. During his seven years' college course he made remarkable progress in scholarship, and July 25, 1814, was ordained priest by Bishop Murray (afterwards archbishop), at Dublin. In the following year he was appointed lecturer, and in 1820 professor of dogmatic theology in the College of Maynooth.

In 1820 Father MacHale published the first of a series of powerful letters over the signature of Hierophilos in defense of Catholic dogma and the freedom of education, which won for him great popularity. From 1821 to 1824 he wrote a number of letters on the state of Ireland to the English people, dealing principally with Catholic Emancipation and education.

In 1825 he was appointed Bishop of Maronia, and coadjutor to the Bishop of Killala, with right of succession to the See of St. Muriedach. He was consecrated June 5, at the College of Maynooth.

His learned work, "The Evidences and Doctrines of the Catholic Church," was published in 1827. This work has passed through two editions, was translated into French and German, and extended his reputation abroad. In 1829 Dr. MacHale laid the foundation of the Killala Cathedral. In 1831 he visited Rome, where he delivered a number of sermons that were afterwards translated into Latin. After making a tour of the continent he returned home, in December, 1832. On the death of Dr. Waldron,

May 20, 1834, he succeeded to the bishopric of Killala, and in August of the same year he was made Archbishop of Tuam.

He was an able supporter of Daniel O'Connell and his pen had long been vigorously employed in behalf of Catholic Emancipation. His forceful and impassioned letters in the newspapers, bearing the familiar signature, "John, Archbishop of Tuam," treated of all the burning questions of the time,—national education, the tithes, poor laws, the charitable bequest act, Catholic Emancipation, the repeal association, tenant rights, and the famine. The "Lion of the Fold of Judah," as the archbishop was called by his friend O'Connell, was perhaps, next to the great Liberator, the most popular public man in Ireland. During the famine of 1847-48 he appealed everywhere for assistance, and was the principal channel through which the Irish in all parts of the world transmitted aid to their perishing countrymen.

With voice and pen he vigorously opposed the system of Queen's Colleges, as he had previously denounced the national schools, as a menace to the religious faith of Catholics. He went to Rome in 1848 and laid the matter before the Cardinals of the Propaganda, and the colleges were later condemned by the Holy See.

Archbishop MacHale translated many works into Irish, among which are many of "Moore's Melodies," 1841 (new edition, 1871); "The Iliad" (eight books, 1841-71); "The Way of the Cross," 1854; five books of Moses, or the Pentateuch, 1861; and prepared a catechism and a book of prayers, 1866.

The same spirit that influenced him to aid O'Connell urged him to assist by his sanction and encouragement the cause of Home Rule advocated first by Isaac Butt. "Come what may," he said, "Ireland must one day be free and self-governed." He died at Tuam, November 7, 1881, and was interred in the cathedral there. Archbishop MacHale was a great church builder, and he labored in the humblest priestly functions as actively as the youngest priest almost to the close of his long life. No Catholic prelate filled a larger place in Irish public affairs, and none approached him in popularity. By his religious zeal and national spirit his name will always be held in great veneration by the Irish people.

Thomas William Croke

Thomas William Croke, R. C. archbishop, was born near Mallow, County Cork, May 19, 1824. His early education was received at home and at the Charleville Endowed School, which he left at the age of fourteen. He then went to Paris, entered the Irish College, and after passing through the usual course of philosophy and theology, was appointed professor in a college in Belgium. In November, 1845, he went to Rome and entered the Irish College, where he remained three years, studying theology under the Jesuit Fathers Perrone and Passaglia.

In 1846 he won the gold and silver medals, the following year took the degree of doctor of divinity, and was ordained priest. Subsequently returning to Ireland, he entered Carlow College, as professor of rhetoric, in 1848. In 1849 he taught theology in the Irish College at Paris. Again returning to his native country, he was engaged in missionary work in the diocese of Cloyne, County Cork, until 1858, when he was appointed president of St. Colman's College, Fermoy. This important position Father Croke filled for seven years with honor to himself and benefit to the Church. In 1865 he was appointed to the pastoral charge of Doneraile and chancellor of the diocese of Cloyne.

In 1870 he accepted the bishopric of Auckland, New Zealand, which he held until 1874. While in New Zealand he labored zealously in building churches, founding missions, and devoted himself especially in christianizing the native Maoris, with whom he became exceedingly popular. In 1875 he was advanced to the Archiepiscopal See of Cashel and returned to Ireland, where he played an important part in the ecclesiastical and political affairs of his country. The indefatigable efforts of the archbishop to better the condition of the tenant farmers and in promoting the Irish Land League and Nationalist movements greatly endeared him to the hearts of his countrymen. He died at Thurles, July 22, 1902. Archbishop Croke was a man of large stature and powerful physique, and in his younger days was a famous athlete.

Daniel Murray

Daniel Murray, R. C. archbishop, was born near Arklow, County Wicklow, April 18, 1768. After an academical training at the University of Salamanca, in Spain, he was ordained priest, and returned to Ireland in 1790. He was pastor at Arklow until 1798; and in 1809, having been appointed coadjutor to Dr. Troy, Archbishop of Dublin, he was consecrated Bishop of Hierapolis. At the instance of his brother prelates he paid a visit to France in the following year, and succeeded in obtaining from the French government the restoration of property belonging to the Irish College in Paris.

He rendered conspicuous service, between 1810 and 1816, by his determined opposition to the proposed royal veto on the appointment of Catholic Bishops in Ireland. He was delegated to accompany Dr. Milner to Rome, to protest against all compromise on this subject; they succeeded in carrying their point, and the veto was eventually condemned by the Holy See in 1814.

On the death of Dr. Troy, May 11, 1823, his mitre devolved upon Dr. Murray, who received the pallium from Rome October 19, 1824. The archbishop was one of the foremost in the struggle for Catholic Emancipation, and in other political movements for national rights. He was appointed a commissioner by the government under the Bequests Act of 1844, and a commissioner of education in 1851. He even consented to act as a visitor of the Queen's Colleges, but when the proceedings of the synod of Thurles, condemning the colleges, were ratified by the Sovereign Pontiff, in 1852, Dr. Murray withdrew from all connection with those institutions. He died at Dublin, February 26, 1852. Dr. Murray was a ripe scholar and polished gentleman. He published some works on political and polemical subjects, and his "Sermons" were published at Dublin in two volumes in 1859.

William Quarter

William Quarter, the first Bishop of Chicago, was born in Kings County, Ireland, January 21, 1806, son of Michael and Anne Bennet Quarter. He studied in the schools of Tullamore preparatory to entering the College of Maynooth. From a priest who had just returned to Ireland, young Quarter learned the condition of Catholic missions in America, and shortly after left his native land. He landed at Quebec in 1822, and, being rejected by the bishop there and at Montreal as an ecclesiastical student, on account of his youth, he went to Emmettsburg, Md., and entered Mount St. Mary's College as a divinity student, September 8, 1822. There, in the following year, though only sixteen years old, he was chosen professor of Latin and Greek.

September 19, 1829, on the completion of his theological studies, he was ordained priest and was sent to New York City, where, in 1832, during an epidemic of cholera, Father Quarter devoted himself assiduously to aiding the sufferers. In 1833 he was appointed pastor of St. Mary's Church, New York City, where he remained until appointed bishop of the newly constituted See of Chicago. He was consecrated March 10, 1844, by Archbishop Hughes, and arrived in Chicago May 5 of that year.

He found but one Catholic Church in the city, and conditions throughout the new diocese unsettled. Bishop Quarter, however, entered upon his new duties with such wisdom and zeal that the new Cathedral of St. Mary's was completed in October, 1845, the University of St. Mary's of the Lake was opened July 4, 1846, and the Sisters of Mercy introduced in the diocese the following September. At the time of his death sixty-eight churches had been erected in the diocese, with fifty-three priests, and the educational institutions brought to a high standard. His administration marked an era of solidity and harmony throughout the diocese. He died at Chicago, Ill., April 10, 1848. His remains were interred in old St. Mary's, the then procathedral.

Anthony O'Regan

Anthony O'Regan, third Bishop of Chicago, was born in County Mayo, in 1809. He received his ecclesiastical training at the College of Maynooth, where he was ordained priest, and appointed professor in the College of St. Jarlath's at Tuam. After serving in this capacity for a number of years, he was appointed president of the latter institution, and won high honors as a theologian and educator. About 1849, having received an invitation from Archbishop Kenrick of St. Louis, he came to America and was placed in charge of the theological seminary at Carondelet, Mo. In 1854 he was nominated Bishop of Chicago, and in July of that year was consecrated at the St. Louis Cathedral by Archbishop Kenrick.

The diocese of Chicago was not in a vigorous condition, there being few priests and ecclesiastical structures and little other diocesan property. His first acts were to build a new episcopal residence and to purchase the land for Calvary cemetery. Bishop O'Regan also brought the Jesuit and Redemptorist Fathers into the diocese. His administration, however, did not long continue successful. He had numerous difficulties with the clergy, and in 1856 went to Rome to present his resignation to the Pope, which, after considerable difficulty, was accepted. He was made Titular Bishop of Dora in 1858, and retired to St. Michael's Grove, near London, England, where he died November 13, 1866. He bequeathed his property toward education in Ireland and to the erection of a Catholic hospital in Chicago; also to the education of ecclesiastical students in the dioceses of Alton and Chicago.

James Duggan

BY WILLIAM J. ONAHAN

James Duggan, fourth Bishop of Chicago, was born May 22, 1825, in Maynooth, County Kildare, where he received a good classical and theological education. As soon as he was out of college he emigrated to the United States, arriving in St. Louis in 1846. He there completed his studies under the Lazarist Fathers at Carondelet, and was shortly after ordained priest. Assigned to parochial duty first as assistant, he was subsequently appointed pastor of the Immaculate Conception, where his capacity and zeal found full scope, and was quickly recognized by Archbishop Kenrick, who showed his appreciation by appointing Father Duggan his vicar-general.

During the interregnum in Chicago in 1853, caused by the resignation of Bishop Van de Velde, Father Duggan came to Chicago to fill the position of administrator of the diocese, in the duties of which he acquitted himself with signal tact and capacity. Upon the removal of Bishop O'Regan, who had succeeded Bishop Van de Velde, Father Duggan was nominated and appointed in 1859 to the vacant see. The new bishop had won general favor in St. Louis by his zeal, his acknowledged ability, and by his winning and gracious manners.

He was known to be an especial favorite of Archbishop Kenrick, who, it was said, sought to retain him in St. Louis as coadjutor.

Bishop Duggan was warmly welcomed in Chicago by all classes—Protestants vying with Catholics in cordiality. The "Bishop's Palace," as it was then styled, was a stately marble front mansion, which had been built by Bishop O'Regan on the corner of Michigan avenue and Madison street—now occupied by the building of Montgomery Ward & Co. Bishop Duggan's house soon became the favorite center of culture for the elite of the city. The bishop's refined taste in literature and art made him an authority amongst the increasing circle of the literary and art loving people of the city. Bishop Duggan was an early and generous patron of George P. Healy, the well-known portrait painter, and many of the artist's finest pictures and studies were to be seen adorning the bishop's elegant library and parlors. When the civil war broke out, Bishop Duggan stood actively and conspicuously for the Union cause, and in public addresses and writings made his power and influence widely felt.

He cordially approved of the organization of the Chicago "Irish Brigade," commanded by the heroic and lamented Colonel Mulligan, and assigned to it as chaplain his own secretary, Rev. Dr. Butler.

He likewise aided the Very Rev. Dr. Dunne, V. G., in the formation of the "Irish Legion," the 90th Illinois, another Chicago Catholic regiment, to which Father Kelly, the first pastor of St. James Church, was assigned as chaplain.

In the management of diocesan and Church affairs he was for many years most successful and fortunate. Churches were multiplied, the new Cathedral of the Holy Name pushed forward towards completion, religious orders of

men, and teaching communities of Sisters introduced throughout the diocese. The bishop's hostile attitude towards the "Fenian Brotherhood"
caused some local friction for a time, and, towards the end of his administration, there was
considerable dissatisfaction manifested by several of the best known and most highly respected
Chicago priests against certain of Bishop Duggan's decisions and appointments: protests and
remonstrances were sent to Rome in regard to
these matters. The condition of the bishop, however, shortly made things clear.

He had for some time shown symptoms of
mental as well as physical disorder, which soon
necessitated his removal to an institution in St.
Louis, and retirement from episcopal duties.
This in 1869. In this sad state of almost constant mental aberration Bishop Duggan continued until death came to his relief, March 27,
1899. His remains were brought to Chicago and
the solemn funeral rites held in the Cathedral
of the Holy Name. The newly appointed Auxiliary Bishop McGavick delivered the sermon on
the occasion. Those who remember Bishop Duggan speak of him as a man of exceptionally attractive manners, a scholar of rare ability and
culture, especially well equipped in classical
knowledge and in general literature. He possessed one of the choicest private libraries in the
city. Bishop Duggan was a pleasing preacher and
lecturer, and, until the closing year of his administration, he was held in the most affectionate
regard by priests and people.

The Church in Chicago made notable progress in his time. Bishop Duggan's local clergy
and assistants included several of the ablest
priests known in diocesan history—Very Rev.

Denis Dunne, V. G., Rev. Dr. McMullen, later
Administrator of Chicago, and subsequently
Bishop of Davenport; Rev. Joseph P. Roles,
long time pastor of St. Mary's; Rev. Dr. Butler,
nominated Bishop of Concordia, who died in
Rome on the eve of the day appointed for his
consecration; Rev. Father P. W. Riordan, now
Archbishop of San Francisco, and Rev. Dr. Mc-
Govern, the present pastor of Lockport, who was
the first priest ordained in Rome for the diocese
of Chicago.

Patrick Augustine Feehan

Patrick Augustine Feehan, first Archbishop
of Chicago, was born in Killenaule, County Tipperary, August 29, 1829. His parents were people of culture, and descended from families noted
for their scholarly attainments. At the age of
sixteen, young Patrick was sent to the Ecclesiastical Seminary at Castleknock, where he remained
two years. In 1847 he entered the College of Maynooth, and during the five years as a student
there made unusual progress in the study of philosophy and theology. Plans were being arranged for him to enter the Dunboyne establishment, when, by invitation from Archbishop Kenrick of St. Louis, he decided to select America
as the scene of his future activity.

He came to the United States soon after
and was ordained priest at St. Louis, Mo., November 1, 1852, and for six months taught in the
diocesan seminary. In July, 1853, Father Feehan
was appointed assistant pastor at St. John's
Church, and in 1854 succeeded the Rev. Anthony
O'Regan as president of the theological seminary
at Carondelet, where he remained three years.

In 1857 he was made pastor of St. Michael's Church, St. Louis, and in the following year was transferred to the Church of the Immaculate Conception in the same city.

The See of Nashville became vacant in 1864, by the resignation of Bishop Whelan, and Father Feehan was nominated for the vacancy. He at first declined, owing to his mother's poor health. The next year his mother died; the office was again offered to him; he accepted, and was consecrated November 1, 1865. The diocese of Nashville presented at the time numerous difficulties for the young bishop. The civil war had just ended, and the church was left in the same condition of debt and confusion as the city. While Bishop Feehan was struggling to build up his diocese, with the aid of the new priests he had gathered about him, the city of Nashville was visited by an epidemic of cholera and yellow fever. On three different occasions the plague visited the diocese, and Bishop Feehan labored constantly amid scenes of trouble and misery. He saw many of his priests fall victims to the pestilence, but he fearlessly carried on his work in the fever-stricken city until the plague had been stamped out.

In 1866 he took part in the second plenary council of Baltimore and in the Ecumenical council of the Vatican. In 1880, shortly after the death of the Right Rev. Thomas Foley, D. D., Chicago was created an archiepiscopal see, and Bishop Feehan was appointed the first archbishop. He was given a notable reception on his arrival in Chicago, and, November 28, 1880, the installation services were held at the Cathedral of the Holy Name. The archdiocese comprised eighteen counties in the northern part of

Illinois, in which there were 194 churches, attended by 204 priests.

Archbishop Feehan entered upon his labors in Chicago when the immigration of Catholics from many lands to the archdiocese was at its height, but by establishing churches and schools, and providing for the religious needs of the different nationalities, he preserved unity and harmony. The establishment of schools, even before the erection of churches, was a policy on which the archbishop insisted. In 1883 he was invited to Rome, with other archbishops, to formulate the schemata of the third plenary council of Baltimore. In 1899 the Rev. A. J. McGavick was consecrated auxiliary bishop, and July 25, 1901, the Rev. Peter J. Muldoon was consecrated Titular Bishop of Tamassus.

During his administration Archbishop Feehan created numerous new parishes in Chicago, founded homes for the aged, hospitals, orphan asylums, and established the Chicago Industrial School for Girls and the great St. Mary's Training School for Boys at Feehanville. He introduced into the archdiocese very many religious orders of nuns devoted to teaching, all of whom were placed in charge of academies and parochial schools. He regularly visited all parts of the archdiocese, and at the close of two decades had confirmed about 200,000, ordained more than 250 priests, laid the corner-stones of and dedicated more than 150 churches.

An important event in the administration of Archbishop Feehan, and in the history of the Church in America, was the Catholic educational exhibit at the World's Columbian Exposition in 1893, which attracted wide attention and was greatly admired. He died at Chicago, after a short illness, July 12, 1902, and was succeeded by the Most Rev. Edward Quigley. Archbishop Feehan was noted for his great piety and for his kindly disposition. He was an authority on matters of church discipline and on all questions of theology. At the time of his death there were 298 churches in the archdiocese (150 in Chicago) and 538 priests. In no diocese were the affairs of the Church, it may be said, better managed or more extensively developed than in Chicago during the administration of Archbishop Feehan.

Francis Patrick Kenrick

Francis Patrick Kenrick, R. C. archbishop, was born in Dublin, December 3, 1797. At the age of eighteen, after receiving a classical education at home, he went to Rome and pursued his theological studies at the College of the Propaganda. Here young Kenrick applied himself diligently to the study of the Sacred Scriptures and the writings of the early Fathers. In 1821 he was ordained priest and was selected to take charge of the new theological seminary at Bardstown, Ky., founded by Bishop Flaget. During his residence at Bardstown he attended the bishop in his visitations to the widely scattered missions of the diocese, aiding greatly by his ability and energy. He also succeeded in establishing the diocesan seminary upon a firm basis.

In 1828 he entered the field of theological controversy, in defense of his religion, and in which he was an able champion throughout life. In 1829 he was theologian to Bishop Flaget at the Provincial Council of Baltimore and was appointed secretary to the assembly. At this council he was appointed coadjutor to the Bishop of Philadelphia, the diocese of which was, at the time, under the domination of the trustee system. He was consecrated bishop June 6, 1830, at Bardstown, Ky., by Bishop Flaget. The consecration sermon was delivered by Bishop England.

The trustees of St. Mary's Church, Philadelphia (the bishop's cathedral), refused to recognize him in the exercise of his pastoral authority, but he finally overcame all opposition, and one of his first acts was to establish an order that all diocesan property was to be vested in the bishop. To Bishop Kenrick is due much of the credit of rescuing the Church in the United States from trustee dictatorship. There being no college for the education of priests in his diocese, which left many congregations in the widely scattered districts without regular pastors, he founded the Seminary of St. Charles Borromeo at Philadelphia about 1833. In 1838 he obtained a charter for the college under the name of the Philadelphia Theological Seminary of St. Charles Borromeo.

On the death of Bishop Conwell, in 1842, he succeeded to the bishopric of Philadelphia. That same year he introduced the order of St. Augustine into the diocese and assisted them in founding the College of St. Thomas at Villanova. In 1844, during the anti-Catholic riots in Philadelphia, he was compelled to suspend temporarily all public worship. During these outbreaks of vandalism, in which priests were often compelled to conceal their clerical dress, much church property was destroyed and several people killed. He continually preached against acts of retaliation by his own people, and took immediate steps to restore the churches and institutions destroyed by the mob.

In August, 1851, shortly after the death of the Most Rev. Samuel Eccleston, he was made Archbishop of Baltimore. He was also appointed Apostolic Delegate by the Pope to preside over the first National Council of all the archbishops and bishops in the United States, convened at Baltimore in May, 1852. By a decree signed by Pope Pius IX., July 25, 1858, the primacy of the United States was conferred upon him and his successors,—Baltimore being the oldest Catholic See in this country. He rearranged the parishes of Baltimore; with his approval, the Jesuits built St. Ignatius Church in 1853, and opened Loyola College about 1855. In 1854 he went to Rome and took part in the deliberations that led to the definition of the dogma of the Immaculate Conception.

Besides most of the modern languages, Archbishop Kenrick had a rare knowledge of Hebrew, Latin and Greek. One of the most learned theologians and vigorous writers in America, his pen was constantly employed in defense of his faith; and he was indefatigable in extending the influence and powers of the Church.

While at Bardstown, Ky., he published "Letters from Omicron to Omega," 1828, embodying a defense of the Catholic doctrine of the Eucharist, which had been attacked by Rev. Dr. Blackburn, President of Danville College, Ky., who wrote under the signature of "Omega." He published a series of letters, now in book form, and regarded as of the highest authority, "On the Primacy of the Holy See and the Authority of General Councils," 1837 (in reply to Bishop Hopkins of Vermont), subsequently enlarged and reprinted under the title of "The Primacy of the Apostolic See Vindicated," and another series

of letters, entitled "Vindication of the Catholic
Church." Of the same class of publication were
his "Catholic Doctrine of Justification Explained
and Vindicated," 1841, and "Treatise on Baptism," 1843. His Latin treatises on dogmatic
theology, "Theologia Dogmatica" (four volumes,
1839-40, new edition three volumes, 1857), and
moral theology, "Theologia Moralis" (three volumes, 1841-43), form a complete course of divinity, and are extensively used as text-books in the
Catholic Seminaries of the United States. During the latter part of his life he was engaged
upon a revised English translation of the Scriptures, which is considered to be the greatest of
his literary efforts. At the time of his death
the whole of his version of the New Testament
and the greater part of the Old Testament had
been published with copious notes. He died at
Baltimore, Md., July 6, 1863.

Peter Richard Kenrick

Peter Richard Kenrick, R. C. archbishop,
brother of Francis Patrick, was born in Chancery Lane, Dublin, August 17, 1806. He matricu-
lated at the College of Maynooth in 1827, and
was ordained priest there by Archbishop Murray
of Dublin, March 6, 1832. After serving in the
cathedral parish of Dublin and at Rathmines for
a short time, he came to the United States. In
1835 he was made rector of the cathedral in Philadelphia by his brother, who was coadjutor
bishop of the diocese. Subsequently he was
made president of the Seminary of St. Charles
Borromeo and vicar-general. He also edited the
Catholic Herald, the diocesan paper.

In 1841 he was appointed Bishop of Drasa
and coadjutor to the Bishop of St. Louis. He

was consecrated by Bishop Rosatti at Philadelphia, November 30, 1841. On the death of the latter, in September, 1843, he succeeded him to the See of St. Louis, which then embraced the states of Arkansas, Missouri, and part of Illinois. He introduced many educational and charitable orders into the diocese, and within a few years had completed a number of new churches and institutions, and established a diocesan paper, the Catholic Cabinet.

October 8, 1847, St. Louis was created an archiepiscopal see and Dr. Kenrick became its first archbishop. In September of the following year he received the pallium at the hands of his brother in St. John's Cathedral, Philadelphia. He visited Rome in 1867 and again in 1869 to attend the Vatican Council. Archbishop Kenrick's golden jubilee was celebrated in 1891 with imposing ceremonies, the first in the history of the Catholic Church in the United States. Owing to his declining health, Bishop Kain of Wheeling, W. Va., was made administrator of the diocese in 1893 and created coadjutor archbishop in 1895. Archbishop Kenrick died at St. Louis, Mo., March 4, 1896. During his administration he consecrated many new bishops to the sees that were being continually created out of the original diocese of St. Louis. Among his works are: "Anglican Ordinations" and "The Holy House of Loretto." He ranked among the best as a pulpit orator; his command of language was extraordinary.

John Hennessy

John Hennessy, R. C. archbishop of Dubuque, Iowa, was born in County Limerick,

August 20, 1825. In 1847 he came to the United
States and entered Carondelet Seminary, near
St. Louis, Mo., where he began the study of
theology, and was ordained priest November 1,
1850. His first mission was at New Madrid,
Mo., embracing 6,000 miles of territory, with no
railroad facilities. In 1854 he became professor
of dogmatic theology at Carondelet Seminary
and, in 1857, president of that institution. The
next year he went to Rome as representative of
Archbishop Kenrick. In 1860 he was made pastor at St. Joseph, Mo., where he remained until
appointed Bishop of Dubuque, Iowa. He was
consecrated by Archbishop Kenrick, September
30, 1866; and September 17, 1893, he was made
the first Archbishop of Dubuque. Archbishop
Hennessy was an eminent orator, a profound theologian, and was always ardent in the cause of
religious education. Wendell Phillips declared
that Archbishop Hennessy's oration on Daniel
O'Connell was a masterpiece of eloquence, and
the finest of all those delivered on the occasion of
O'Connell's centenary. He founded St. Joseph's
College and Theological Seminary at Dubuque
in 1873. During his administration the Catholic
Church in Iowa increased in membership from a
few thousand to 250,000. He died at Dubuque,
Iowa, March 4, 1900.

John Baptist Purcell

John Baptist Purcell, R. C. archbishop, was
born in Mallow, County Cork, February 26, 1800.
He was the son of Edmund and Johanna Purcell.
Young Purcell emigrated to Baltimore, Md., in
1818, where he was employed as a teacher in
Asbury College and as a tutor in a private family

in Queen Anne County. From 1820 until 1823 he studied philosophy and theology in Mount St. Mary's College at Emmettsburg, at the end of which time he received minor orders, and in 1824 was sent to France to complete his ecclesiastical studies at the Seminary of Issy, and at St. Sulpice in Paris.

He was ordained priest in the Cathedral of Notre Dame, May 21, 1826, after which he visited his parents in Ireland. Returning to America, he was appointed professor of moral philosophy in St. Mary's College, Baltimore, and in 1828 was made its president. Father Purcell rendered valuable service to that institution. On the death of Bishop Fenwick he was nominated Bishop of Cincinnati and consecrated in the Cathedral of Baltimore, October 13, 1833. His diocese embraced the states of Ohio and Michigan, then for the most part an unsettled wilderness, containing only sixteen churches (one at Cincinnati) and a Catholic population considerably under 10,000. He immediately began to establish academies and parish schools. He built a convent for the Ursulines, organized a German congregation at Cincinnati, and by his vigorous labors the diocese was transformed within a few years from its former frontier condition into one of great importance, containing seventy-five churches and a Catholic population of about 75,000 in 1846.

In 1833 the diocese of Detroit was formed, which embraced the state of Michigan, and in 1847 the diocese of Cleveland was created. In 1850 he was made an archbishop with four suffragan bishops to the metropolitan See of Cincinnati. He received the pallium from the hands of Pius IX., at Rome, in 1851. Archbishop Purcell presided over his first provincial council in 1855

and the second in 1858. He devoted much of his
time to establishing religious orders of education
and charity in his archdiocese, and to the erection of institutions and academies for their use.
He founded Mount St. Mary's of the West for
the education of priests, which subsequently became one of the leading theological seminaries
of the country, established the Catholic Tele-
graph, and built St. Peter's Cathedral at Cincinnati. Archbishop Purcell visited Europe many
times during his episcopate and attended the
Vatican Council in 1869. He was on intimate
terms with many public men, among whom were
Chief Justice Chase, Thomas Ewing and General Sherman. He officiated at the wedding ceremony for the latter's daughter and Thomas W.
Fitch, in the Jesuit Church at Washington, D. C.,
in 1874. In 1876 his golden jubilee was celebrated
at Cincinnati.

The last years of his life were saddened by
great monetary troubles, caused by placing the
financial affairs of the archdiocese in the hands
of his brother, Father Edward Purcell, the vicar-
general, whom he permitted to receive money on
deposit. Both were unacquainted with the principles of business, and when conditions were in-
vestigated, in 1879, it was discovered the liabili-
ties were very large. While the crisis was widely
discussed, no one questioned the integrity of the
archbishop, and it was learned he had been a
bishop for twenty-five years before accepting any
salary. Father Edward Purcell died soon afterwards. In 1880 the archbishop offered his resignation, but instead of being accepted, a coadjutor
was appointed and he retired to St. Martin's Convent, in Brown County, Ohio, where he died July
4, 1883.

Archbishop Purcell met Alexander Campbell in a debate on religion at Cincinnati that lasted seven days, which was later published and extensively read throughout the United States. He ably defended the Catholic Church and did much to soften the prevailing prejudice against his religious faith, and brought many converts to the Church. Among his publications are: "The Roman Clergy and Free Thought," 1870; "Lectures and Pastoral Letters," "Diocesan Statutes, Acts, and Decrees of Three Provincial Councils Held in Cincinnati," and a series of books for parochial schools in the diocese. At the time of his death the archdiocese of Cincinnati had a Catholic population of upwards of 200,000.

James Louis O'Donnel

James Louis O'Donnel, the apostle of Newfoundland and colonial R. C. bishop, was born at Knocklofty, County Tipperary, in 1738. At the age of eighteen he left Ireland and entered the Franciscan Convent of St. Isidore at Rome. He afterwards was sent to Bohemia, and upon the completion of his theological studies was ordained priest at Prague, in 1770. In 1775 he returned to Ireland and settled at Waterford. In 1779 he was appointed prior of the Franciscans there, and subsequently became provincial of the order in Ireland.

In 1784 Father O'Donnel was sent to Newfoundland as prefect and vicar-apostolic, "being the first fully accredited Catholic ecclesiastic who had appeared in Newfoundland since it became a British possession." In 1796 he was consecrated at Quebec, Titular Bishop of Thyatira. On his return to Newfoundland, Bishop O'Donnel made his first episcopal visitation. He established missions at Harbor Grace and in other parts of the island, and in 1801 published a body of diocesan statutes, divided the diocese into missions, and, owing to the scarcity of clergymen, he was often obliged to perform the duties of a mission priest. The missionary duties of Bishop O'Donnel at length wore out his health, and in 1807 he was obliged to resign his see and return to Ireland.

In recognition of his services to the colony of Newfoundland, the British government granted him a life pension of £50 per annum. He spent the last years of his life at Waterford, where he died April 15, 1811. Bishop O'Donnel's name was one of the most honored in Newfoundland during his time, and his position in the island was as exalted as that of the chief executive. His deep religious character and inherent gentleness won the respect of all. It has been said that, through his counsels and activity in promoting Christian work, and by his services to the colony in suppressing a mutiny among the soldiers of the Newfoundland regiment stationed at St. John's in 1800, his arrival in the island was of more importance to the government than a garrison or the advent of a half dozen admiral-governors.

Michael O'Connor

Michael O'Connor, R. C. bishop, was born in the city of Cork, September 27, 1810. He passed his youth in Queenstown, where he received a grammar-school education. At the age of fourteen he was sent to the College of the Propaganda at Rome, by Bishop Coppinger, and here completed his studies in philosophy and theology before reaching the canonical age. For being the most able student in mathematics, he was given a gold medal by the college, and his professor is said to have remarked that had he devoted himself to this department of scholarship, he would have developed into one of the most skilled mathematicians of his time. He won his doctor's degree in a public disputation of great brilliancy, in which the thesis contained all the branches of theology and philosophy that was embraced in the test which made St. Thomas and St. Bonaventure doctors of the University of Paris in the thirteenth century.

He was ordained priest at Rome in 1833 and appointed professor of sacred Scripture and later vice-rector of the Irish College in that city. In 1834, after having spent ten years in Rome, he returned to Ireland and was made pastor of Fermoy. Subsequently he became chaplain to the Presentation Convent at Doneraile. In 1839, Father O'Connor accepted an offer from Bishop Kenrick of Philadelphia to come to America, and was made president of the Seminary of St. Charles Borromeo. While discharging the duties of this office, he visited the missions of Norristown and Westchester twice a month and built St. Francis Xavier's Church at Fairmount.

In 1841 Father O'Connor was sent to Pittsburg, then in the diocese of Philadelphia, as vicar-general, and became pastor of St. Paul's Church. The Provincial Council of Baltimore, which met in 1843, having favored the erection of a new see in the western part of Pennsylvania, Father O'Connor was nominated as its first bishop.

For many years he had desired to join the

Society of Jesus, but as a student of the Propaganda he was unable to do so without the consent of the Pope; hence, in 1843, he hastened to Rome to ask permission and thus escape the episcopal appointment. When he knelt before Gregory XVI., however, he was not permitted to rise until consenting to become bishop of the new diocese, the Pope saying: "You shall be Bishop of Pittsburg first and Jesuit afterwards." He was consecrated by Cardinal Franzoni, August 15, 1843, at St. Agatha's, the Church of the Irish College at Rome. Before his return to this country, he visited Ireland, where he was joined by a number of ecclesiastical students and sisters of the newly created order of Our Lady of Mercy, who came with him to America.

His diocese had thirty-three churches (some unfinished), two religious institutions, fourteen priests, and a Catholic population of about 25,-000. Bishop O'Connor held his first diocesan synod in 1844, and the same year he founded a female academy and orphan asylum, under the care of the Sisters of Charity, Sunday Schools, total abstinence societies, and a circulating library. The Sisters of Mercy opened an academy for young ladies, and a school for boys was established under the charge of Rev. J. Mullen, afterwards Bishop of Erie. In 1844 a paper known as The Catholic was started, and St. Michael's Seminary, for the education of candidates for the priesthood, was founded. He visited Europe in 1845 to secure priests for his diocese, and returned to Pittsburg in December of that year with four Presentation Brothers, who established an institution of their order and took charge of a school for boys. In 1847 he purchased a large piece of land on a hill south of

Birmingham, for $16,000, which was afterwards sold and assessed for $162,000.

From 1847 to 1850 twelve churches were erected in the diocese, and in 1855 the new cathedral was completed, being one of the largest in the United States at that time. Archbishop Hughes delivered a brilliant sermon at the dedication ceremonies. The consecrating prelate was Archbishop Kenrick of Philadelphia. In 1852 Bishop O'Connor again visited Europe and returned with a colony of Passionists, who founded their first establishment in the United States at Pittsburg. In 1853 the See of Pittsburg was divided and the diocese of Erie was erected. Bishop O'Connor, at his own request, was transferred to the new diocese, but was soon recalled by the Pope, who had been petitioned by the people of Pittsburg for the return of their old bishop. In 1854 he was summoned to Rome by Pope Pius IX. to take part in defining the dogma of the Immaculate Conception, and it is claimed that changes in the wording of the decree were due to his suggestions.

Bishop O'Connor's resignation was accepted May 23, 1860, when he sailed for Europe, and in December following he entered a Jesuit monastery in Germany. After remaining there two years, he was allowed, by special dispensation, to take the four vows at once. Returning to the United States, he taught theology in Boston College, subsequently became socius to the provincial of the Jesuits, and delivered lectures in many parts of the United States. The latter office he held until his death. He was an eloquent pulpit orator and a brilliant linguist. He was an ardent worker among the colored people, and through his efforts St. Francis Xavier's Church in Baltimore was secured for them. He died in the college at Woodstock, Md., October 18, 1872. His remains were interred there with other deceased members of the Society of Jesus. His brother, James O'Connor, who was associated with him in Pittsburg, became afterwards Bishop of Omaha.

Thomas Francis Hendricken

Thomas Francis Hendricken, R. C. bishop, was born in Kilkenny, May 5, 1827. He was the son of John and Anne Maher Hendricken. In 1844 Thomas entered St. Kieran's College, Kilkenny, and in 1847 was admitted as an ecclesiastic student in the Royal College of Maynooth, where he graduated six years later. In addition to theology he acquired a thorough knowledge of other branches of learning in this famous Catholic institution. In 1853, after having completed his studies, Hendricken was ordained by Bishop O'Reilly of Hartford, Conn., who was on a visit to Ireland. He induced the young priest to select America as his field of labor. While on the voyage some of the passengers became affected with a malignant disease, and when Father Hendricken undertook to aid the sick, despite the orders of the captain, he was saved from violence only by the intervention of a fellow-passenger.

His first service in America was at the cathedral in Providence, R. I. Later he officiated at Newport and Woonsocket. In January, 1854, he was sent to St. Joseph's Church at West Winsted, Conn. In 1855 he was promoted to the Church of the Immaculate Conception at Waterbury, where he ministered for seventeen years. Here he built a costly Gothic church, a school and a pastoral residence, and laid out a beautiful cemetery. Father Hendricken also introduced the Sisters of the Congregation of Notre Dame, established the convent of the Immaculate Conception, and for a number of years was an active member of the public board of education, taking a keen interest in the education of poor children of all denominations. In 1866 he received the degree of D. D. from Pope Pius IX.

When the diocese of Hartford was divided, in 1872, and a part (which embraced the state of Rhode Island and a part of Massachusetts) was erected into the See of Providence, Father Hendricken was appointed bishop of the newly created diocese. He was consecrated at Providence by Cardinal McCloskey of New York on April 28, 1872. The next year Bishop Hendricken visited Rome, and again in 1878. During his administration numerous churches were erected, including a new cathedral (in 1878), to meet the demands of a rapidly increasing Catholic population, which ranks among the foremost structures of its kind in the United States. He also erected many other churches and schools in different parts of his diocese. The Jesuit Fathers were placed in charge of St. Joseph's parish, Providence; the Ladies of the Sacred Heart established their house at Elmhurst, the Ursulines came to teach in the parish schools, and the Sisters of Jesus and Mary opened a branch in Fall River, Mass. An orphan asylum and hospital were erected, the priests and parishes doubled, and the opportunities for a Catholic education greatly improved and extended.

During all these labors Bishop Hendricken was a constant sufferer from asthma and was often confined to his bed. During the twenty-four years of his ministry he paid for church property valued at $1,000,000. He died at Providence, R. I., June 11, 1886, and was buried beneath the main altar of the new cathedral, which had just been completed.

Thomas Galberry

Thomas Galberry, R. C. bishop and educator, was born at Naas, County Kildare, in 1833. When he was three years old his parents emigrated to the United States, settling at Philadelphia, Pa. He entered Villanova College, near the latter city, in 1847, and December 20, 1856, after completing his theological studies, was ordained priest by Bishop Neumann of Philadelphia. He was then made one of the professors at Villanova College, two years later was appointed to the pastoral charge of the Augustinian mission at St. Dennis' Church, nearby, which was founded by the order in 1825, and styled by the Augustinians as "our training school for bishops." Many distinguished clergymen of the United States received their early training there. He was transferred to Lansingburg, N. Y., in 1860, where he erected a beautiful Gothic church, the cornerstone of which was laid by Bishop McCloskey in June, 1864, and also built a convent for the Sisters of St. Joseph.

While still pastor at Lansingburg he was appointed superior of the Commissariat of Our Lady of Good Council, the Augustinian mission in the United States. Father Galberry continued to act as pastor at Lansingburg until 1870, when he was transferred to the Augustinian Church at Lawrence, Mass. Here he assumed charge of completing the building of a new church, which, however, was finished by his successor.

In 1872 he was elected president of Villanova College, to succeed Rev. Dr. Stanton, O. S. A. While president of that institution he erected a new college building and rearranged and improved the course of studies. In 1874, when the Augustinian order decided to erect the Commissariat of Our Lady of Good Council in the United States into a religious province, under the patronage of St. Thomas of Villanova, Father Galberry was elected provincial. This was the first election of a superior by the Augustinians in this country.

March 15, 1875, he was nominated Bishop of Hartford, but owing to his attachment to the monastic life, he forwarded his resignation to Rome, but was forced to accept, and he was accordingly consecrated, at Hartford, Conn., March 19, 1876, by Archbishop Williams. Shortly after his consecration he visited Rome and other parts of Europe. Bishop Galberry founded the Connecticut Catholic, the official paper of the diocese, and built two churches and a new cathedral. His constitution, never strong, was being gradually weakened by his new duties, and, in failing health, he set out for Villanova to seek rest, but was seized with hemorrhages at New York City, where he died October 10, 1878.

James Whelan

James Whelan, R. C. bishop, was born in Kilkenny, December 8, 1823, and came to the United States with his parents when a boy. In 1839 he entered the Dominican Seminary at Springfield, Ky., and took the vows in 1842. He then entered the Dominican Convent at Somerset, Ohio, where he completed his theological studies, and was ordained priest by Archbishop Purcell, August 2, 1846. In 1852 he was elected president of St. Joseph's College, Perry County, Ohio, and in 1854 was appointed provincial of the Dominican province, which embraced all of this country except the Pacific coast.

While provincial he was chosen coadjutor to Bishop Miles of Nashville, Tenn., and consecrated Bishop of Marcopolis at St. Louis, May 5, 1859. After the death of Bishop Miles, February 21, 1860, he succeeded to the bishopric of Nashville. Bishop Whelan immediately began to establish an academy, a boarding school, and an orphan asylum, all of which he placed under the care of the Dominican Sisters. During the civil war, being allowed to pass through the lines of the Federal army, he visited Bishop Spalding at Louisville, and upon his return was accused by the Confederates of making remarks, while in the lines of the enemy, which had influenced the movements of the Union army.

This loss of favor with the Southern people and the state of chaos in which his diocese had fallen by the subsequent campaigns, affected him greatly, and in February, 1864, he resigned his see and retired to St. Joseph's Convent. The latter part of his life was spent at St. Thomas' Church and parochial residence, Zanesville, Ohio, where he died, February 18, 1878. He was the author of "Catena Aurea, or a Golden Chain of Evidence Demonstrating that Papal Infallibility Is No Novelty," 1871.

Denis Mary Bradley

Denis Mary Bradley, R. C. bishop, was born at Castleisland, County Kerry, February 25, 1846. He came to the United States with his parents when eight years old and settled at Manchester, N. H., where he received his early education. He subsequently entered Holy Cross College, Worcester, Mass., and graduated in 1867. That same year he entered St. Joseph's Theological Seminary, Troy, N. Y., where he was ordained priest, June 3, 1871. He then became rector of the Cathedral at Portland, Me., and also chancellor of the diocese under the administrations of Bishops Bacon and Healy.

In 1880 he was appointed pastor of St. Joseph's Church at Manchester, N. H., and four years later became the first bishop of the newly-constituted See of Manchester. Bishop Bradley's energy and zeal in the promotion of religious and educational institutions throughout his diocese greatly improved the condition of his people. He died at Manchester, N. H., December 13, 1903.

Patrick Nieson Lynch

Patrick Nieson Lynch, R. C. bishop, was born at Clones, County Monaghan, March 10, 1817. He was the son of Conlan P. and Eleanor McMahon N. Lynch, who, in 1819, emigrated to America and settled at Cheraw, S. C. Patrick received his early education at the Seminary of St. John the Baptist at Charleston, and in 1834 was sent to Rome by Bishop England to complete his studies at the College of the Propaganda. He remained at the latter institution for six years, became one of its most brilliant scholars, graduated with honors, and received the degree of D. D. by a public thesis.

In 1840 he was ordained priest, returned to America, and was appointed assistant pastor in the Cathedral of St. Finbar at Charleston. In

1844 he was made pastor of St. Mary's Church by Bishop Reynolds, and in 1847 principal of the Collegiate Institute, subsequently serving as vicar-general of the diocese. In 1848, when an epidemic of yellow fever raged in Charleston, Father Lynch took personal charge of one of the hospitals. He caught the disease himself, but by excellent care and nursing his life was saved.

On the death of Bishop Reynolds, in 1855, he was made administrator of the diocese, which office he held for three years, when he was appointed bishop, and consecrated March 14, 1858, by Archbishop Kenrick of Baltimore. The Bahama Islands were subsequently added to the diocese.

Soon after the opening of the civil war a fire destroyed a portion of Charleston, including the new cathedral Bishop Lynch had built, and other church property. Sherman's march to the sea, and the burning of Columbia, with its college and convent, further augmented the distress of the once prosperous diocese. The sympathies of Bishop Lynch were naturally with the South and he was sent to France on a mission of peace by the Confederate government, as had Archbishop Hughes of New York been sent by the North. At the close of the war the diocese was left in a state of chaos, being over $200,000 in debt, $100,000 of which represented savings of the poor who had deposited their money with Bishop Lynch. He devoted the remainder of his life to restoring the diocese to its former prosperity. Churches and institutions were rebuilt and all but $15,000 of the debt was paid at the time of his death. The greater part of this money was secured by his own efforts outside the state of South Carolina.

In 1871 yellow fever again broke out in Charleston, and, although weakened by excessive labor, he hastened to Charleston and courageously exposed himself to the dangers of the plague by ministering to the sick and dying. His powerful constitution gradually declined in the last years of his life, and he died at Charleston, S. C., February 26, 1882.

From the time of his ordination until his death he had attended the councils of Baltimore, both provincial and plenary. He was a profound scholar, a brilliant orator and lecturer, and a learned scientist. He had been for several years editor of the United States Catholic Miscellany. Bishop Lynch contributed a number of interesting articles to the periodicals and revised and edited the American edition of Deharbe's "Series of Catechisms." His letters on the "Vatican Council" (written for the Catholic World) and "The Miracle of St. Januarius" were published in book form.

Francis Alison

Francis Alison, educator and Presbyterian divine, was born in County Donegal, in 1705. He was educated in the schools of his native country and at the University of Glasgow, coming to America in 1735. He was ordained minister in 1737 and taught in various parts of the colonies previous to the revolutionary war.

Alison was one of the best classical scholars of his time in the colonies and assisted in the education of many of the leading men of that period. He was vice-provost of the College of Philadelphia from 1755 until 1777 and pastor of the First Presbyterian church. He delivered a remarkable sermon on "Peace and Unity Recommended." By his will all his slaves were emancipated. He received the degree of A. M. from Princeton and Yale colleges in 1755 and that of D. D. from Glasgow University in 1758. He died at Philadelphia, November 28, 1799.

Francis Makemie

Francis Makemie, Presbyterian clergyman, distinguished in the early history of the American colonies, was born in Ramelton, County Donegal, in 1658. He studied for the ministry at Glasgow. After being ordained he came to this country, in 1682, and began preaching and trading, principally in Maryland, Virginia, the Carolinas and in Barbadoes. In 1690 he settled in Accomac County, Virginia, where he was engaged in the West India trade, and where, in 1692, a large tract of land was granted him. He shortly afterwards went to the Barbadoes and held a pastorate for several years, but returning to Virginia in 1698, he organized a congregation, which he served for some time.

In 1704 Makemie went to England and returned with several ministers. In 1706 he organized, at Philadelphia, the first presbytery in America, and is, therefore, regarded as the father of Presbyterianism in this country. In January, 1707, he was arrested at Newton, Long Island, on a warrant issued by Governor Cornbury for preaching on the 19th of that month, without a license, in a private house in New York. He was kept in prison until the following March, when he was released on bail. In June of the same year he was tried in New York and was acquitted of the charge of transgressing the toleration act,

on producing the license to preach which he had
received in Barbadoes.

The opposition of Governor Cornbury, however, continued, and in justifying his action, he
wrote of Makemie as "a preacher, a doctor of
physic, a merchant, an attorney, a counselor-at-
law, and, which is worst of all, a disturber of
governments." Makemie printed a "Narrative"
of this affair, and many tracts, some of which
have since been republished. His "Answer to
George Keith's Libel" (Boston, 1692) was characterized by Increase Mather as the work of "a
reverent and judicious minister." Two of
Makemie's letters, addressed to Mather, dated
1684 and 1685, are still extant and preserved in
the library of the Massachusetts Historical Society. He married Naomi Anderson, the daughter of a wealthy Virginia merchant. Makemie
died in Virginia, in the summer of 1708.

John Murray

John Murray, Presbyterian clergyman, was
born in Antrim, May 22, 1742. He was educated
at Edinburgh, came to America in 1763, and held
several pastorates in the colonies prior to the
revolution. He entered with enthusiasm into the
patriotic cause, and such was his eloquence that
on one occasion, after an address, a company was
raised for the Continental army in a few hours.
He acquired great influence over the people of
his district by his powers as a preacher and his
patriotic activity throughout that sanguinary
struggle. In 1780 he published a volume of
"Sermons on Justification," and in 1791 "Sermon
on Original Sin." The latter part of his life was

passed at Newburyport, Mass., where he died, March 13, 1793.

James Waddel

James Waddel, Presbyterian clergyman, was born at Newry, County Down, in July, 1739. He was brought to America by his parents in infancy, who settled on White Clay Creek, in Pennsylvania. He was educated at Dr. Finley's "log college" at Nottingham, Pa., of which he was made a tutor, and afterwards became an assistant in the school of Rev. Robert Smith, at Pequea, Pa.

At the age of nineteen he went to Hanover County, Va., and became the friend of Colonel Henry, father of Patrick Henry, and the Rev. Samuel Davies. He subsequently taught in the school of Rev. John Todd at Louisa, and devoted his spare time to the study of theology. He was licensed to preach April 2, 1761, and June 16, 1762, was ordained minister at Prince Edward. He accepted a call from Lancaster and Northumberland counties, where he remained until about 1778, when he removed to Tinkling Spring, in the Shenandoah valley. During the revolutionary war he addressed, prior to their departure to engage in the battle of Guildford Courthouse, a company formed principally of his congregation.

In 1786 he purchased an estate in Louisa County, Va., near Gordonsville, which he named Hopewell, where he continued to preach, and opened a private school in his own residence. He became totally blind in his latter years, but this affliction did not weaken his intellectual powers nor diminish his activity of body. Possessed of great eloquence and controversial abilities, he had few equals as an orator among his contemporaries in America. These qualities are attested by William Wirt in an article published by him in the British Spy. He had listened to a sermon by the "blind preacher" while passing through Orange County, Virginia, and says in part: "It was a day of the administration of the sacrament, and his subject . . . . was the passion of our Savior. I had heard the subject handled a thousand times. . . . . Little did I suppose that in the wild woods of America I was to meet a man whose eloquence would give to this topic a new and more sublime pathos than I had ever before witnessed."

The honorary degree of D. D. was conferred on him by Dickinson College in 1792. About 1768 he married Mary Gordon, daughter of Colonel James Gordon, by whom he had a numerous family. He died at his residence in Louisa County, Virginia, September 17, 1805. His "Memoir" was published by his grandson, James W. Alexander, in the Watchman of the South, 1846.

John Hall

John Hall, Presbyterian clergyman, was born at Ballygorman, County Donegal, July 31, 1829, where his family had been settled for six generations. He was educated at Belfast College, which he entered at the age of thirteen, and while a student there repeatedly won the prizes for Hebrew scholarship and theology. After graduating, in 1849, he was licensed to preach, in June of that year, and sent to the West of Ireland. In 1852 he became pastor of the First

Presbyterian Church at Armagh, where he remained five years, when he accepted a call from
the Church of St. Mary's Abbey (now Rutland
Square), Dublin, in which charge he continued
from 1858 until 1867. Here he edited the Evan-
gelical Witness, built a new church, and received
the honorary appointment of commissioner of
education for Ireland. While on a visit to this
country, in 1867, as a delegate to the Presbyterian Assembly of the United States, he delivered a sermon at the old Fifth Avenue Church
in New York City. He made such a favorable
impression upon the congregation that he received a call from that body, which he accepted
after his return to Ireland. He delivered his
first sermon at the old church on Nineteenth
street, November 3, 1867, and soon became one
of the leading preachers of his denomination in
the United States. A new church was built in
1873-74, at a cost of $1,000,000, and missions and
charitable institutions were established in different parts of New York City. Under Dr. Hall
the Fifth Avenue Church reached the height of
its power, and became one of the most affluent
and influential Presbyterian institutions in the
world. He presided over this congregation for
more than thirty years, and the church was
known throughout the country as "Dr. Hall's
Church." His speeches and sermons were distinguished for their logic and simple eloquence.
Dr. Hall was trustee of Princeton College, the
Union Theological Seminary of New York, and
of Wellesley College, Massachusetts; chairman
of the Presbyterian Board of Home Missions,
and of the Church Extension Committee. He
received various honorary degrees, among which
was that of LL. D., from Columbia University

in 1886, and LL. D., from Trinity College, Dublin, in 1891. From 1881 to 1891 he was Chancellor of the University of the City of New York. Dr. Hall resigned his pastorate in January, 1898, but withdrew his resignation on the urgent request of his congregation.

He was a prolific writer on religious topics, contributed to weekly publications, and edited a series of Sunday school lessons which were widely used. He published "Family Prayers for Four Weeks," 1868; "Papers for Home Reading," 1871; "Questions of the Day," 1873; "God's Word Through Preaching," 1875; "Familiar Talks to Boys," 1876; "Foundation Stones for Young Builders," 1879; "A Christian Home," 1883; and, in conjunction with George H. Stuart, "American Evangelists," 1875. June 15, 1852, he married Emily Bolton, of Dublin, Ireland, by whom he had three sons and one daughter. Dr. Hall died at Bangor, County Down, September 17, 1898, while on his annual visit to Ireland. His remains were returned to New York and interred in Woodlawn cemetery. His eldest son, Robert W. Hall, became professor of analytical chemistry in the University of the City of New York; Richard J. Hall, a prominent physician on the Pacific coast, died at Santa Barbara, Cal., June 23, 1897; Thomas C. Hall, pastor of the Fourth Presbyterian Church at Chicago for some years, is now professor of theology in the Union Theological Seminary; Bolton Hall, a stepson, is a well-known lawyer and lecturer.

William Homes

William Homes, clergyman, was born in the North of Ireland, in 1663. He received a

good education, and when a young man removed
to New England and taught school at Martha's
Vineyard, Mass., for three years. He then re-
turned to Ireland and was ordained minister at
Strabane, in 1692. Again removing to New
England, in 1714, he became a pastor at Chil-
mark, Martha's Vineyard, where he died, June
20, 1746. He was the author of sermons on
"The Sabbath," "Church Government," and
other theological works. His son, Captain
Robert Homes, married a sister of Benjamin
Franklin.

Gilbert McMaster

Gilbert McMaster, Presbyterian clergyman
and theological writer, was born in the parish
of Saintfield, County Down, February 13, 1778.
While he was still a child his father emigrated
to America, and settled in Pennsylvania. Gilbert studied theology and was ordained pastor
of the Reformed Presbyterian Church at
Duanesburg, N. Y., in 1808, where for thirty-
two years he exercised his ministry, and afterwards for six years at Princeton, Ind. In 1846,
he resigned, owing to poor health. The degree
of D. D. was conferred on him by Union College
in 1828.

McMaster was the author of "The Shorter
Catechism Analyzed," 1815; "The Moral Character of Civil Government Considered," 1832,
and many other theological works. He was married in 1803 to Jane Brown. He died at New
Albany, Ind., March 15, 1854.

His son, Erasmus D. McMaster, was ordained minister in 1831; became president of
South Hanover College, Indiana, in 1838; presi-

dent of Miami University in 1845; professor of
theology in the Theological Seminary at New
Albany, Ind., in 1850, and of the Northwestern
Theological Seminary at Chicago in 1866,
where he died, December 11th of that year.

Another son, James A. McMaster, became a
Catholic, and in 1848 purchased the Freeman's
Journal and Catholic Register. He was con-
sidered during his time the foremost Catholic
journalist in the United States. He was a life-
long Democrat, but opposed the candidacy of
Samuel J. Tilden. He died at Brooklyn, N. Y.,
December 29, 1886.

John Henry Hopkins

John Henry Hopkins, Episcopal bishop,
was born in Dublin, January 30, 1792. He came
to America with his parents in 1801. After receiving a classical education, he spent a year in
a counting house at Philadelphia, assisted Wilson, the great ornithologist, to prepare plates for
one of his works, and about 1810 embarked in
the manufacture of iron in western Pennsylvania with James O'Hara. He became bankrupt
in 1817; subsequently studied law, and was admitted to the bar at Pittsburg, where he practiced for a time with excellent success. In November, 1823, he entered the Episcopal ministry,
and became rector of Trinity Church, Pittsburg.
He then studied architecture, and built a new
church. In 1831 he removed to Boston, and
the next year was consecrated the first Bishop
of Vermont. He was afterwards involved in
financial difficulties by the failure of the Vermont Episcopal Institute, opened under his re-
sponsibility. He took a prominent part in the

Pan-Anglican Synod at Lambeth, and was made
a D. C. L. of Oxford. He was an accomplished musician and artist. Besides innumerable pamphlets, he published many books,
among which are "Christianity Vindicated,"
New York, 1833; "Essay on Gothic Architecture," 1836; "Twelve Canzonets," words and
music, 1839; a refutation of Milner's "End of
Controversy," 1854, and "A Scriptural, Historical and Ecclesiastical View of Slavery," 1864, in
which he advocates the Southern view of slavery. He died at Rock Point, Vt., January 9,
1868.

Of his five sons, all born in this country,
John Henry became a noted clergyman and
author, Edward Augustus a merchant, Casper
Thomas a journalist, Charles Jerome a musician,
and Frederick Vincent a physician.

Thomas Barton

Thomas Barton, clergyman, was born in
County Monaghan, in 1730. After graduating
from Dublin University he emigrated to America, and in 1751 opened a school at Norriston,
Pa. He later became tutor at the Academy in
Philadelphia (now the University of Pennsylvania). In 1753 he married a sister of David
Rittenhouse, the distinguished mathematician
and astronomer.

In 1754 Barton went to England, where he
was ordained in the established church. He returned to America as a missionary of the Society for the Propagation of the Gospel, and
settled at Lancaster, Pa., where he was made
rector of St. James's Church, remaining for
nearly twenty years. His adherence to the roy-

alist party after the Declaration of Independence compelled him to leave his post and remove to New York, where he died, May 25, 1780. He was the father of Benjamin Smith Barton, American physician and naturalist.

Charles Elliott

Charles Elliott, Methodist clergyman, was born in County Donegal, May 16, 1792. He studied in Dublin, emigrated to the United States in 1814, and was received into the traveling connection of the Ohio Conference in 1818. In 1822 he was appointed superintendent of the Wyandotte Indian mission at Upper Sandusky, Ohio. He was presiding elder of the Ohio district for five years, and from 1827 until 1831 professor of languages in Madison College at Uniontown, Pa. Stationed at Pittsburg in 1831, he was presiding elder of that district, subsequently editing the Pittsburg Conference Journal and the Western Christian Advocate.

About 1856 he became president of the Iowa Wesleyan University, which office he retained until 1860, when he resigned, and was made editor of a religious paper at St. Louis, Mo. During the civil war he was a strong supporter of the Union cause. He was the author of numerous important works, principally dealing with the history of the Methodist Church and against slavery. He died at Mount Pleasant, Iowa, January 6, 1869.

John Bowden

John Bowden, clergyman, was born in Ireland, January 7, 1751. He was brought to

America by his father (a soldier in the British army), and attended school for two years, when he returned to Ireland. He again came to America in 1770, graduated at King's College two years later, and subsequently studied divinity. Bowden then went to England, where he was ordained, and, returning to this country in 1774, was made assistant minister at Trinity Church, New York City, where he officiated for some years. He also held pastorates in other parts of the United States, and the West Indies. In 1796 he was chosen bishop of Connecticut, but declined the position owing to physical disability.

In 1797 he received the degree of S. T. D. from Columbia College, New York, in which institution he was professor of moral philosophy belles-lettres, and logic, from 1802 until his death. He was the author of "Portrait of Calvinism," two letters addressed to Ezra Stiles, president of Yale College, "Concerning Church Government," 1788; "The Apostolic Origin of Episcopacy," 1808, and other theological works. Bowden was not in sympathy with the American cause in the revolutionary war. He died at Ballston Spa, N. Y., July 31, 1817.

Joseph Banigan

Joseph Banigan, manufacturer and philanthropist, was born in County Monaghan, June 7, 1839. At the age of eight he came to the United States and settled at Providence, R. I. After learning the jeweler's trade he became identified with the rubber goods business in 1860, in which line he continued the remainder of his life, and became known as the "American Rubber King." He organized the Woonsocket

Rubber Company in 1866, and at different times numerous other companies of the same nature. He was made president of the United States Rubber Company upon its organization, from which office he retired in 1896. Banigan was also an officer in numerous mercantile corporations, and acquired a fortune of many millions.

He was a munificent donator to the fund for building the new cathedral in Providence, established a Home for the Aged Poor in 1884, was the principal benefactor towards establishing St. Joseph's Hospital, St. Joseph's Orphan Asylum, Home for Working Girls, and St. Xavier's Convent, all Catholic institutions, but accessible to Protestants on uniform terms. He bequeathed a large fortune to charity. For his benevolent acts he was made a Knight of the Order of St. Gregory by Pope Leo XIII.

Banigan was a member of the Rhode Island Historical Society. He was twice married—first, in 1860, to Margaret Holt, by whom he had three children. After her death he married Maria T. Conway, in 1873. He is described as being of sturdy frame, with a quiet, unassuming manner—a man who owed his success to hard work, a clear head, and good, sound sense. He died at Providence, R. I., July 28, 1898.

Thomas Francis Walsh

Thomas Francis Walsh, capitalist and mine owner, was born near Clonmel, County Tipperary, April 2, 1851. He was educated in the public schools of Ireland and later learned the millwright's trade. In 1870 he came to the United States, and after working at his trade in Worcester, Mass., for a time, he removed to Colorado, in 1871. He located at Central City in 1874, and became a practical miner. The next year he went to the Black Hills, shortly after the discovery of gold there; located first at Custer City, and subsequently at Deadwood, S. D., where he accumulated $100,000.

Returning to Colorado in 1878, he went to Leadville, where carbonate silver ore had been discovered, and purchased a hotel, but devoted most of his time to mining enterprises. By close study he acquired an intimate knowledge of geology, metallurgy, and the deposition of ore bodies. Walsh not only became an expert mining engineer, but, in 1890, introduced into Colorado the Austin pyritic process of smelting ores. In 1892 he built a smelter at Kokomo, Colo., operated the Black Hawk group of mines at Rico in 1894, and subsequently built the Walsh smelter at Silverton.

In 1896 Walsh located in the San Juan district, near Ouray. Here he discovered ore that was rich in gold, on property where formerly there had been a number of silver mines. Walsh purchased this land, known as the Camp Bird Mine, which became one of the richest mines in the world, and laid the basis of his great fortune. Here he installed extensive machinery, erected smelters for reducing ores, built comfortable quarters for his employees, and began to develop the mines on a broad and systematic scale. Within three years the yield was $3,000,000.

In the winter of 1898 Walsh removed to Washington, and in 1902 sold the Camp Bird mine to an English syndicate for approximately $6,000,000. At Washington he erected a palatial residence, one of the most beautiful in the national capital, and built the Ouray and Colorado office buildings. Walsh and his family became prominent socially at Newport, Washington and Paris. Wolhurst, his beautiful country home near Denver, Colo., was rechristened Clonmel by President Taft in 1909, in honor of his place of birth.

In 1900 Walsh was commissioner from Colorado to the Paris Exposition, and, while at the French capital, gave a series of social entertainments which were the talk of Europe. While abroad he formed the acquaintance of King Leopold of Belgium, with whom he later became associated in the development of mines in the Congo. Walsh was a member of the American Association for the Advancement of Science, the Washington Academy of Science, and of the National Geographic Society. He was elected president of the National Irrigation Congress in 1900, of the Transmississippi Congress in 1908, and was a member of the executive committee of the Washington Board of Trade.

Walsh married Carrie B. Reed at Leadville, in 1879, by whom he had a son and a daughter. His son, Vinson Walsh, was killed in an automobile accident at Newport, R. I., August 19, 1905. His daughter, Evalyn Walsh, in 1908 married Edward B. McLean, only son of John R. McLean, owner of the Cincinnati Enquirer and the Washington Post. In memory of his son, Walsh established in the Colorado School of Mines, at Golden, a fund to be used in the free examination of ores thought to contain radium.

He died at Washington, D. C., April 8, 1910. He was buried in Rock Creek cemetery at the national capital. His wealth has been variously estimated at from ten to fifteen million dollars.

Alexander Brown

Alexander Brown, banker, was born in Ballymena, County Antrim, November 17, 1764. He came to the United States in 1800 and settled in Baltimore, Md., where he soon became an extensive importer of Irish linens. He ultimately merged into the commission and banking business, in which he built up an extensive foreign trade. His early education had been limited, but with marked talent for business he and his sons founded large banking houses in Liverpool, London, Philadelphia and New York City. The business integrity of the firm made the name of Alexander Brown & Sons respected both in America and Europe. He died December 17, 1834, leaving his son George in control of the Baltimore house. John A. Brown, another son, born at Ballymena, May 21, 1788, was placed at the head of the Philadelphia house, which he managed for twenty years. He died December 31, 1872. James Brown, the youngest son, opened the New York house and was also the American representative of his brother, William (see Volume II.), who established the Liverpool and London houses.

Patrick Joseph Healy

Patrick Joseph Healy, the son of James and Catherine Sheehan Healy, was born at Mallow, County Cork, March 16, 1840. He came to America when ten years of age, and after attending school at Boston a few years, he secured employment as errand boy in the music house of Henry Tolman & Co. in that city. Shortly after the close of the civil war Healy came to Chicago,

where, in May, 1864, he established, with George
W. Lyon, the music house of Lyon & Healy.
Sheet music and text-books was the scope of the
business at first, but within six years the firm
absorbed the piano and organ house of Smith &
Nixon, and established a wholesale department
of musical instruments.

In 1870 the establishment was destroyed by
fire, and again in the great fire of 1871. Healy
found new quarters, however, and from that
time the business steadily increased, until the
concern was recognized as one of the leading
music houses in the world. Healy was engaged
in the music trade in Chicago for more than
forty years and became known as the dean of
that business in America. He was made president of the concern in 1890.

Healy was married twice—first, in 1863, to
Mary Griffith (who died in 1877); and again in
1882, to Francis Hannah, who died in 1892. He
died in Chicago, April 3, 1905, and was interred
in Calvary cemetery. James, Raymond and
Paul Healy, sons, became identified with the
business founded by their father.

John Vaughn Clarke

John Vaughn Clarke, banker, was born at
Union Hall, County Cork, in 1825. He was a
son of William Clarke, a man of affluence, who,
owing to financial reverses, left Ireland and removed to Kingston, Canada, when young Clarke
was twelve years of age. The boy was apprenticed to a grocery firm in Kingston, but removed
to New York a few years later and entered the
wholesale grocery house of Dater & Co.

In 1849 Clarke removed to Chicago and es-

tablished the wholesale grocery firm of Warren,
Clarke and Dater. In 1863 the firm closed its
business in Chicago and Clarke went back to
New York. Returning to Chicago in 1867, he
established the Mercantile Association, the
name being changed to the Hibernian Banking
Association in 1869. Clarke was its first president and continued in that capacity until the
time of his death. His institution was regarded
as the financial center of Irish-Americans in Chicago, where Clarke was one of the influential
men of his race, being identified with its business
interests for over a quarter of a century.

He was married to Elizabeth Bertrand,
August 14, 1857. He died August 8, 1892, and
his remains were interred in Calvary cemetery.
Clarke left property valued at over a million
dollars. His wife and all the children—four
sons and three daughters—survived him. One
of his daughters, Anne M. Clarke, is the wife of
ex-Mayor Hempstead Washburne. John V.
Clarke, a son, born in Chicago, October 15, 1863,
entered the Hibernian Bank in 1880 and rose
through the different grades of the institution,
till, on the death of his father, he succeeded to
the presidency. He successfully piloted the
bank through the panic which came soon after,
and since then has greatly increased his business. Two other sons, Henry B. and Louis B.
Clarke, are vice-presidents and directors of the
same institution. It is the oldest savings bank
in Chicago.

John Elliott Cairnes

John Elliott Cairnes, political economist,
was born at Castlebellingham, County Louth,
December 26, 1823. After leaving school he

spent some time in his father's counting-house, but was eventually permitted to follow his natural disposition, and enter Trinity College. In 1851 he took the degree of M. A. He engaged in the study of law and was called to the Irish bar. Cairnes did not have much inclination for the legal profession, and during some years occupied himself to a large extent with contributions to the daily press, chiefly relating to various Irish social and economic questions. Political economy he studied with great thoroughness and care; this led to a friendship with Archbishop Whately, and in 1856 he was appointed to the professorship of political economy, founded in Trinity College by that prelate.

In 1857 appeared his "Character and Logical Method of Political Economy," which forms a most admirable introduction to the study of economics as a science. Able articles in Frazer's Magazine and the Edinburgh Review on the gold question as relating to prices next occupied his attention. In 1861 he was appointed to the professorship of political economy and jurisprudence in Queen's College, Galway.

From the first he took much interest in the American civil war of 1861-65, and combated Confederate sympathies by the publication of "The Slave Power," in 1862, a work that rapidly went through two editions, and had considerable influence in modifying opinion in Great Britain. The Encyclopedia Britannica styles it "one of the finest specimens of applied economical philosophy." His health, at no time very good, was further weakened, about 1863, by a fall from his horse, and an acutely painful malady gradually crept over him that ultimately rendered physical exertion impossible.

In 1866 he was appointed to a professorship in University College, London. He spent the season of 1866-69 in Italy. His health soon rendered it impossible to further discharge public duties, and he resigned his post in 1872, retiring with the honorary title of Emeritus Professor of Political Economy. Next year the Dublin University conferred on him the degree of LL. D.

The last years of his life were spent in the collection and publication of papers contributed to various reviews and magazines, and in the preparation of his great work, published in 1874, "Some Leading Principles of Political Economy Newly Expounded," "beyond doubt a worthy successor to the great treatises of Smith, Malthus, Ricardo and Mill." A careful summing up of the results of these contributions will be found in the Encyclopedia Britannica, showing the advances in economic doctrine established by him, in (1) his exposition of the province and method of practical economy; (2) his analysis of cost of production in its relation to value; (3) his exposition of the natural or social limit to free competition, and of its bearing on the theory of value; (4) his defense of the wages fund doctrine. Professor Cairnes died in London, July 8, 1875, and was interred at Willesden.

Edward George Ryan

Edward George Ryan, jurist, was born at Newcastle House, County Meath, November 13, 1810, the son of Edward and Abby Keogh Ryan. He began the study of law in Ireland, but before completing his course he came to the United States, in 1830, and resumed his studies in New York City, where he supported himself by teaching until he was admitted to the bar, in 1836. He then removed to Chicago, began the practice of his profession, and from 1839 to 1841 edited a paper called the Tribune, the commencement of the present Chicago paper of that name.

In 1842 Ryan located at Racine, Wis., where he remained until 1848, when he removed to Milwaukee. He was prosecuting attorney at Chicago, 1840-41; represented Racine County at the first Wisconsin State Constitutional Convention of 1846, was a delegate to the Democratic National Convention of 1848, and as chairman of a committee of the Democratic State Convention, in 1862, drew up an address to the people of his adopted state which became known as the "Ryan Address."

He was one of the most powerful advocates at the Wisconsin bar, being engaged in many noted legal battles, among which was the impeachment trial of Judge Levi Hubbell, before the State Senate, in 1853. He was city attorney of Milwaukee from 1870 until 1872, and in June 1874, upon the resignation of Luther S. Dixon, he was appointed by Governor Taylor chief justice of the State Supreme Court, to fill the vacancy, an office which he held until his death. In 1842 he married a daughter of Captain Hugh Graham. Ryan died at Milwaukee, Wis., October 19, 1880.

Robert Emmet

Robert Emmet, lawyer, eldest son of Thomas Addis Emmet, the distinguished Irish patriot, was born in Dublin, September 8, 1792. He was with his father at Fort George during the latter's imprisonment, and there received his

early education through teachings from the
state prisoners. After his father's release he resided with his parents for some time in France
and subsequently came with them to America,
at the age of thirteen. After graduating at Columbia College, New York, in 1810, he studied
law, was admitted to practice, and rose to eminence at the New York bar. He served one term
in the State Legislature in 1828; was corporation counsel in 1836, Register of the Court of
Chancery for a long period, and from November,
1852, to December, 1854, was a judge of the New
York State Superior Court. In 1848 Emmet
was one of the leaders of the association formed
in New York to aid the proposed insurrection in
Ireland, and after the leaders of the uprising had
been sentenced to penal servitude, a ship was
chartered by Mr. Emmet and others of a committee and sent to Van Diemen's Land, in which
John Mitchell, Thomas Francis Meagher and
others made their escape in May, 1852. He was
a Democrat up to the time the parties became
divided on the question of slavery, and subsequently became one of the organizers of the Republican party in the state of New York. He
presided at the convention, in 1856, when John
C. Fremont was made the Republican presiden-
tial nominee. Mr. Emmet married Rosina Hubley, daughter of Adam Hubley, an officer in the
American army during the revolutionary war.
She died June 1, 1849. Emmet died at New Ro-
chelle, N. Y., February 15, 1873. He was the
father of eight children.

Thomas Addis Emmet

Thomas Addis Emmet, brother of Robert,
was born in Dublin, May 29, 1797, and remained

in Ireland until his father had settled in New York, when he joined him. He was educated at Columbia College, New York, afterwards studied law, and was admitted to practice, and for many years held the position of master in chancery. March 4, 1823, he married Anna Riker Tom, stepdaughter of William J. Mac-Nevin, by whom he had ten children. Emmet died August 12, 1863. His son, Temple Emmet, died in August, 1862, from exposure, while serving in the Irish brigade under Thomas Francis Meagher. Another son, Richard R. Emmet, was also with the Irish brigade, and died of fever at Fredericksburg, Va., in February, 1863.

Richard Busteed

Richard Busteed, jurist, was born in Cavan, February 16, 1822. His father was a colonel in the British army, subsequently a barrister at Dublin, and at one time chief secretary of the Island of St. Lucia, which office he lost through his efforts in behalf of emancipation. Returning to Ireland, he emigrated to Canada, where he started a paper called the True Patriot. Richard learned the compositor's trade in his father's office.

After coming to the United States he continued to work at his trade for some time. Subsequently he studied law, was admitted to the bar in 1846, and rose rapidly in his profession. In 1856 he was elected corporation counsel of New York City. He supported Douglas for president in 1860, but when war had been declared he joined the Union army, was appointed brigadier-general of volunteers, and commanded a brigade at Yorktown, Va.

His former attitude on the slavery question,
however, caused strong opposition to his appointment, and he sent his resignation to President Lincoln, in 1863. The same year he was
appointed United States District Judge of Ala-
bama and the next year his appointment was
unanimously confirmed by the Senate. The test-
oath enjoined by Congress, as exercised by at-
torneys practicing before the United States
courts, he decided was unconstitutional—a decision that was afterwards affirmed by the Supreme Court. Judge Busteed resigned his position in 1874 and resumed the practice of law in
New York City, where he died, September 14,
1898.

William Joyce Sewell

William Joyce Sewell, soldier and United
States Senator, was born at Castlebar, County
Mayo, December 6, 1835, and came to this country in 1851, having been left an orphan at an
early age. After making several voyages in the
merchant marine service to Australia and Asia,
he settled in Chicago, Ill., and later at Camden,
N. J. At the opening of the civil war he entered
the army as captain in the 5th New Jersey regiment. He served in many battles with the army
of the Potomac; was severely wounded at
Chancellorsville, where he commanded a brigade,
and was again wounded at the battle of Gettysburg. At the close of the war he was mustered
out of the service as brigadier-general of volunteers, and March 13, 1865, was brevetted major-
general.

From 1872 until 1881 he was a member of
the New Jersey Senate, of which he was president, in 1876, 1879 and 1880. In 1881, he was

elected to the United States Senate, of which body he was a member for twenty years and until his death, serving at different times on the military affairs, appropriations, and other committees.

Sewell was National Commisioner of New Jersey to the World's Columbian Exposition in 1893, and headed the New Jersey delegation in every Republican national convention from 1876 until 1900. Shortly after the civil war he became connected with the Pennsylvania railroad, and at the time of his death was an officer or director in many commercial, steamship and railroad companies. Sewell was married twice, the second time to Helen L. Heyl. He died at Camden, N. J., December 27, 1901, being survived by two sons and three daughters. His sons, Robert and William Joyce Sewell, were officers in the Spanish-American war.

Robert Adrain

Robert Adrain, mathematician, was born at Carrickfergus, September 30, 1775. He commanded a company of patriots in the rebellion of 1798, and was dangerously wounded, but managed to escape to America. He taught school successively at Princeton, N. J., and at York and Reading, Pa. He was professor of mathematics and natural philosophy at Rutgers College from 1810 to 1813, then until 1825 at Columbia College, and at the University of Pennsylvania from 1827 to 1834. He was a member of many scientific bodies in Europe and America. He edited the "Mathematical Diary" from 1825 till 1828, prepared an edition of "Hutton's Mathematics," and contributed to the maga-

zines. He died at New Brunswick, N. J., August
10, 1843.

His mathematical powers and knowledge
of the work of French geometers were displayed
in two papers communicated to the American
Philosophical Society in 1817 entitled "Investigation of the Figure of the Earth and of the
Gravity in Different Latitudes," and "Research
Concerning the Mean Diameter of the Earth."

His son, Garnett B. Adrain, was admitted
to the New Jersey bar and represented that state
in Congress from 1856 to 1858. He died at New
Brunswick, N. J., August 17, 1878. His grandson, Robert Adrain, also became an eminent
lawyer and publicist of New Jersey.

James E. Boyd

James E. Boyd, governor, was born in
County Tyrone, September 9, 1834, the son of
Joseph and Margaret Boyd. He came to the
United States with his parents in 1844, and settled first at Belmont and later at Zanesville,
Ohio. In 1856 James went to Nebraska with
his brother, where he became interested in stock-
raising, the packing business, and in the grad-
ing of the Union Pacific railroad. He was a
member of the first state legislature in 1866,
when Nebraska was admitted into the Union,
and also a member of the state constitutional
conventions of 1871 and 1875.

Boyd was elected mayor of Omaha in 1881
and again in 1885. He was a delegate to the
Democratic National Conventions of 1884, 1888
and 1892. In 1890 he was elected governor of
Nebraska by the Democratic party, but was removed from office in May, 1891, it being alleged

his father had never properly completed his naturalization, and therefore his son was an alien. He was, however, declared a citizen by the United States Supreme Court and reinstated as governor February 8, 1892, and served until January 1, 1893. The latter part of his life was devoted to the grain commission business. Boyd was a member of the Chicago Board of Trade and of the New York Stock Exchange. He died in 1906.

John G. Warwick

John G. Warwick, congressman, was born in County Tyrone, December 23, 1830. He came to America in 1850 and settled in Stark County, Ohio, where for several years he was employed as a dry goods clerk. He finally entered into business for himself, and for many years was identified with coal mining and manufacturing enterprises, from which he amassed a comfortable fortune. In 1883 he was elected lieutenant-governor of Ohio on the Democratic ticket; and in 1890 defeated William McKinley (afterwards President of the United States) for Congress in the Sixteenth Ohio district. He died at Washington, D. C., August 14, 1892. A wife and one son survived him.

David Wark

David Wark, father of the Canadian Senate, was born near Londonderry, February 19, 1804. He emigrated to New Brunswick in 1825 and was for many years engaged in mercantile pursuits, in which he acquired a comfortable fortune. In 1843 he was elected from Kent County to the New Brunswick Assembly, and in 1851 was appointed to the Legislative Council, where he remained until the confederation of British North America, in 1867. In that year he was made a Dominion Senator, a life position. He was a Liberal in politics, and a Presbyterian in religion.

Wark published "The Future of Canada and Its Relation to the British Empire," 1894. He also wrote in behalf of Imperial Federation, and Reciprocity of Trade between Canada and the United States. In 1897 he received the honorary degree of LL. D. from New Brunswick University. He married, in 1860, Anne E. Burpee, of Sunbury, N. B. Wark died at Fredericton, N. B., August 20, 1905, at the remarkable age of 101 years and 6 months, being, it is said, the oldest member of any legislative body in the world at the time of his decease.

Arthur Dobbs

Arthur Dobbs, colonial governor of North Carolina, was born in Ireland, April 2, 1689. He was the son of Richard Dobbs of Castletown, who was high sheriff of Antrim in 1694. He succeeded to the family property on the death of his father, in 1711, and in 1727 was returned to the Irish Parliament for Carrickfergus. In 1730, he was appointed engineer-in-chief and surveyor-general in Ireland by Sir Robert Walpole.

Dobbs took an active part in promoting the search for a northwest passage to India, China and Japan. He laid the matter before Admiral Wager and the Hudson's Bay Company. Eventually the admiralty provided two small vessels for the service, which left England in May, 1741, under the command of Captain Christopher Middleton. They wintered at Churchill river, in Hudson's Bay, and the next year penetrated farther north than any of their predecessors. At Repulse Bay the expedition was stopped by ice, and they returned home in September, 1742.

In 1754 Dobbs was appointed governor of North Carolina. He adopted measures to conciliate the Indian tribes, and commissioned Colonel Hugh Waddell to treat with the Catawabs and Cherokees. He was one of the colonial governors who attended the council at Hampton, Va., summoned by General Braddock in April, 1755. Superior courts of justice were established in the districts of the colony, to be held semi-annually, by the chief justice and one associate. His administration of ten years, however, was a continual contest between himself and the legislature, arising from his energy in behalf of the royal prerogative, and the stubborn resistance on the part of the colonists when he endeavored to introduce unpopular acts. He died at his seat on Town Creek, N. C., March 28, 1765. Dobbs was the author of "An Essay on the Trade and Improvement of Ireland," Dublin, 1729; "Captain Middleton's Defense," 1744, and "An Account of the Countries Adjoining Hudson's Bay," London, 1748.

John Beresford

John Beresford, statesman, was born in Dublin, March 14, 1738. He was the second son of Marcus, Earl of Tyrone, whose ancestors first settled in Ireland in 1574. His mother was Barroness Le Poer, heiress and representative of a long line of barons, descending in direct male

succession from Roger Le Poer, a knight who
accompanied Strongbow to Ireland.

From Kilkenny School, John Beresford proceeded to Trinity College, Dublin, where he graduated A. B. in 1757. He then entered at the Middle Temple, studied law for nearly three years,
and was admitted to the bar in 1760. In April,
1761, he was elected member of the Irish Parliament for County Waterford, which constituency
he continued to represent uninterruptedly till
his death,—for forty-four years. He applied
himself with great assiduity to the discharge
of his parliamentary duties, and soon became a
power in the House. In 1768 he was sworn
on the Privy Council, and in 1770 was appointed
a Commissioner of Revenue. Eventually he succeeded to the post of First Commissioner, and
it was under his administration, and much at
his instance, that the new Custom House in
Dublin was built, between 1781 and 1791. It
was also largely through his exertions that the
widening and extending of the Dublin quays,
and the opening up of Sackville and other streets,
were accomplished.

His political position was strengthened in
the year 1774 by his taking as his second wife
Barbara Montgomery, a celebrated beauty, sister of Lady Mountjoy and of the Marchioness
of Townshend. During the administrations of
the Duke of Portland and Lord Temple (1782
to 1783) he confined himself to routine duties,
but on the arrival of the Duke of Rutland, to
whom Pitt had entrusted the government of Ireland, he threw his whole energies into political
affairs.

Holding opinions diametrically opposed to
Grattan and the national party on almost all

questions, he strenuously supported Orde's Trade Propositions, and sided with Pitt in the matter of the Regency. The almost overwhelming power and influence which the Beresfords attained in the government of Ireland was signally put to the test in 1795, when Lord Fitzwilliam went over to Ireland, January 4th, as Lord-Lieutenant, to inaugurate a policy of concession both on religious and political questions. He took Grattan and the leaders of the liberal party into his councils, and Beresford was immediately dismissed from his various offices, although still left in the enjoyment of his salary.

Beresford immediately proceeded to London, where his influence with the Ministry was so great that within a few weeks Lord Fitzwilliam was recalled. The illness of Mrs. Beresford, who expired near London, May 19th, deferred until June 28th a hostile meeting with Lord Fitzwilliam, provoked by strictures made by the latter in letters to Lord Carlisle. The duel was interrupted by a peace officer. Next month Beresford returned to Dublin, and was restored to all his offices.

In the events that soon followed,—the insurrection and the Union,—he sided with Lord Castlereagh and Clare; and few contributed more than he to the successful carrying through of the Union, or had more to do with the fiscal arrangements consequent thereupon. It was a bitter mortification to him that his son, John C. Beresford, threw up a good government appointment and voted against the measure. Before many years were over, however,—in November, 1804,—in a letter to a friend, we find him deploring many of the results of the change. He entered the British Parliament for Waterford.

In 1802 he was, at his own request, relieved from official duties, and the three remaining years of his life were spent between his London residence and Walworth, his seat in County Londonderry. He was all through life devoted to gardening and agriculture. He died, after a short illness, on November 5, 1805. A portion of his correspondence, edited by a grandson, and published in two volumes in 1854, contains valuable information on current events, and remarks upon public characters.

His brother became Marquis of Waterford in 1789, and his grand-nephew, the third Marquis, killed out hunting in 1859, was a nobleman of great sporting notoriety. The influence of the Beresfords is further shown by the fact that among his descendants, within fifty years of his decease, may be counted an archbishop, a bishop, a governor of a colony, a colonial secretary, an M. P., a colonel, a lieutenant-colonel, a knight of the Legion of Honor, a privy-councilor, and several officers of rank; while he had one brother an earl, another an archbishop and a baron; one nephew an archbishop and primate, and another a lieutenant-general.

Richard Southwell Bourke

Richard Southwell Bourke, statesman, Earl of Mayo, was born in Dublin, February 21, 1822. The Bourkes of the County of Kildare, whom he represented, were connected by ties of family and property with the county since the war of 1641-52, when their ancestor, having held a captaincy of horse under the Marquis of Ormond, settled at Kill. Bourke was educated at Trinity College, taking his degree of B. A. in 1844;

LL. D. was subsequently conferred upon him. He traveled in Russia in 1845, and published his experiences in a work entitled "St. Petersburg and Moscow."

In 1849, on the death of his uncle, and his father becoming Earl of Mayo, the honorary title of Lord Naas devolved upon himself. During more than twenty years he sat in parliament,— for Kildare from 1847 to 1852; Coleraine, 1851 to 1857; and Cockermouth, 1857 to 1867,—when, upon the death of his father, August 12, he became Earl of Mayo.

He was an earnest and consistent Conservative, and as such held the post of Chief Secretary for Ireland in each of the three Derby administrations,—March to December, 1852; February, 1858, to June, 1859; June, 1866 to 1868. In 1868 he was appointed Governor-General of India, and Knight of St. Patrick.

He proved to be one of the most able administrators that ever ruled India. In the prime of middle life, and possessed of vigorous health, he evinced great activity of body as well as mind, and was constantly on the alert visiting the portions of his viceroyalty that required inspection. In 1872 he went to the penal settlement at the Andaman Islands, concerning which there had been reports of abuses and maladministration. Returning to embark in the dusk of the evening of February 8, he was assassinated by a convict named Shere Ali, who declared that "he had no accomplices, that it was his fate, and that he had committed the act by the order of God." He had long threatened that he would take the life of some distinguished European in revenge for having been imprisoned for murdering a man in a "blood-feud." Bourke was only able to totter against a truck, and say faintly to his secretary, "They've hit me, Burne," before he expired. The assassin was executed at Calcutta. Lord Mayo's remains were brought back to Ireland, were received in military state in Dublin, and deposited in the family mausoleum near Naas.

A man of genial manners, he was very popular among his associates. He was an enthusiastic sportsman, as well in Ireland as in the fiercer and more dangerous sports of India. (See W. W. Hunter's "Life of the Earl of Mayo," London, 1875.)

John Hely-Hutchinson

John Hely-Hutchinson, lawyer and Provost of Trinity College, Dublin, son of Francis Hely of Gortore, was born in Ireland in 1724. On his marriage to an heiress named Hutchinson in 1751 he assumed the name of Hely-Hutchinson. He was admitted to the bar in 1748, elected to parliament for Lanesborough in 1759, and for Cork in 1761; appointed Prime-Sergeant in 1762, Provost of Trinity College in 1774, Secretary of State for Ireland, and Keeper of the Privy Seal in 1777. In 1783 he obtained a peerage for his wife as Baroness of Donoughmore.

He was at one and the same time Secretary of State, Major of Horse, Provost of Trinity College, and Searcher, Packer, and Gauger of the Port of Strangford. His appointment as provost created some turmoil. As a layman he was considered unsuitable for the post, and became involved in constant disputes with the Fellows and students. Dr. Duigenan wrote a book in opposition to his appointment; a series of satirical pamphlets appeared against him; and he was also involved in several duels. He died at Buxton, September 4, 1794.

He wrote an excellent treatise on the "Commercial Restraints of Ireland." In "Grattan's Life" it is stated that he supported nearly every good measure,—the Claim of Right, free trade, Catholic emancipation and Reform. Taylor, in his "History of the University of Dublin," while admitting that his appointment to the provostship was ill-advised, considers that his administration conferred great benefits on the university.

One of his sons became an earl, another a baron, and others of his numerous descendants were distinguished in the senate, the Church, and the army. His eldest son, Richard, created Earl of Donoughmore, was the untiring advocate of Catholic emancipation. At his death, in 1825, the title devolved upon his brother John, a distinguished general, who succeeded Abercrombie in command of the British army in Egypt. He sat in the Irish Parliament in 1800, voted for the Union, and was created Baron Hutchinson, with a pension of £2,000 per annum. He died in 1832. Richard W. J. Hely-Hutchinson, the present representative of the family, is the sixth Earl of Donoughmore.

Hugh McCalmont Cairns

Hugh McCalmont Cairns, Lord Chancellor, first Earl of Cairns, was born in County Down in December, 1819. He was educated at Belfast Academy and afterwards at Trinity College, Dublin. He received the degree of B. A. in 1838 and went to London to prepare for the bar. He was admitted to the bar of the Middle Temple in January, 1844, and shortly afterwards mi-

grated to Lincoln's Inn, where he soon gained
an extensive practice. In July, 1852, he entered
parliament as member for Belfast and continued
to represent that city as long as he remained at
the bar. In 1856 he was made a Q. C. and a
bencher of Lincoln's Inn.

In February, 1858, when Lord Derby took
office, he was appointed solicitor-general and
knighted, enjoying from this period an enormous
practice. When the Conservatives returned to
power in 1866 he was made attorney-general and
the same year a lord justice of appeal. In 1867
he was created a privy-councillor and Baron
Cairns of Garmoyle, County Antrim. He now
took a very active part in the discussions upon
the Reform bill and made no less than twenty-
four speeches on that bill in the House of Lords.
In February, 1868, upon the resignation of Lord
Derby and the accession of Benjamin Disraeli as
Prime Minister, the latter appointed Cairns Lord
Chancellor. On the defeat of the Conservatives
at the general election, Cairns resigned with Disraeli, and after Lord Derby's death, in 1869, led
the opposition in the House of Lords. His resistance to the disestablishment of the Irish Anglican Church was always vigorous. His speech
on Gladstone's Suspensory bill was printed and
widely circulated. Shortly after this he resigned
the leadership of the Conservative party in the
House of Lords, but again resumed it in 1870.

On the return of the Conservatives to power
in 1874, Cairns was again made Lord Chancellor.
In September, 1878, he was created Viscount
Garmoyle and Earl Cairns in the peerage of the
United Kingdom; but after the Conservative
defeat and his resignation in 1880, he took no
very active part in public life. His health, never

strong, had long been failing, and he spent much of his time on the Riviera, having erected a house at Bournemouth, where he died April 2, 1885, of congestion of the lungs. He received the degree of LL. D. from Cambridge in 1862, D. C. L. from Oxford in 1863, and LL. D. from Dublin in 1867.

He married, in 1856, Mary Harriet MacNeile of Parkmount, County Antrim, by whom he had five sons and two daughters. His second son, Arthur W. Cairns, succeeded to the peerage. Cairns was considered by many the greatest lawyer of his time; his especial characteristic was lucidity. As a speaker he was generally cold and unimpassioned, though in public addresses there were traces of repressed fire. His grasp of political subjects was so sure and his language so clear and forcible that the Conservative party wavered between selecting him or Lord Salisbury or Sir Stafford Northcote for its leader.

William McArthur

Sir William McArthur, Lord Mayor of London, was born at Malin, County Donegal, July 6, 1809. He received his early education at a school in his native county, where Isaac Butt was a fellow pupil. In 1821 he was apprenticed to a woolen draper at Enniskillen. In 1825 he removed to Lurgan and was engaged in mercantile pursuits until 1831, when he formed a partnership in the woolen draper business at Londonderry. In 1835 this partnership was dissolved and McArthur continued the business alone. In 1841 his brother went to Australia and opened a branch of the concern at Sydney. After the discovery of gold the business rapidly increased; other branch houses were opened in Australia, the headquarters of the firm transferred to London, and the McArthurs became wealthy.

In 1857 William McArthur settled in London, and was member of parliament for Lambeth, 1868-85; chosen sheriff of London, June 24, 1867; alderman, September 3, 1872, and Lord Mayor of London, September 29, 1880. He was one of the founders of the London Chamber of Commerce in 1881. In the House of Commons he took an active interest in colonial, educational, and Irish affairs. November 17, 1882, he was made K. C. M. G.

McArthur married Marianne McElwaine, September 5, 1843. He died at London, November 16, 1887, and was interred in Norwood Cemetery. He left about £150,000 to charitable institutions, chiefly connected with the Methodist Church, to which he had belonged.

Frederick William Burton

Sir Frederick William Burton, painter in water-colors and director of the National Portrait Gallery, was born at Corofin House, County Clare, April 8, 1816. He was the son of Frederick and Hannah Mallet Burton. The family removed to Dublin in 1826, where young Burton received his elementary instruction in drawing under the brothers Brocas. His progress in art was so rapid that in 1837, when only twenty-one years of age, he was elected an associate of the Royal Hibernian Academy, of which he became a full member in 1839, acquiring distinction as a painter of miniatures and water-color portraits.

In 1840 he exhibited his picture, "The Blind Girl at the Holy Well," and in the following year, "The Arran Fisherman's Drowned Child."

In 1842 he exhibited at the Royal Academy in London his famous painting, "A Connaught Toilet," which was afterwards burned, with a number of other pictures, at an exhibition in London. Burton spent seven years on the continent, dating from 1851, establishing his headquarters at Munich, where he began the thorough study of German masters. He also found numerous subjects in his wanderings through the forests of Franconia, Nuremberg, and Bamberg, and completed several drawings which he brought with him to London on his annual visits.

In 1855 he was admitted an associate of the Royal Water-Color Society and to full membership in 1856. In 1874 Burton was appointed director of the National Gallery in London. During his administration of twenty years some of the most valuable paintings were added to the British collection, there being some 450 pictures of foreign artists secured within that period.

From the time of his appointment as director of the National Gallery, Burton laid aside the brush and did not even complete work that was well advanced and would have, if completed, added much to his reputation as an artist. On his retirement in 1894 he was knighted, and in 1896 the degree of LL. D. was conferred on him by Trinity College, Dublin.

Burton was a clever writer and deeply interested in antiquarian research, being long a member of the London Society of Antiquarians. A portrait by him of George Eliot is in the National Portrait Gallery. Among his other more important pictures are: "Peasantry of Franconia Waiting for Confession," "The Widow of Wohlin," and "The Meeting of the Turret Stairs." Burton died unmarried at Kensington, England, March

16, 1900, and was interred in Mount Jerome Cemetery, Dublin.

Martin Archer Shee

Sir Martin Archer Shee, author, portrait painter and president of the Royal Academy, was born in Dublin, December 20, 1769. His mother died a few months after his birth. His father becoming blind, and in consequence reduced in circumstances, was compelled to retire to a cottage near the Dargle, where many of young Shee's early years were spent. He evinced a taste for drawing, was admitted to the schools of the Royal Dublin Society, and shortly was enabled to support himself in Dublin by painting portraits.

In 1788, after his father's death, he removed to London, where he studied with the utmost diligence, Edmund Burke's personal introduction to Sir Joshua Reynolds procuring for him admission to the schools of the Royal Academy. His first picture was exhibited in 1789. In 1798 he was elected an associate and in 1800 a member of the academy. His reputation as a portrait painter soon became widely extended.

On the death of Sir Thomas Lawrence, in 1830, he was elected president of the Royal Academy, and was knighted the same year. He was also elected a fellow of the Royal Society, and other honors were showered upon him to which, at that time, Catholics in England were little accustomed.

Shee wrote several poetical pieces, and two novels, "Harry Calverley" and "Old Court," in which were embodied many reminiscences of the neighborhood of Bray. He was instrumental in

procuring the charter for the Royal Hibernian
Academy. In 1845, when at the age of seventy-
six, he resigned as president at the Royal Academy; but a unanimous address was presented
to him by the academicians and associates to continue in office, which he felt unable to refuse.
He continued, therefore, to hold the office until
his death, at Brighton, August 19, 1850. A civil
list pension of £200 a year was conferred upon
him shortly before his death.

Two of his paintings, "The Infant Bacchus"
and a portrait of Morton, the dramatist, are in
the National Gallery, London. He married, December 19, 1796, Mary Power of Youghal, by
whom he left three sons and three daughters.
His "Life," by his son, was issued in two volumes, London, 1860.

Peter Paul Duggan

Peter Paul Duggan, artist, was born in Ireland about 1810, and in early life came to the
United States, devoting his time to the study of
crayon drawing, but occasionally painting in
oils. His portraits were "delicate and truthful."
He subsequently became professor of drawing
in the New York Free Academy, but on account
of poor health was compelled to resign his position. He went to London and later to Paris,
where he died October 15, 1861.

George Barret

George Barret, landscape painter, was born
in Dublin, about 1728. He became a teacher of
drawing in his native town, and gaining the attention of Edmund Burke, upon whose recom-

mendation he was induced to study and design the scenery around Dublin, and shortly afterwards received the prize offered by the Dublin Academy for the best landscape painting. He removed to London in 1762; received £1,500 for three pictures from Lord Dalkeith; was a member of the Incorporated Society of Artists, and in 1764 gained the Society of Arts' premium for the best landscape. He was an active organizer and one of the original members of the Royal Academy, founded in 1768.

He achieved eminent success as an artist, but spent more than he realized, and became bankrupt when his annual income was £2,000. Through the influence of his friend, Edmund Burke, he was appointed master painter of Chelsea Hospital. His principal landscapes were secured by the Dukes of Portland and Buccleuch, but his most important work was the decoration of a room at Norbury Park, which ranks among the most celebrated productions of the art. His works are true delineations of nature and executed with admirable taste. Three of his watercolors are in the National collection at South Kensington. He died at Paddington, England, May 29, 1784. His son George became a successful water-color painter; exhibited chiefly landscapes at the Royal Academy after 1795, and at the Society of Painters in Water-Colors, 1805-42. Another son and daughter were also painters of considerable merit.

Hugh Hamilton

Hugh Hamilton, portrait painter, was born in Dublin, about 1734. He was a student in the Dublin Art School and commenced his career as an artist in crayons at an early age. He settled for a time in London, where he achieved success, and was overwhelmed with orders. In 1771 he exhibited some portraits at the exhibition of the Incorporated Society of Artists, of which he was a member. In 1778 he went to Rome, where he remained for twelve years. By the advice of Flaxman, he turned his attention to oil painting, and subsequently confined himself to painting portraits in that method.

He painted the portraits of many distinguished Irishmen. His picture in the Royal Dublin Society of Dean Kirwan is one of the best known of his works. About 1791 he returned to Dublin, where he resided until his death, in 1806.

Augustus Saint Gaudens

Augustus Saint Gaudens, sculptor, was born in Dublin, March 1, 1848. His mother, Mary McGuinness Saint Gaudens, was a native of that city. His father, Bernard Paul Ernest Saint Gaudens, was born in the Department of Haut Garonne, in the Pyrenees. When only six months old he was brought to the United States by his parents, who settled in New York City. At the age of thirteen he was apprenticed to a cameo-cutter, and for three years worked at this trade. After studying for some time at the art school in Cooper Union and the Academy of Design, he went to Paris, in 1867, to complete his art studies.

He studied at the Petite Ecole for some time, and then entered the studio of Jouffroy, in the Ecole des Beaux Arts, where he worked with Mercier and other noted sculptors of the last century. After three years of study he went to

Rome, where he executed his statue of Hiawatha, which laid the foundation of Saint Gaudens' fame as a sculptor. This masterpiece was purchased by ex-Governor E. D. Morgan of New York. About 1873 Saint Gaudens returned to New York City and made a marble bust of William M. Evarts. His first public commission was for a bronze statue of Admiral Farragut, which was unveiled in Madison Square, New York, in 1880. While still in plaster it was exhibited at the Paris Salon, winning the highest praise from the French critics, and considered to be one of the world's masterpieces.

His other more important productions are his Lincoln, in Lincoln Park, Chicago; the Shaw Memorial, in Boston; the Peace of God, in Rock Creek Cemetery, Washington, D. C.; Diana, on the tower of Madison Square Garden, New York City; Adoration of the Cross, in St. Thomas' Church, New York City; Deacon Chapin, in Springfield, Mass.; John A. Logan, in Grant Park, Chicago, and of General William T. Sherman, in New York City.

Chicago claims two of Saint Gaudens' greatest figures,—those of Abraham Lincoln and General John A. Logan. With his Lincoln statue he won success where other sculptors had failed. It is the resurrection of the great emancipator about to address the people. The Shaw Memorial, unveiled in 1897, occupies a position on Boston Common, and exhibits clear evidence of his genius in illustrating an actual fact in history.

The figure of Deacon Chapin at Springfield, Mass., is one of the most striking pieces of modeling accomplished by Saint Gaudens. The work is called the Puritan and represents a rough-hewn, elderly man in a long coat and steepled hat with a broad brim shading his determined features. The equestrian statue of General William T. Sherman, in New York City, is another high example of Saint Gaudens' art. From every point of view, the whole work is compact with dignity, alive with elevated and inspiring energy.

Saint Gaudens was one of the first American sculptors to produce portraits in bas-relief. Two of his most attractive reliefs are those of Robert Louis Stevenson and the noted French artist, Bastine Le Page. Among other figures that have gone far to make Saint Gaudens famous are his Peter Cooper, in New York City; the portrait reliefs of Dr. James McCosh, in the chapel of Princeton University; of Dr. Bellows, Mrs. Schuyler Van Rensselaer, and Miss Violet Sargent. He also produced a statue of Captain Robert R. Randall, at Sailors' Snug Harbor, Staten Island; of Hamilton Fish and Phillips Brooks, the latter for the city of Boston. He has produced many works of art for private residences, and for churches, libraries and other public institutions. He designed the medal for the Columbian Exposition of 1893. In 1898 Saint Gaudens removed his studio to Paris, France.

Probably the last completed work to leave the hands of the sculptor was his design of the new gold coins for the United States Government in 1907. The latter part of his life was spent in America. He married Augusta F. Homer in 1877. Saint Gaudens was a member of the Society of American Artists, the Architectural League, the National Academy, corresponding member of the Institute of France, and an officer of the Legion of Honor. He received the honorary degree of LL. D. from Harvard, and that of L. H. D. from Princeton. He died at

Cornish, N. H., August 3, 1907, where he had removed and established his studio.

His brother, Louis Saint Gaudens, sculptor, was born at New York City, January 8, 1854; studied at the Ecole des Beaux Arts, Paris, and assisted his brother in many of his productions. He also has executed numerous original works. He is a member of the National Sculpture Society and resides at Windsor, Vt.

George Buchanan Armstrong

George Buchanan Armstrong, founder of the railway mail service, was born in Armagh, October 27, 1822. His mother was a Buchanan and is said to have been distantly related to James Buchanan, fifteenth president of the United States. Young Armstrong came to this country with his parents at an early age and passed his youth in Baltimore, Md. In 1854 he was appointed assistant postmaster at Chicago, Ill., but resigned in 1856 to go into business in New York City. The panic of 1857, however, forced him to close his establishment, and the next year, returning to Chicago, he was given his old position of assistant postmaster. In the spring of 1862, shortly after the Civil War broke out, Armstrong was sent to Cairo, Ill., to superintend the work of forwarding tons of "war mail" which had accumulated at that point. Under his supervision the mail was quickly distributed, and in recognition of his services he was appointed colonel of Illinois volunteers. For a long time Armstrong had conceived the idea of mail distribution on railways. He presented his plan to the government, and July 1, 1864, was authorized by Postmaster-General Montgomery Blair to equip a car for testing the practicability of the new service.   In a compartment car provided for that purpose, on the Chicago and Northwestern Railroad, the first railway postoffice was established by Armstrong, August 28, 1864, and placed in service between Chicago, Ill., and Clinton, Iowa.   Other complete cars were also built by the same company in 1867, from plans furnished by Armstrong, and ran between Boone and Council Bluffs, Iowa.   The advantage of the new system of mail distribution early became apparent and other railroads speedily followed in establishing postal cars on their lines.   When the system had extended to most of the leading roads in the United States, a new department was created at Washington, of which Armstrong was placed in charge as General Superintendent of the Railway Postal Service, April 4, 1869.   He continued in that office until May 3, 1871.   He died at Chicago two days later, May 5, 1871.   In May, 1881, the postal clerks erected a bronze bust to his memory in the Custom House Square at Chicago.

Thomas Byrnes

Thomas Byrnes, famous detective and superintendent of the New York City police, was born in Ireland in 1842.   When a child he was brought to the United States, the family settling in New York City.   After serving in the Civil War with a New York regiment, he joined the police force in December, 1863; became a roundsman in 1867, sergeant two years later, and captain in 1870. His abilities as a leader were displayed in coping with the Orange rioters in 1871.   In 1879 he captured the notorious band of burglars who had looted the vaults of the Manhattan Savings Institution of securities valued at $2,747,700, on the night of October 27, 1878. The criminals were sent to prison for long terms, and Byrnes was appointed to the rank of chief inspector. It was while in this capacity, in charge of the detective bureau in Mulberry street, that Byrnes won his greatest fame. He originated the "third degree" method of securing confessions from criminals. His skill in keeping in touch with the movements of criminals and his wide familiarity with the underworld made Byrnes the most feared man among thieves in America. He did more perhaps to prevent and detect crime than any other man of his time. He established the famous "dead line" in the financial district of New York City, and by instructing his detectives to arrest any man with a criminal record seen south of Fulton street, he rid Wall street and Maiden Lane of professional thieves. He became the intimate friend of Jay Gould, and one of his noteworthy achievements was the capture of a blackmailer who had been trying to extort money from the great financier. Gould showed his appreciation for this service by keeping Byrnes in touch with the stock market, in which operations the inspector cleared an ample fortune.

In April, 1892, Byrnes succeeded William Murray as superintendent of the New York police, from which office he retired in May, 1895. His thirty-two years of service in the police department brought many improvements in handling the criminal classes of the metropolis; and while at the head of the New York Detective Bureau he became well known all over the civilized world.

Byrnes was offered the decoration and title

of chevalier and officer of the Order of the Crown of Italy by King Humbert, but he declined the offer. He died at New York City, May 7, 1910. In religion he was a Catholic. Byrnes compiled a work entitled "The Professional Criminals of America," New York 1886, which has passed through several editions, and is considered a standard publication on criminology.

Kane O'Hara

Kane O'Hara, musician, author of several burlettas or comic operas, was born in Ireland, about 1714. He attained a foremost position in Dublin, and was elected the Vice-President of the Musical Academy, founded mainly through his exertions, in 1758. Next year appeared his burletta of "Midas," written to throw ridicule on Italian operas, and shortly afterwards "Golden Pippin," "Tom Thumb," "April Day," and a musical farce, "The Two Misers." He died in Dublin, June 17, 1782, having been totally blind for some time previous.

Patrick Sarsfield Gilmore

Patrick Sarsfield Gilmore, musician and bandmaster, was born near Dublin, December 28, 1829. In his early youth he became a member of the brass band at Athlone, where he had obtained employment in a mercantile establishment. At the age of nineteen he went to Canada with an English band, and from there to Salem, Mass., where he soon became leader of a military band. In 1858 he organized Gilmore's band at Boston, which speedily made a national reputation. After some short tours the Civil War broke out; he attached his band to the Twenty-fourth Massachusetts Regiment, and upon his arrival at New Orleans was made master of all the bands in the Department of the Gulf by General Banks.

After the close of the war he was the projector of the monster peace jubilees held at Boston in 1869 and 1872. These jubilees, at which he assembled 20,000 singers and 2,000 instrumentalists in specially erected concert halls, spread the name of Gilmore far and wide, and his reputation became international. He made a tour through Europe with his band in 1878, and upon his return was made bandmaster of the 22nd New York Regiment. He traveled through the United States giving concerts, at which he introduced many musical innovations, and became the most "picturesque" leader in the American world of music.

Among his best known compositions, words and music, are: "The Voice of the Departed Soul; or, Death's at the Door," a National Anthem, and "Columbia." His song, "Good News from Home," written during the war, attained a world-wide popularity. He wrote "When Johnny Comes Marching Home Again" (under the pen name of Louis Lambert), which was extremely popular, not only during the war, but many years after its close. Gilmore also wrote a history of the Peace Jubilee of 1869, and a work on scales for the cornet.

To his qualities as a leader he added marvelous industry, executive ability of a high order, and the faculty of attaching to himself his associates by strong and lasting ties. Gilmore's love for the ancient minstrelsy of Ireland made him extremely popular in the United States. In New

York his music deeply touched the people's hearts, and he was himself so well beloved in the community that fourteen years after his death 15,000 people assembled in Madison Square Garden to pay tribute to his memory. His daughter, Mary Sarsfield Gilmore, has written many touching poems on Irish subjects.

Gilmore died of heart failure at St. Louis, Mo., September 24, 1892, during an engagement of his band at the St. Louis Exposition. In religion he was a Catholic. His remains were removed to New York, and interred in Calvary Cemetery, with both military and civic honors.

Garrett Wellesley

Garrett Wellesley, Viscount Wellesley, of Dangan Castle, and Earl of Mornington, was born in Ireland, July 10, 1735. He was the son of Richard Colley, whose aunt married Garrett Wesley of Dangan, County Meath, descended from a family said to have been settled in Ireland since the reign of Henry II. Her son, Garrett Wesley, died childless in 1728, and bequeathed to Colley all his real estate, upon condition that "he and his sons, and the heirs male of his body, assumed and took upon him and them the surname and coat-of-arms of Wesley." Richard Colley changed his name accordingly, and was created Baron Mornington, in 1746. He died January 31, 1758. His descendants, about the year 1796, reverted to what was considered the more correct form of the name,—Wellesley. The Colleys (otherwise spelled Cowley or Cooley) came to Ireland in the reign of Henry VIII. and were granted estates in the neighborhood of Carbery. Henry Colley of Castle Carbery, a captain in

Queen Elizabeth's Irish army, an ancestor of Richard, was knighted by Sir Henry Sidney.

Garrett Wellesley entered Trinity College, Dublin, received the degree of B. A. in 1754, and M. A. in 1757. He succeeded his father as Baron Mornington in 1758, and was created Viscount Wesley (or Wellesley) and Earl of Mornington in 1761. From his earliest years he displayed an aptitude for music. At fourteen he played the harpsichord and organ, and within a short time was able to extemporize fugues on the latter. The degree of Doctor of Music was conferred on him by Trinity College in 1764. Among his other compositions were "Here in Cool Grot" and "Come, Fairest Nymph." He died May, 22, 1781.

By his wife, Anne, daughter of Arthur Hill, Viscount Dungannon (whose family had been settled in Ireland for more than one hundred years), he had seven sons and two daughters. One son, Arthur Wellesley, became the famous Duke of Wellington. Lady Mornington, a somewhat cold and severe woman, who had a difficult struggle to bring up her large family on a small property, heavily encumbered, lived to witness the eminence to which her son attained, and died September 10, 1831.

David Bailie Warden

David Bailie Warden, physician and author, was born in Ireland, in 1778. He was a member of the Society of United Irishmen, and being implicated in the insurrection of 1798, was permitted to go into exile. He came to this country and became distinguished for his scientific attainments and varied learning. For some time Secretary of the United States Legation in France, he was subsequently, for forty years, United States Consul in Paris, where he became a member of the French Academy.

He was the author of numerous works, both in French and English, among which are: "Moral Faculties and Literature of the Negroes," 1810; "Statistical, Political and Historical Account of the United States," 1819; "Bibliotheca Americana," 1831; and "History of the Silk Ball," 1837. Dr. Warden died in Paris, October 9, 1845.

Robert Adams

Robert Adams, surgeon, was born in Ireland about 1791. He entered Trinity College, received the degree of B. A. in 1814, that of M. A. in 1832, and M. D. in 1842. He was elected a fellow of the Royal College of Surgeons in 1818, and subsequently spent some time on the continent to perfect his medical and surgical knowledge. On his return to Dublin he was elected surgeon successively to the Jervis Street and the Richmond Hospitals. He took part in founding the Richmond (afterwards called the Carmichael) School of Medicine, and lectured there on surgery for a number of years.

Adams was three times president of the Royal College of Surgeons, and in 1861 was appointed surgeon to the Queen in Ireland, and regius professor of surgery in the University of Dublin. He gained a high reputation as a surgeon and pathological anatomist. He published a "Treatise on Rheumatic Gout" (London, 1857), which is considered an authentic work on the subject; also he issued an essay on "Disease of the Heart," and contributed articles on "Abnormal Conditions of the Joints" to Todd's Cyclopedia of Anatomy and Physiology. He died January 13, 1875.

Barry Edward O'Meara

Barry Edward O'Meara, surgeon to Napoleon Bonaparte at St. Helena, was born in Ireland in 1786, educated at Trinity College, and at an early age appointed Assistant Surgeon to the 62nd Regiment. He served for some years in Sicily, Egypt and Calabria. In consequence of a duel, he was obliged to quit the army, but soon received an appointment in the navy. He was serving in the Bellerophon when, on July 14, 1815, Napoleon surrendered on board of that vessel. His professional skill and knowledge of Italian gained the favor of the former Emperor, at whose request he was sent with him to St. Helena, as his medical attendant. O'Meara appears to have agreed tolerably well with Sir George Cockburn and Sir P. Malcolm, Governors of St. Helena; but soon after the arrival of Sir Hudson Lowe, misunderstandings arose, and he returned to England in 1818. O'Meara was at first well received by the Admiralty, but having preferred accusations against Lowe for tyrannical and oppressive treatment of Napoleon, his name was erased from the list of naval surgeons. In 1822 he published "Napoleon in Exile; or, A Voice from St. Helena," in which he feelingly depicted the petty annoyances and degrading restrictions to which, he claimed, Napoleon was subjected. He became exceedingly popular, his view of the case being supported by public opinion. He died in London, June 3, 1836, the result of a cold caught while attending one of O'Connell's meetings. O'Meara was twice married.

His granddaughter, Kathleen O'Meara, born in Dublin in 1839, removed to Paris at an early age and adopted a literary profession, becoming well known as a writer of works of fiction under the pen name of Grace Ramsay. Her biographical work also won her a high reputation.

Bryan Higgins

Bryan Higgins, M. D., physician and chemist, was born in County Sligo, about 1737. After obtaining his medical degree, he went to London, where he practiced with considerable success. He early devoted his attention to chemistry, and opened a school for its practical study at London in July, 1774. In 1786 he published his best known work, "Experiments and Observations on Chemical Philosophy." Between 1780 and 1790 he visited Russia, and enjoyed the favor of the Empress Catherine. In 1789 he obtained a patent for a cheap and durable cement. On his return from Russia he resumed his chemical lectures. Dr. Higgins died on his estate of Walford, in Staffordshire, in 1820. His biographer, W. K. Sullivan, gives a full analysis of his works.

William Higgins

William Higgins, chemist, nephew of Bryan Higgins, was born in County Sligo. He graduated at Oxford and received instructions from his uncle in the science in which he afterwards became eminent. In 1791 he was appointed chemist to the Apothecaries' Company of Ireland, at what was then considered a high salary

—£200. In 1795 he was made chemist and librarian to the Royal Dublin Society. He was a man of peculiar habits, with little energy. His style of lecturing was very peculiar, and a number of anecdotes were long remembered of incidents the result of his quaintness. His life was singularly uneventful; he died in 1825.

W. K. Sullivan gives a full account of his discoveries in chemistry, more especially the law of multiple proportion, in which he is said to have anticipated by many years some of Dalton's greatest achievements. Indeed, he may be said to have led the way in the discovery of the atomic theory.

Francis Barker

Francis Barker, M. D., chemist and physician, was born in Waterford the latter part of the eighteenth century. He obtained his degree from the University of Dublin in 1793, and completed his medical education in Edinburgh, where he became intimate with Sir Walter Scott. Previous to the discovery of the voltaic battery, he suggested the identity of the nervous fluid with dynamical electricity. Returning to his native city, he practiced for five years, and took part in the establishment of what has been said to be the first Irish fever hospital. Afterwards, in Dublin, as a chemical lecturer, he became deservedly popular, and started the first medical journal in Ireland.

In 1821, in conjunction with Dr. Cheyne, he published a treatise on "Epidemic Fevers in Ireland," in two volumes; and in 1826 he edited the Dublin Pharmacopœia. Until 1852 he continued Secretary of the Irish Board of Health. He died about 1859.

Richard Barter

Richard Barter, M. D., hydropathic physician, was born in Cooldaniel, County Cork, in 1802. He entered on the duties of his profession as a dispensary physician at Inniscarra, where he was elected honorary secretary of the County of Cork Agricultural Society, and contributed materially to improve the husbandry of the south of Ireland. About the year 1842 Cork was visited by Captain Claridge, an advocate of hydropathy. Dr. Barter, who had been for some time inclining towards the new system, now openly advocated it, and despite the opposition of members of his profession, devoted his talents and energy to its practice. He opened the celebrated water-cure establishment at Blarney. It was mainly through his exertions that Turkish baths were introduced into the British Isles. He died at Blarney, October 3, 1870.

O'Bryen Bellingham

O'Bryen Bellingham, surgeon, was born in Dublin, December 12, 1805. He received his medical education in Dublin. In 1833 he became a member of the College of Surgeons, and not long after examiner in pharmacy and professor. Two years later he was appointed surgeon to St. Vincent's Hospital, where he assiduously labored until his death. He was one of the founders of the Dublin Natural History Society. He died October 11, 1857, and was laid in the burying-place of his ancestors at Castlebellingham. His advocacy of the cure of aneurisms by pressure gained for him European fame.

David MacBride

David MacBride, M. D., one of the most eminent Dublin physicians of his time, was born at
Ballymoney, County Antrim, April 26, 1726. He
served for many years as surgeon in the navy,
and made those observations which resulted in
his valuable treatise on scurvy, published in 1767.
After the peace of Aix-la-Chapelle he left the
service, and studied anatomy under Hunter, and
obstetrics under Smellie. He studied at Ballymoney in 1749, and removed to Dublin in 1751,
where his modesty kept him in the background
for many years.

In 1764 he published his "Experimental Essays on the Fermentation of Alimentary Mix-
tures," a work which, translated almost immediately into French and German, gained for him
a European reputation. The value of his im-
improvements in the art of tanning was recognized by the presentation of medals from more
than one learned society. The results of his
medical experience were given to the world in
1772, in his valuable "Methodical Introduction to
Medicine," afterwards translated into Latin, German, French, and Dutch. Dr. MacBride died at
his home in Dublin, December 28, 1778.

Henry Marsh

Sir Henry Marsh, physician, was born in
Loughrea, County Galway, in 1790. He was line-
ally descended from Francis Marsh, Archbishop
of Dublin. Sir Henry graduated at Trinity College in 1812, but having attached himself to a
sect known as the Walkerites, abandoned the
studies which he had been pursuing, with a view

of entering the church. He turned his attention to medicine and was apprenticed to Philip Crampton.

In 1818 he took his degree, practiced in the Paris hospitals, and in 1820, having settled in Dublin, was appointed physician to Dr. Steevens' Hospital. Henceforth his progress in the medical profession was rapid. He enjoyed an increasing private practice, and held some of the most important and honorable positions connected with Dublin medical charities, and in 1839 he and Surgeon Crampton were created baronets. He died at his residence in Merrion Square, Dublin, December 1, 1860, and was buried in Mount Jerome Cemetery.

Bernard Flaherty

Bernard Flaherty, actor (whose stage name was Barney Williams), was born in Cork in 1823. He came to the United States when a boy, and in 1836 was employed at the old Franklin Theater in New York City. He later became a member of the company, and in 1845 made his appearance at Philadelphia as Mad Sampson in "The Heroic Struggle of 1776." That same year he became manager of Vauxhall Garden in the Bowery, New York City. In 1850 he married Maria Pray, widow of Charles Mestayer, who thereafter appeared with him, chiefly in Irish comedy, with great success.

In company with his wife, he went to San Francisco, in 1845, and the next year sailed for England and made his debut at the Adelphi Theater, London, June 30, 1855, as Rory O'More. After a very successful engagement, he traveled on the continent. Returning to this country in

1859, he played at Niblo's Garden, and subsequently managed Wallack's old Broadway Theater in New York City. He afterwards made annual tours throughout the United States, became one of the most affluent actors of his time, and attained wide popularity as a comedian. He died in New York City, April 25, 1876. He owed much of his success to his wife, who had been an actress of considerable talent from childhood.

John Drew

John Drew, actor, was born in Dublin, September 3, 1825. He came to this country when a boy, and after a somewhat adventurous career, including a voyage at sea, he made his first appearance as an actor at the Richmond Hill theater, New York City. After traveling through the West, he reappeared at the latter city as Dr. O'Toole in "The Irish Tutor." July 27, 1850, he married Louisa Lane Mossop, one of the most noted actresses then on the American stage, and at one time leading lady for Edwin Forrest, Junius Booth, and other noted actors. After their marriage, Drew and his wife acted throughout the United States. In 1852 they began an engagement at the old Arch Street Theater, Philadelphia, appearing in "She Would and She Would Not," and other comedies, with a company which included Frank Drew, brother of John and an actor of much ability.

August 20, 1853, in conjunction with William Wheatley, Drew undertook the management of the Arch Street Theater, but the venture not meeting with success, he made a tour throughout the United States and England. In 1859 he again went abroad, going to Australia and Europe, returning to this country in 1862.

Shortly before his return to the United States, his wife assumed the entire management of the Arch Street Theater, Philadelphia, and there John Drew played several of his roles, such as O'Bryan in "The Irish Emigrant," and Sir Lucius O'Trigger in "The Rivals." He made his last appearance on the stage May 9, and died at Philadelphia May 21, 1862.

Among his most successful characters were Goldfinch in "The Road to Ruin," and Flutter in "The Bell's Stratagem." Mrs. Drew continued in the management of the Arch Street Theater for thirty years after her husband's death, and her house became famous throughout the country as the home of comedy. Some of the most noted performers on the American stage appeared there, among whom were Edwin Booth, Lester Wallack, and Charlotte Cushman. Mrs. Drew died at Larchmont, N. Y., July 2, 1897.

The most distinguished member of the family now living is the son, John Drew, one of the foremost comedians in America at the present time. His sister, Georgiana Drew, married Maurice Barrymore in 1876. Their children, Ethel, John and Lionel Barrymore, occupy prominent places on the stage. No family has, perhaps, produced so many distinguished players or holds a higher place in the annals of the American stage than do the descendants of John Drew.

Patrick Donahoe

Patrick Donahoe, journalist and publisher, was born in County Cavan, March 17, 1811. He came to the United States with his parents at the age of ten, and, at Boston, Mass., where the family settled, young Donahoe received his early education. He subsequently learned the compositor's trade and, while serving in this capacity on several Boston papers, acquired a knowledge of journalism. In 1836 he founded the Boston Pilot, a Catholic weekly paper, which became a a great success, and attained a wide circulation. In addition to his paper Donahoe established a publishing house, and a Catholic book and church goods store.

In the banking and publishing business he acquired wealth and influence. He was a generous subscriber to charity, and took a leading part in organizing several Irish-American regiments for service in the Union army during the Civil War. His misfortunes began in 1872, when the great Boston fire of that year destroyed his property, the loss of which amounted to more than $300,000. Immediately resuming business, he was burned out the second and third time within a few years, and as most of the insurance companies had also failed, his loss was almost total. The failure of friends, whose paper he had indorsed, cost him $200,000 more. In 1876 his bank suspended payment, with a heavy indebtedness to depositors, which obliged him to place his entire possessions at the disposal of his creditors.

The Pilot passed into the hands of Archbishop Williams of Boston and John Boyle O'Reilly. Donahoe, at the advanced age of sixty-five, began business anew, resumed his foreign exchange and passenger agency, established Donahoe's Magazine in 1878, and shortly after the death of John Boyle O'Reilly, he again came into the possession of the Pilot. The Laetare medal, an honor given once a year to Catholic laymen for distinguished service, by the University of Notre Dame, Ind., was conferred on him in 1890. He died in Boston, Mass., March 18, 1901. In May, 1894, three hundred of Boston's most influential citizens assembled at the Tremont House to felicitate him on the completion of his eightieth year.

Hugh O'Brien

Hugh O'Brien, journalist and politician, was born in County Fermanagh, July 13, 1827. He came to the United States with his parents at the age of five and received a common-school education at Boston, Mass. At the age of twelve he was apprenticed to learn the printer's trade in the office of the Boston Courier, and became foreman in a book and job establishment at fifteen. Several years later he founded the Shipping and Commercial List, of which he was long the editor and publisher, and for many years was an authority on matters relating to the trade and commerce of Boston.

He was a member of the Board of Aldermen, 1875-77, 1879-81 and 1883, and was chairman of the board for four years. In December, 1884, he was elected Mayor of Boston, and held that office four terms, until 1888. As Alderman and Mayor, covering a period of eleven years of active service, he carried out various reforms and improvements in the city government. O'Brien was president of the Union Institution of Savings, treasurer of the Franklin Typographical Society for fifteen years, and trustee of St. Vincent's Orphan Asylum. He died at Somerville, Mass., in 1895.

James Jeffrey Roche

James Jeffrey Roche, editor and poet, was born at Mountmellick, Queens County, May

31, 1847, son of Edward and Margaret Doyle Roche. His parents removed to Prince Edward Island the same year young Roche was born, where the boy received a classical education at St. Dunstan's College, Charlottetown. James came to the United States in 1866 and engaged in commercial pursuits at Boston, and contributed articles to several newspapers and periodicals. In 1883 he became assistant editor of the Boston Pilot, of which John Boyle O'Reilly was editor, and on the latter's death, in 1890, Roche was made editor-in-chief.

He was a member of the Metropolitan Park Commission, Boston, in 1893. Roche was the author of "Songs and Satires," 1886; "Life of John Boyle O'Reilly," 1891; "The Story of the Filibusters," 1891; "Ballads of the Blue Water," 1895; "Her Majesty the King," 1898; "By-ways of War," 1899. In 1904 Roche was appointed United States Consul at Genoa, Italy, and in 1907 Consul at Berne, Switzerland, where he died April 3, 1908. His remains were returned to America and interred at Boston. Roche received the honorary degree of LL. D. from the University of Notre Dame in 1891.

Patrick Walsh

Patrick Walsh, journalist and United States Senator, was born at Ballingarry, County Limerick, January 1, 1840, son of Michael and Mary Hays Walsh. He came to the United States with his parents at the age of twelve, the family settling at Charleston, S. C., where young Walsh was apprenticed to the printer's trade. He subsequently studied at Georgetown College, D. C., until the Civil War broke out, when he returned to South Carolina and served for a short time in the army. He removed to Augusta, Ga., in 1862, obtained employment as a printer on the Daily Constitution, and rose steadily in the newspaper business until, in 1877, he became editor and proprietor of the Augusta Chronicle. Previously, in 1866, he was made southern agent of the New York Associated Press.

In 1872 Walsh was elected to the State Legislature, and in 1880 was a delegate to the National Democratic Convention which nominated General W. S. Hancock for President. In 1884 he was a delegate-at-large to the National Convention held at Chicago, that nominated Grover Cleveland. For four years he was the Georgia member of the National Democratic Executive Committee, and member-at-large of the World's Columbian Exposition in 1893. In April, 1894, Walsh was appointed by the governor to fill the unexpired term as United States Senator of Alfred H. Colquitt, who died, and served in the Senate until March 4, 1895. He was elected Mayor of Augusta in 1897. Walsh was married, in 1866, to Anna I. McDonald of South Carolina. He died at Augusta, Ga., March 19, 1899.

John Binns

John Binns, journalist, was born in Dublin, December 22, 1772. His father, who died when he was two years old, left considerable property and John received an excellent education. At the request of his elder brother, who inherited the estate of his father, he accompanied him to London in 1794. Shortly after his arrival he became a member of the London Corresponding Company, which was afterwards an influential

political association. He later became a member
of the United Irishmen, was arrested, but was
acquitted. February 21, 1798, he left London,
bound for France, but was rearrested at Margate, and after an examination by the privy council, was committed to the Tower of London. At
Maidstone Binns was tried, with Arthur O'Connor, for high treason, but acquitted. Shortly
afterwards he was again arrested and confined in
Clerkenwell prison, whence he was transferred
to Gloucester, where he remained until March,
1801.

In July of that year he emigrated, with his
brother, Benjamin, to Baltimore, Md. Proceeding to Northumberland, Pa., he founded, in
March, 1802, the Republican Argus, which gave
him great influence with the Democratic party.
From 1807 to 1829 Binns conducted, at Philadelphia, the Democratic Press—the leading
paper in the state, until, in 1824, it opposed the
election of Andrew Jackson. In December, 1822,
he was chosen alderman of the city of Philadelphia, an office which he held until 1844. In
1850 he published "Binns' Magistrate's Manual,"
and in 1854, "Recollections of the Life of John
Binns." He died in Philadelphia, June 16, 1860.

Joseph Burbridge McCullagh

Joseph Burbridge McCullagh, journalist,
"Father of the Interview," was born in Dublin,
in 1843. He came to the United States at the
age of eleven and secured employment as an ap-
prentice in the office of a weekly paper in New
York City. In 1858 he went to St. Louis, where
he served first as a compositor and later as a
reporter on the St. Louis Democrat. Shortly

afterwards he became connected with the Cincinnati Commercial, and on the outbreak of the civil war was made war correspondent for that paper at Washington, D. C. His letters, signed "Mack," soon made him very popular.

McCullagh was with Grant's army in the early part of the war, and the general and correspondent grew to be fast friends, their intimacy continuing until the former's death. He was on one of the boats that ran the shore batteries past Vicksburg to cut off supplies coming up the Mississippi river. McCullagh was also with Sherman's army on its march through Georgia.

It was after the war that he became famous as an interviewer for the press. He traveled through the South and wrote up his observations for the Cincinnati Commercial. During the tour he sent a long article, containing an interview with Alexander H. Stephens, ex-vice-president of the Confederacy, which is said to have been the first interview of the kind ever given to the public. He was also a frequent visitor at the White House during the administration of President Johnson and for some time was chief medium of communication between the president and the public.

From 1868 to 1870 he was managing editor of the Cincinnati Enquirer. In the latter year he purchased an interest in the Chicago Republican (now the Inter Ocean), which was burnt out during the great fire of 1871. Removing to St. Louis, McCullagh became editor of the Democrat, but when the managers disagreed as to the policy of the paper he founded and edited the Globe. In 1873 the two papers were consolidated as the Globe-Democrat, of which Mc-

Cullagh was made editor-in-chief, a position which he occupied at the time of his death.

McCullagh was considered one of the best newspaper correspondents of the country and is credited with being the originator of the modern style of newspaper interviewing. He was a writer of force and ability, a tireless worker, possessed of striking genius in gathering news. He died as a result of a fall from a second story window at the residence of his sister-in-law, at St. Louis, Mo., December 31, 1896. His remains were interred in Bellefontaine cemetery.

Peter Fenelon Collier

Peter Fenelon Collier, publisher, was born in Myshall, County Carlow, December 12, 1849, son of Robert and Catherine Fenelon Collier. At the age of seventeen he came to this country and secured employment in the car shops at Dayton, Ohio. By thrift and economy he was soon able to save sufficient money out of his small wages to enter St. Mary's Seminary, at Cincinnati, Ohio, where he remained four years.

On leaving school he obtained a position as book salesman in the publishing house of Sadlier & Co., of New York. He canvassed from door to door and prospered from the start. Before long he embarked in the publishing business on his own account, and with only a few hundred dollars' capital, he purchased the electrotype plates of "Father Burke's Lectures," a popular Catholic work. Though obliged to borrow money for materials and printing, he made such a success of the venture that his profits the first year amounted to nearly $100,000. In 1874 he published the "Life of Pius IX.," and his business grew to such an extent that branch houses were established in several large cities.

Collier was exceedingly successful in publishing the complete works of popular standard authors, issued in a series of volumes comprising extensive sets for the household library, including the best of fiction, poetry, essays, histories, encyclopedias, and several editions of the Bible. A pioneer in the installment plan of payment for these popular editions, he was able to reach a large number of people, and by this method sold millions of volumes throughout the United States and Canada.

His first venture in the periodical field, Once a Week, was ultimately transformed into Collier's Weekly, with which he made a fortune. The energy and fearlessness of this paper, both in editorial and business departments, gives it a foremost position in current topics and national affairs. He was an enthusiast on out of door sports, being an expert polo player, and almost daily was in the saddle. At his home in New Jersey he kept a pack of hounds, with which he hunted in the surrounding country. He married, in 1875, Catherine Louise Dunn. Collier was a member of the Ohio Society, the American Academy of Political and Social Science, the United States Catholic Historical Society, the New York Historical Association, and many clubs. He died in New York City, April 24, 1909, being survived by his wife and only child, Robert J. Collier.

As founder of Collier's Weekly and the head of P. F. Collier & Son, he ranked as one of the most successful publishers in America. His son, Robert, born in New York, June 17, 1876, graduated A. B. at Georgetown University, Washington, D. C., and afterwards studied at Oxford University, England, and at Harvard College in this country. He succeeded his father as head of the publishing house of P. F. Collier & Son.

Edwin Lawrence Godkin

Edwin Lawrence Godkin, journalist, was born in Moyne, County Wicklow, October 2, 1831. His father, Rev. James Godkin, a Presbyterian clergyman, was a supporter of the Young Ireland party and the cause of Home Rule. In 1848, he was forced out of his pulpit, when it became known that he was the author of "Repeal Essays." Lawrence graduated at Queens College, Belfast, in 1851, and in the same year went to London and began the study of law in Lincoln's Inn. He began his journalistic career in 1853, and served as war correspondent for the London Daily News in the Crimean War. In 1856 he came to the United States and made a tour of the South, writing up the country for the London Daily News. Godkin returned to New York City in the spring of 1857, studied law, and was admitted to the bar, February 6, 1858. During the civil war he was on the editorial staff of the New York Times and correspondent for the London Daily News. In July, 1865, he founded and became editor of the Nation, a weekly journal. When the Nation was made the weekly edition of the New York Evening Post, in 1881, he continued as one of the editors, and on the retirement of Carl Schurz, in 1883, he was made editor-in-chief, which office he continued until 1899, when he retired on account of ill health. Godkin was eminently distinguished for his work of exposing the spoils system in American politics.

The ardor and fearlessness with which he fought against political corruption brought him a great reputation. He was a lifelong Home Ruler, and was present in the House of Commons when Gladstone's Home Rule bill passed its third reading. In 1870 he declined the Chair of History at Harvard University. He served for some time as civil service commissioner under Mayor Strong of New York. Godkin was married twice—first, in 1859, to Frances E. Foote, of New Haven, Conn., who died April 11, 1875. In 1884 he married Katherine Sands. He was the author of "The History of Hungary and the Magyars: From the Earliest Period to the Close of the Late War," in 1853, second edition, 1856; "Reflections and Comments," 1895; "Problems of Democracy," 1896, and "Unforeseen Tendencies of Democracy," 1898. He died at Greenway, Devon, England, May 21, 1902, being survived by his second wife and by his son, Lawrence Godkin, who rose to prominence at the New York bar.

Edmund Bailey O'Callaghan

Edmund Bailey O'Callaghan, historian, was born at Mallow, County Cork, February 29, 1797, where he was carefully educated. About 1820 he went to Paris and began the study of medicine. In 1823 he immigrated to Canada and completed his medical studies at Quebec, where he was admitted to practice, in 1827. He also became active in public affairs and joined in organizing the Society of the Friends of Ireland. In 1830 he removed to Montreal, where he took a prominent part in public meetings and wrote political articles. In 1834 he became editor of the Vindicator, the organ of Canadian independence, and in 1835 was elected for Yamaska to the Assembly of Lower Canada.

After the insurrection of 1837 he removed to Albany, N. Y., where he practiced medicine and also edited the Northern Light, an industrial journal. Impressed with the richness of the colonial documents and old Dutch records preserved at Albany, he determined to translate and edit this valuable material on the early history of New York state. In 1846 appeared the first volume of his "History of New Netherlands, or New York Under the Dutch." This work, which has since gone through several editions, marked an epoch in historical research in the United States. It was the first authentic history of early New York.

For some years O'Callaghan was attached to the office of the secretary of state at Albany and edited the records embodied in the fourteen volumes of "The Documentary History of the State of New York," 1849-51. One of the results of this work was J. R. Brodhead's mission to consult the archives of the chief European countries for additional material on the colonial history of New York. O'Callaghan was requested to edit data thus secured, and he did so, producing eleven volumes of "Documents Relative to the Colonial History of the State of New York" (procured in Holland, England and France, by John Romeyn Brodhead, Albany, 1855). These may well serve as a monument to his rare skill and ability.

In 1870 he removed to New York City, and there undertook the translation and arrangement of the municipal archives, but the city later refused to supply the requisite money, and the work was discontinued. He died in New York City, May 27, 1880. Among his other works are: "Jesuit Relations," 1847; "The Register of New Netherland" (1626 to 1674), Albany, 1865; "A Calendar of Historical Manuscripts in the Office of the Secretary of State," Albany, 1866; "A List of Editions of the Holy Scriptures and Parts Thereof Printed in America Previous to 1860, with Notes," Albany, 1861, and "The Voyage of George Clark to America," 1867.

O'Callaghan was a member of the Catholic Union and a donor to St. Mary's Church at Albany. In 1846 he was made honorary M. D. by the University of St. Louis, and later LL. D. by St. John's College, Fordham, N. Y.

John Daly Burk

John Daly Burk, historian and dramatist, was born in Ireland, said to be descended from the ancient House of Clanricard. He received his education at Trinity College, Dublin, where his republican principles made him obnoxious to the government. He came to America in 1796. The same year he established in Boston, Mass., a paper called the Polar Star and Daily Advertiser, which was discontinued the next year, whereupon he removed to New York City. Here he began the publication of the Time Piece, but being arrested under the sedition law for publishing a libel, he removed to Petersburg, Va., and devoted himself to literature and the practice of law.

His principal works are: "Bethlem Gabor," a historical novel; "Bunker Hill," a tragedy; "History of the Late War in Ireland," Philadelphia, 1799, and a "History of Virginia from

Its First Settlement" (three volumes, 1804), down to the commencement of the revolutionary war. Burk was killed in a duel with Felix Coquebert in consequence of a political dispute, April 11, 1808. His son, John Junius, born in Virginia, became a prominent lawyer and subsequently judge of the State Court of Louisiana. (See a Memoir of Burk by Charles Campbell, Albany, 1868.)

Ossian or Oisin

Ossian, or Oisin, the heroic poet of the Gael, was born in Ireland in the third century. Although his name is constantly to be met in the legends of the time, there is very little definitely known concerning him. In Gaelic story, Ossian was the son of Finn MacCool, a celebrated hero, who flourished in the third century, A. D. Finn gathered about him a band of warriors like himself, who were collectively termed the Feni or Fenians. The adventures and exploits of these heroes, and especially of the principal figures in the group,—of Finn himself, magnanimous and wise; of his grandson Oscar, chivalrous and daring; of his nephew Dermot, handsome and brave; of his rival Goll, the one-eyed; and Conan, the villain of the band—their jealousies, dissensions, and final overthrow, constitute the literature of the Feni.

Ossian himself fought at Gawra, where the Fenian power was entirely broken. He is fabled after the battle to have been spirited away to the land of perpetual youth and not to have appeared again on earth until the days of St. Patrick. One of the Fenian lays (published with a translation by the Ossianic Society in 1857) gives an ac-

count of his interview with the Saint, his longing
for the great pagan past, his grief at the loss of
his heroic Fenian companions, and his contempt
for the new religion and its professors.   There
are two earlier cycles.   The first of these extended from unknown antiquity until the settlement of the Gael in Ireland.

The legends of this period preserve traditions of the old divinities of the race, notably the
Tuatha De Danann, under the guise of earlier
colonists whom the Gael conquered and displaced.   Several tales of this cycle are preserved,
among which the fate of the Children of Turenn
and the fate of the Children of Lir are the best
known.   The second, and perhaps the richest
epoch in Gaelic romance, is that of the hero
Cuchullin.   The date is about the commencement
of the Christian era, when Conor MacNessa
ruled Ulster and Queen Meave ruled Connaught.
The great literary product of this period is the
Cattle Spoil of Cooley, the Iliad of the Gael.

Eventually the legends of the Feni partly absorbed and totally eclipsed the earlier traditions;
so the Ossianic literature is now but another
name for the heroic literature of the Gael.   These
traditions have come down from the misty past
in tale and ballad.   They were early reduced to
writing, and as time goes on we observe great
development in incident and detail.   The leader
of the Feni is at one time a god, at others a hero,
a king, a giant, but usually a great warrior, as
wise as brave.   But the literary forms in which
the legends are preserved remains practically un-
changed.   A Gaelic tale is of a distinct type—
narrative prose with verse interspersed.   Gaelic
poetry, older and later, is ever rhymed lyric verse.

To the majority of people Ossian is known

through the publications of James Macpherson,
a Scotch writer. In 1760-63 he published
"Fingal," an epic poem, in six books; "Temora," another epic, in eight books; with a number of shorter pieces, epic and dramatic—
all purporting to be translations of poems composed by Ossian, the son of Fingal. In 1780 Dr.
Smith of Campbeltown issued a volume of Sean
Dana, or ancient poems composed by Ossian, and
in 1787 Baron Edmund de Harold, an Irishman
in the service of the Elector Palatine, printed at
Dusseldorf seventeen so-called Ossianic poems
in English.

The genuineness of Macpherson's Ossian
was early called in question by Dr. Johnson and
others. It is maintained that Macpherson had
jumbled together persons and periods to an un-
warrantable extent; that his originals, so far as
he had any, were not Scottish, but Irish. If this
were all that could be said one would feel justified in regarding, with Professor Windisch of
Leipzig, Macpherson's Ossian as a legitimate development of the old traditions. For the legends
of the Feni are the common property of the Gael,
whether in Ireland, Scotland, or Man. It is no
doubt absurd to represent Finn, whom Macpherson, after Barbour, calls Fingal, as a mighty
monarch, at one time successfully fighting the
Roman legions in the third century—at another
assisting Cuchullin, who lived in the beginning
of the first century, to expel from Ireland the
Norsemen, who made their appearance for the
first time in the end of the eighth. According to
the Gaelic tale, his father, Cool, sets up as king
of Alba, and the kings of Ireland and Scandi-
navia combine to effect his overthrow, while the
son is ever fighting Norsemen.

Gaelic literature supplies material for epics and dramas, but the epic and dramatic, as literary forms, were unknown to the people. The dim and shadowy characters of Macpherson are in sharp contrast to the clear-cut features of the Gaelic heroes. Rarely does this author make a definite statement of fact; but when he does, as when, for example, he arms the old Gaels with bows and arrows, he blunders hopelessly. In the opening of Book III. of Cathloda, the author inquires regarding the origin and issue of things, but he is indebted for his answer rather to Bishop Berkeley than to the son of Finn.

The only Gaelic printed in the author's lifetime was Temora, Book VII. Ossian was published in all the languages of Europe before he appeared in his own. And when at length the edition of 1807 did appear there were Gaelic texts for only one-half of the poems, and for about three-fourths of the matter published by Macpherson in English forty-five years previously. For the others, no "original," ancient or modern has ever yet been found. The idioms and constructions are colorless, and show traces of classical training rather than of the turns of phrase characteristic of native authors. The archaic orthography of the seventh book of Temora is adduced by Dr. Clark of Kilmall as proof of the antiquity of the writing. The truth seems to be that these so-called translations were essentially the compositions of James Macpherson, and that the Gaelic texts were prepared with or without aid from his friends, but how and when we do not know. (See the poems of Ossian, 1762-63; Brook's "Reliques of Gaelic Poetry," 1789, "Ossian," 1807; "Transactions of the Ossianic Society of Dublin," 6 volumes, 1854-61;

"Dean of Lismore's Book," 1862, and Clerk's "Ossian," 1870.)

William Allingham

William Allingham, poet, was born at Bally-shannon, County Donegal, March 19, 1824. He entered the bank with which his father was connected at the age of thirteen, and strove to perfect the scanty education he had received at a boarding school by a vigorous course of self-improvement. At the age of twenty-two he received an appointment in the customs, successfully exercised for several years at Donegal, Ballyshannon, and other towns in Ulster. He nevertheless paid almost annual visits to London, the first in 1843, about which time he contributed to Leigh Hunt's "Journal," and in 1847 he made the personal acquaintance of Leigh Hunt, who introduced him to Carlyle and other men of letters.

Through Coventry Patmore he became known to Tennyson as well as to Rossetti. The correspondence of Tennyson and Patmore attests the high opinion which both entertained of the poetical promise of the young Irishman. His first volume, entitled simply "Poems," published in 1850, with a dedication of Leigh Hunt, was, nevertheless, soon withdrawn, and his next venture, "Day and Night Songs," though reproducing many of the earlier poems, was on a much more restricted scale. Its decided success justified the publication of a second edition next year, with the addition of a new title-piece, "The Music Master," an idyllic poem which had appeared in the volume of 1850, but had undergone so much refashioning as to have become almost a new work.

A second series of "Day and Night Songs" was also added. The volume was enriched by seven very beautiful wood-cuts after designs by Arthur Hughes, as well as one by Millais and one by Rossetti, which rank among the finest examples of the work of these artists in book illustration. Allingham was at this time on very intimate terms with Rossetti, whose letters to him, the best that Rossetti ever wrote, were published by Dr. Birkbeck Hill in the "Atlantic Monthly" for 1896. Allingham afterwards dedicated a volume of his collected works to the memory of Rossetti, "whose friendship brightened many years of my life, and whom I never can forget." Many of the poems in this collection obtained a wide circulation as halfpenny ballads.

June 18, 1864, he obtained a pension of £60 on the civil list, and this was augmented to £100, January 21, 1870. In 1863 Allingham was transferred from Ballyshannon, where he had again officiated since 1856, to the customs house at Lymington. In the preceding year he had edited "Nightingale Valley" (reissued in 1871 as "Choice Lyrics and Short Poems, or Nightingale Valley"). In 1864, he edited "The Ballad Book" for the "Golden Treasury" series, and in the same year appeared "Laurence Bloomfield in Ireland," a poem of considerable length in the heroic couplet, evincing careful study of Goldsmith and Crabbe, and regarded by himself as his most important work.

Another reprint from "Fraser" was the "Rambles of Patricius Walker," lively accounts of pedestrian tours, which appeared in book form in 1873. In 1865 he published "Fifty Modern Poems," six of which had appeared in earlier collections. Except for "Songs, Ballads and

Stories" (1877), chiefly reprints, and an occasional contribution to the Athenaeum, he printed little more verse until the definitive collection of his poetical works in six volumes (1888-93); this edition included "Thought and Word," "An Evil May-Day: A Religious Poem," which had previously appeared in a limited edition, and "Ashley Manor" (an unacted play), besides an entire volume of short poems entitled "Blackberries," which had been previously published in 1884.

In 1870, Allingham retired from the civil service, and removed to London as sub-editor of "Fraser's Magazine," of which he became editor four years later. August 22, 1874, he married Miss Helen Paterson, known under her wedded name as a distinguished water-color painter. He conducted the magazine with much ability. His editorship was made memorable by the publication in the magazine of Carlyle's "Early Kings of Norway," given to him as a mark of regard by Carlyle, whom he frequently visited. After the termination of his connection with "Fraser," in 1879, he took up his residence in Surrey, whence in 1888 he removed to Hampstead with a view to the education of his children. His health was already much impaired by the effects of a fall from horseback, and he died about a year after his settlement at Lyndhurst Road, Hampstead, November 18, 1889. His remains were cremated at Woking.

Allingham was an excellent poet, simple, clear and graceful, with a distinct, though not obtrusive, individuality. His best work is concentrated in his "Day and Night Songs" (1854), which, whether pathetic or sportive, whether expressing feeling or depicting scenery, whether upborne by simple melody or embodying truth in symbol, always fulfil the intention of the author and achieve the character of works of art. Two portraits, one representing Allingham in middle, the other in later life, are reproduced in the collected edition of his poems. A collection of prose works entitled "Varieties in Prose" was posthumously published in three volumes in 1893.

Edmund O'Donovan

Edmund O'Donovan, war correspondent, was born at Dublin, September 13, 1844, son of Dr. John O'Donovan, the eminent Irish scholar. Edmund was educated at St. Francis Xavier's College and at the Royal College of Science, Dublin. He subsequently studied medicine at Trinity College, but never graduated. He began his journalistic career by contributions to the Irish Times and other Dublin papers. From 1866 to 1870 he made several journeys to France and the United States, and, while in this country, continued his medical studies at New York City.

When the Franco-German war broke out he joined the French army, took part in the battles around Orleans, was wounded and made prisoner. While confined at Straubing, in Bavaria, he gave the account of his experiences to several Dublin and London papers. He went to Spain during the Carlist rising of 1873, and his letters were published in the London Times and London Hour.

When Bosnia and Herzegovina rose against the Turks in 1876 he went to the seat of war as correspondent of the London Daily News, and the following year went to Asia Minor as representative of the same paper during the war between Russia and Turkey.

In 1879, as representative of the London
Daily News, O'Donovan undertook his famous
journey to Merv—a most daring and perilous
feat. After remaining some time with the Russian advanced posts on the southeastern shores
of the Caspian sea, he traveled through Khoras-
san, and finally, with great difficulty, accompanied by two native servants, he penetrated to
Merv. Suspected by the Turcomans of being an
emissary of the Russians, he was for several
months not permitted to leave and in danger of
death at any time, with no prospects of release.
He finally managed to send a message to John
Robinson, manager of the Daily News, explain-
ing his position, and immediate steps were taken
to effect his release. But meanwhile, by his own
courage and diplomacy, he succeeded in extricat-
ing himself from this perilous position.

On returning to London he was received
with enthusiasm, and in 1882 O'Donovan described his experiences in a work entitled "The
Merv Oasis—Travels and Adventures East of
the Caspian During the Years 1879, 1880 and
1881." The work is skillfully written, and his
courage and ingenious resources merit warm
admiration.

O'Donovan went to the Soudan in 1883,
again as representative of the Daily News, and
attached himself to the army of Hicks Pasha on
its march to Obeid. November 3, 1883, the army
fell into an ambush and was annihilated. No
news was ever received of O'Donovan's fate, but
there can be no doubt that he perished with the
rest. Probate of his will, however, was not
granted until eight years later, as there was a
hope among some that he might yet be alive.
O'Donovan was a tall, fine-looking man, **very**

genial and popular. With a restless spirit and striking courage, he was ever in search of adventure. He was a good linguist, speaking several languages, had a knowledge of medicine, was a fair draughtsman, and a good surveyor.

Richard Robert Madden

BY WILLIAM DILLON

Richard Robert Madden, physician, politician and writer, was born in Dublin, August 22, 1798, the youngest son of Edward Madden, a silk manufacturer of that city. My maternal grandmother, Mrs. Hart (born Teresa O'Hara), was born in the same year as Dr. Madden. The O'Hara and Madden families lived near one another in the city of Dublin. The young people of both families were much together, and hence it came about that Dr. Madden and my grandmother formed in their early youth a friendship which lasted through life.

Young Madden was educated in a private school in Dublin, and studied medicine in Paris, Naples and London. From 1824 to 1827 he traveled in the Levant, returning to England in 1828. The following year he was elected a member of the College of Surgeons, and made a fellow in 1855. In 1833 he was sent to Jamaica as one of the special magistrates appointed to abolish slavery on the plantations. His zeal in behalf of emancipation was met with bitter opposition by the planters of his district and the supporters of the system in England, and he resigned in November, 1834. After a tour of the American continent he returned to England, and, in 1836, was made superintendent of liberated Africans and judge arbitrator in the mixed court of commission, at Havana, Cuba. He remained there until 1840, when he accompanied Sir M. Montefiore on his philanthropic mission to Egypt.

In 1841 he was appointed special commissioner to investigate the slave traffic on the west coast of Africa and exposed the iniquitous method known as the "pawn system," which amounted to slavery under disguise. From 1843 to 1846 he was special correspondent of the London Morning Chronicle at Lisbon, and in 1847 was appointed colonial secretary of Western Australia. Returning to Ireland in 1848, on furlough, he resigned his Australian office two years later, in order to accept the secretaryship of the Loan Fund Board in Dublin Castle. This office he held until 1880.

As an author he is best known by his work entitled "The United Irishmen—Their Lives and Times" (1845-46, new edition 1874), a work of great importance, giving in detail the causes and events that led to the rebellion of 1798; also an authoritative account of the principal actors in that memorable struggle.

Among his other publications are: "Travels in Turkey, Egypt, Nubia and Palestine in 1824-27," 1829; "The Mussulman" (a novel), 1830; "The Infirmities of Genius," 1833; "Twelve Months' Residence in the West Indies, During the Transition from Slavery to Apprenticeship," 1835; "The Slave Trade and Slavery," 1843; "Connection of the Kingdom of Ireland with the Crown of England," 1845; "History of the Penal Laws Enacted Against Roman Catholics," 1847; "The Island of Cuba—Its Resources, Progress and Prospects," 1849; "Shrines and Sepulchres of the Old and the New World," 1851; "The Life and Martyrdom of Savonarola," 1853; "The Literary Life and Correspondence of the Countess of Blessington," 1855; "The Turkish Empire in Its Relation with Christianity and Civilization," 1862, and "History of Irish Periodical Literature from the End of the Seventeenth to the Middle of the Nineteenth Century," 1867.

Dr. Madden was a member of the Royal Irish Academy and a corresponding member of the Society of Medical Science. He was a zealous Catholic and an ardent and patriotic supporter of the interests of Ireland. He married Harriet Elmslie, of Jamaica, in 1828, by whom he had three sons.

As a boy, and afterwards as a young man, I knew Dr. Madden very well, and used to see him frequently. Having traveled much, he was a most interesting talker. I can clearly remember how I used to listen with delight as he talked to my grandmother or to my father or mother, and gave an account of some of his varied experiences. He was very tall, about six feet two or three inches, and quite a handsome man. I have heard my grandmother say that he improved with age and was handsomer in after life than he had been as a young man. I left Ireland in December, 1879. Dr. Madden was then over eighty years of age, but he was still quite vigorous and in full possession of his mental faculties. Dr. Madden died at his home near Dublin, February 5, 1886, and was buried in Donnybrook cemetery.

Mayne Reid

Captain Mayne Reid (originally Thomas Mayne Reid), writer of boys' stories and soldier

of fortune, was born at Ballyroney, County
Down, in April, 1818. At the age of sixteen he
was sent to college to prepare for the ministry,
but, disliking that profession, at twenty he emigrated to America, where he led a roving and adventurous life, trading and hunting with the
trappers and Indians along the Red and Missouri
rivers. He, in turn, became storekeeper, negro
overseer, schoolmaster, actor and journalist.

In 1843 he settled in Philadelphia, devoted
his time to literature, and became the friend of
Edgar Allan Poe. When the Mexican war broke
out he obtained a commission in a New York volunteer regiment and sailed for Vera Cruz, in December, 1846. He distinguished himself at the
storming of Chapultepec, where he was severely
wounded. Returning to the United States in
1848, he remained in Ohio until the next year,
when he sailed for Europe, intending to assist
the Hungarians in their struggle for independence, but was too late to render any assistance
before their subjection was accomplished, and
their leader, Kossuth, forced to fly to Turkey.

He then settled down to a literary life, first
at London and later in Buckinghamshire, where
he began the publication of those marvelous tales
which made him famous. The truthfulness of
his scenery and his excellent narrative style have
often been overlooked by his breathless readers,
whom he delighted with a profusion of hair-
breadth escapes and desperate adventures.
Among his best known works are "The Rifle
Rangers" (1850), "The Scalp Hunters" (1851),
"The Boy Hunters" (1853), "The Bush Boys"
(1856), "The War Trail" (1857), and "The
Headless Horseman" (1866).

He returned to the United States, in 1867,

and began the publication of the Onward magazine, but after fourteen months it was abandoned, owing to his ill health, and he returned to England. He died October 22, 1883, and was buried at Kensal Green cemetery, near London. (See "A Memoir of His Life," by his widow, London, 1890, for a full list of his works.)

John Zephaniah Holwell

John Zephaniah Holwell, a writer on Indian affairs, was born in Dublin, in September, 1711. He went to India in 1732 as a surgeon, and in 1736 became a member of the Court of Calcutta. In 1756 he defended Fort William, Calcutta, against Surajah Dowla, Nabob of Bengal, but was obliged to surrender on the 20th of June, after a gallant defense. He and one hundred and forty-six companions were, the evening of the surrender, shut in the memorable "Black-hole" of Calcutta, a room some twenty feet square, where the wretched prisoners soon became frantic with suffocating heat and insufferable thirst. But twenty-three survived a night's confinement. They were liberated from captivity by Clive a few months afterwards. It is from Holwell's narrative we learn the particulars of this imprisonment. In after years he raised a monument at his own expense to his fellow-prisoners who died in the Black-hole. After a short visit to England, he succeeded Clive, in 1758, as Governor of Bengal, in which office he was superseded about the end of 1760. He died in England, November 5, 1798. In his various works he treated especially of some of the native systems of religion—believing them to be of divine origin. His principal books are: "Indian Tracts," 1764;

"Historical Events Relative to Bengal and Indostan," and "Mythology of the Gentoos," 1765-71.

Julia Kavanagh

Julia Kavanagh, novelist and biographer, was born at Thurles, in 1824. Her parents early removed to Paris, where she gained that minute insight into French life displayed in her works. In 1844 she went to London, and embraced literature as a profession. Her first work, "The Three Paths," a tale for children, was published in 1847; and in 1850, "Woman in France During the Eighteenth Century," perhaps her best known work, appeared. She traveled through France, Germany and Switzerland, and works of travel, fiction and general literature flowed from her pen. Among her other works are: "Madeleine," 1848, a tale from real life; a romance, "Nathalie," 1851; "Women of Christianity Exemplary for Acts of Piety and Charity," 1852, and "Daisy Burns" (a novel), 1853. Many of her novels passed through more than one edition, and were reprinted in America. Her writings are remarkable for their delineation of character and graceful simplicity of style. She was subjected to severe attacks of neuralgia the latter years of her life, and died at Nice, October 28, 1877. Her portrait by Chanet is in the National Gallery of Ireland.

John Francis Maguire

John Francis Maguire, politician and writer, the son of a merchant in Cork, was born about 1815. He was admitted to the Irish bar in 1843, was member of Parliament for Dungarvan from

1852 to 1865, and for Cork from that date until his death. He actively supported the Liberal party, especially in its legislation regarding the disestablishment of the church, and the land question. It was known that he was not in affluent circumstances, and it was expected that he would soon be offered a government position of some description, so that his sincerity was strikingly shown in 1870, when he joined the Home Rule party, led by Isaac Butt, and thereby sacrificed all his prospects of an official career. A series of articles on the question of Home Rule, which appeared in his paper, the Cork Examiner, was published in a collected form in 1871.

Maguire was the author of "Rome and Its Ruler," 1857; "Life of Father Mathew," 1862; "Irish in America," 1868; "The Next Generation" (a novel), 1871, and other works. He was a brilliant narrator, was a prominent advocate of woman suffrage, and for his defense of the position of the Pope was created a Knight Commander of St. Gregory. He died near Cork, November 1, 1872. His character for earnestness and sincerity stood high.

Jonah Barrington

Sir Jonah Barrington was born in 1760, the fourth of sixteen children of John Barrington of Knapton, near Abbeyleix, Queens County. His pleasing presence, lively conversation, talents, and pushing activity contributed largely to his advance in public life. He was admitted to the bar in 1788, and two years afterwards, as member for Tuam, he entered Parliament, where, he says, "I directed my earliest efforts against Grattan and Curran, and on the first day of my

SIR JONAH BARRINGTON

rising exhibited a specimen of what I may now call true arrogance." He was rewarded by government for his arrogance, in 1793, by a sinecure in the Custom-house, worth £1,000 a year, and a silk gown. He lost his seat in 1798, but sat for Bannagher in 1799. He boldly voted against the union, though it deprived him of his sinecure and stopped his further advancement. Nevertheless, most inconsistently, he acted as government procurer for bribing at least one member to vote for it.

In 1803 he was an unsuccessful candidate for the city of Dublin in the Imperial Parliament, although Grattan, Curran, Ponsonby and Plunket voted for him. The government now thought he was worth buying again, and accordingly made him judge in the Admiralty Court, and knighted him. In 1809 he published, in five parts, the first volume of the "Historic Memoirs of Ireland." It is thought that he was induced to delay the second volume—the government shrinking from the exposure of their conduct in carrying the union, and it was understood that to purchase his silence he was permitted to reside in France from about 1815, and act as judge by deputy.

In 1827 he published two volumes of "Personal Sketches of His Own Time." In 1830, by an address from both houses of Parliament, he was removed from the bench, in consequence of well-proven misappropriation of public moneys. In 1833 appeared the third volume of "Personal Sketches," and in the same year the delayed volume of his "Historic Memoirs." This book was subsequently reproduced in a cheaper form as "The Rise and Fall of the Irish Nation." His works are interesting, racy, and valuable, containing much of personal incident, related in a fascinating style. He died at Versailles, April 8, 1834.

Michael O'Clery

Michael O'Clery, the chief compiler of the Irish Annals, commonly called "The Annals of the Four Masters," was born in the parish of Kilbarron, near Ballyshannon, County Donegal, about the year 1575. He was descended from a learned family who had been for centuries hereditary historians of the O'Donnells, princes of Tirconnell. He was a lay brother of the Franciscan order, and originally had borne the name of Teige of the Mountain, but on his admission to the order of St. Francis he assumed that of Michael.

Soon after joining his order at Louvain, he was sent to Ireland by his countryman, the learned Hugh Ward, to collect manuscripts and documents, for the purpose of rescuing the annals and antiquities of his country from the comparative oblivion into which they had fallen. O'Clery, who was skilled in the Irish language and eminently qualified for the task, pursued his research for many years, during which time he visited the best Irish scholars then living, and transcribed from ancient manuscripts many lives of Irish saints, genealogies, martyrologies, and other literary monuments. All this material he transmitted to Hugh Ward in 1635, who, however, did not live to avail himself of them; but they proved of great use to the Rev. John Colgan, jubilate lecturer of theology at Louvain, who took up the same subject after the death of Ward.

During O'Clery's stay in Ireland he compiled the following works: "A Catalogue of the Kings of Ireland, and the Irish Calendar of Saints' Days"; "The Book of Conquests"; and "The Annals of Ireland," called "The Annals of the Four Masters," as he and his assistants— Peregrine O'Clery, Conary O'Clery and Peregrine O'Duigenan, a learned antiquary of Kilronan—were named. He also had help from two members of the old and learned family of the O'Mulconrys, hereditary historians of the kings of Connaught. In the "Testimonials" prefixed to the work it is stated that it was entirely composed in the monastery of the Franciscan Brothers of Donegal, who supplied the necessary requirements of the transcribers while their labors were in progress. Fergal O'Gara, a member for Sligo in the Parliament of 1634, is also said to have liberally rewarded O'Clery's assistants, while it was his advice and influence that prevailed on O'Clery to bring them together and proceed with the work. The first volume was started January 22, 1632, and the last finished August 10, 1636.

After the completion of the "Annals of the Four Masters," O'Clery returned to Louvain, where, in 1643, he published a glossary of difficult and obsolete Irish words, which Lloyd embodied in his Irish dictionary. He died at Louvain, in 1643. The first complete printed edition of the "Annals of the Four Masters" (the Irish original, with an English translation and ample notes), was issued by Dr. John O'Donovan, at Dublin, in seven quarto volumes, in 1851, being the main source of information, and, perhaps, the most important single contribution ever made to the study of Irish history. The "An-

nals" begin long before the Christian era and
continue down to A. D. 1616.   An English translation of the "Annals" from 1172 to 1616 made
by Owen Connellan from a copy of the auto-
graph in the Royal Irish Academy, with extensive notes by Dr. MacDermott, was published
in Dublin in 1846.

Michael O'Clery's life was one disinterested
devotion to Gaelic learning.   He regretted the
ruin of the ancient families and religious houses,
but never complained of his own discomforts or
boasted of his performances.   His only reward
for long and faithful service was the esteem of
every friend of Irish learning.

Donough O'Brien

Donough O'Brien, King of Munster, son of
Brian Boru, was away during the battle of Clontarf, April 23, 1014, but returning immediately
afterwards, although the youngest surviving son
of Brian, he assumed command of the Dalcas-
sians, and prepared to return to Thomond.   At
Mullaghmast, Donough and his brother Teige
were opposed by their relative Cian, one of the
chiefs of the Eugenian line, who demanded that
Donough should resign the crown.   The difference was adjusted through the intervention of
Donald, chief of the O'Donoghues.   The Dalcas-
sians had not proceeded much farther on their
way home when they were attacked by Fitz-
Patrick, Chief of Upper Ossory, who thought the
death of Brian a favorable opportunity to re-
nounce his dependency on Munster, and to demand hostages.

According to legend, this treachery so en-
raged Donough's army that even the wounded
demanded to be tied to stakes interspersed
amongst their comrades to assist in opposing
FitzPatrick's onset. This bold front so intimi-
dated the men of Ossory that they refused to
attack, and confined their hostilities to cutting
off a few stragglers. Donough had scarcely settled at home when he was obliged to repel the incursions of the neighboring chiefs. In 1016 Kincora and Killaloe were demolished by the men
of Connaught. Some years later Donough and
Teige fought between themselves; the former
was defeated, and shortly afterwards, in 1023,
procured the assassination of Teige.

After Malachy's death, the same year, Donough advanced pretensions to the supreme power
in Ireland, and the country was devastated by
apparently aimless wars, in which Donough and
his nephew Turlough, son of Teige, figured on
opposite sides. Eventually Donough was defeated, and, according to the annals of Clanmac-
nois, retired to Rome, where he died, in 1064.

Turlough O'Brien

Turlough O'Brien, King of Munster, nephew
of Donough, son of Brian Boru, was born about
1009, and upon the defeat of his uncle, Donough,
assumed the sovereignty. In 1067 he and his
allies marched against Connaught, but were
caught in an ambush and defeated. Next year
Turlough was without a competitor, his cousin,
Murrough, having been killed in a predatory excursion into Teffia. In 1073 he made preparations to reduce Ulster to obedience, but was defeated near Ardee. Better fortune awaited him

in 1076, when he invaded Connaught and compelled the submission of Roderic O'Conor.

October 29, 1084, his son Murtough, with several allies, including the Danes of Dublin, fought an indecisive battle with the opposing Munstermen in Leinster. Four thousand were left dead on the field, including many princes of the O'Brien blood. In 1085 Turlough led a successful incursion into Ulster. He died at Kincora, in 1086. He was twice married—to a princess of Ely, and to a daughter of the prince of Ossory. Turlough O'Brien is said to have presented to William Rufus the oak with which the roof of Westminster Hall is constructed.

Murtough O'Brien

Murtough O'Brien, King of Munster, succeeded his father, Turlough, in 1086. He signalized his accession by ravaging the territories of such of the surrounding chiefs as were obnoxious to him. He defeated the men of Leinster and the Danes of Dublin at Rathedair, near Howth, in 1087. This victory was counterbalanced next year by the invasion of Thomond. Roderic O'Conor marched into Munster and took possession of an island in the Shannon, from which Murtough in vain endeavored to dislodge him.

Murtough was also assailed by Donald MacLoughlin, Prince of Aileach, who, with O'Conor, entered Munster, burned Limerick, and laid waste the country as far as Emly, Lough Gur, and Bruree. They then demolished Kincora, and returned home with hundreds of prisoners, both Irish and Danish. In 1089 Murtough made reprisals in Connaught, but had ultimately to waive his pretensions to the crown of Ireland, and rest satisfied with his position as a provincial king. A conference was held in 1090, and it was agreed by O'Brien and O'Conor to acknowledge O'Melaghlin as monarch; yet, soon afterwards, war was renewed. In 1101 the supremacy of Murtough O'Brien was recognized. It was about this time that he made a grant of the royal residence of Cashel to the Church. A contest between Murtough and Magnus, King of Norway, who arrived off the Irish coast with a large fleet, was averted by Murtough giving his daughter, with a large dowry, to Sigfried, son of Magnus.

In 1114 ill health obliged Murtough to resign the sceptre to his brother Dermot for a time. Murtough O'Brien died March 11, 1119, and was buried at Killaloe. The character of this prince ranks high, not only among the chroniclers of his own nation and time, but also among contemporary writers in England. Malmesbury says that he was held in such respect by the English king, Henry I., that the latter frequently availed himself of the wisdom and advice of Murtough. His reign appears as a career of persevering energy, unnerved by defeat, and only stimulated by reverses to still greater efforts.

Donald O'Brien

Donald O'Brien, King of Munster, succeeded to the throne about 1167. On the advent of the Anglo-Normans he turned against the monarch Roderic O'Conor, and was among the first to pay homage to Henry II. He surrendered Limerick to King Henry, and agreed to render tribute as to his sovereign lord, but took the first occasion to turn against the Anglo-Normans. In 1174 Earl Strongbow marched south to reassert his authority, but was intercepted at Thurles by forces under Roderic O'Conor and Donald O'Brien, and defeated with great loss.

According to the Annals of Inisfallen, four knights and 700 of Strongbow's troops were killed, and the Four Masters say: "He returned in sorrow to his house in Waterford, and O'Brien proceeded home in triumph." On his return from victory Donald blinded and put to death several of his relatives, to prevent the possibility of trouble from their designs upon the crown. Soon afterwards, Strongbow and Raymond Fitz-Gerald besieged and took Limerick, and Roderic O'Conor making an incursion about the same time, Donald again submitted to the Anglo-Normans.

When FitzGerald hastened to Dublin in 1177, on receiving the news of Strongbow's death, O'Brien, forgetful of all his engagements, cut down the bridge over the Shannon, and fired the town, stored with supplies of all kinds, declaring that it should no longer be a nest for foreigners. Henry II. shortly afterwards granted Donald's dominions to Philip de Braosa, and in 1192 two bands of English settlers entered his territory, but were defeated near Killaloe, driven across the Shannon, and again defeated near Thurles. Donald O'Brien died in 1194.

Murtough O'Brien

Murtough O'Brien, King of Munster, succeeded his father in 1194. One of his first acts was to put to death his cousin, Donough, who advanced pretensions to the crown. In 1196, with O'Conor and MacCarthy, he marched upon Cork, obliged the Anglo-Normans to evacuate it, and afterwards defeated them at Limerick, and at Kilfeacle, where they had erected a castle. The Irish allies, however, soon fought among themselves. In 1201, De Burgo led a large army of O'Briens and MacCarthys into Connaught, and devastated the monastery of Athdalaarg, on the River Boyle. After this the O'Briens again fell out among themselves, and also fought against the Anglo-Normans, by whom, in 1208, Murtough was taken prisoner and blinded. He died in 1239.

Donough C. O'Brien

Donough Cairbreach O'Brien, King of Munster, was upon the deposition of his brother, in 1208, allowed by the Anglo-Normans to succeed him, and submitting to King John, Thomond was conferred on him and his heirs, with the fortress and lordship of Garrigogonnell, which had belonged to William de Braosa. Donough fixed his residence at Clonroad, near Ennis, and commenced the erection of the beautiful Franciscan abbey, the ruins of which still remain. He was engaged in constant wars with the princes of Connaught. His death took place in 1242.

Conor O'Brien

Conor O'Brien, King of Munster, succeeded his father in 1242. With twenty other Irish princes, he was summoned by Henry III. to aid him in an expedition against the Scots, and afterwards, the Four Masters record that "a great battle broke out between him and the English of Munster." The territories of all the Irish princes but the O'Neills, the O'Conors and the O'Briens had long before this been partitioned among the descendants of the Norman invaders. In 1258 a conference was held at Narrow-water on the Erne, between Hugh O'Conor and Teige O'Brien, on behalf of their respective fathers, and Brian O'Neill, to concert measures for mutual safety. They made peace with each other, and conferred the sovereignty of the island upon Brian O'Neill.

Little practical result followed this compact; several Irish princes were soon detached from the alliance by the Anglo-Normans, and next year, when O'Neill and O'Conor collected their forces, no representative of the O'Briens joined them. The battle of Drumdearg, near Down-patrick, ensued, in which the Irish were defeated with the loss of Brian O'Neill and a large number of Ulster and Connaught chieftains. On the other hand, O'Brien defeated the English at Kil-barron, in Clare, where many of the Welsh settlers of Mayo were slain. He was then strong enough to compel several of the ancient tributaries of his house to acknowledge his authority. He fell at the battle of Siudan, in Clare, in 1267, in an expedition against the O'Loughlins and O'Conors of Corcomroe.

Brian Roe O'Brien

Brian Roe O'Brien, King of Munster, second son of Conor O'Brien, succeeded on the death of his father, in 1267. Violent contentions immediately ensued between him and his nephew, Turlough, in the course of which Brian called to his assistance Thomas de Clare, a young knight, to whom Edward I. had granted Thomond. When, in 1277, De Clare, armed with Edward's grant, arrived at Cork from England with a numerous band of followers, Brian met him on landing and conveyed to him as the price of his assistance the district comprised in the present barony of Lower Bunratty.

According to a note in the Four Masters, they swore to be true to each other forever, and for confirmation of this bond of perpetual friendship they drew blood from each other, which they mixed and put in a vessel. De Clare immediately erected Bunratty Castle. The same year O'Brien and De Clare were defeated by the De Burgos of Connaught and the Irish of Burren in a bloody engagement at Maghgresain, and fled to Bunratty. There, in vexation at his defeat and at the instigation of his wife, De Clare caused O'Brien to be put to death.

Murrough O'Brien

Murrough O'Brien, first Earl of Thomond, was a descendant of Brian Roe, King of Munster. In 1540, he met O'Neill, O'Donnell and O'Conor at Fore in West Meath, and concerted joint operations against the Anglo-Irish power, but they were shortly afterwards defeated by Sir William Brereton, Lord-Justice. This defeat and one at Bellahoe, the previous year, opened the way for a general pacification through the submission of the Irish chieftains. A Parliament in Dublin, in 1541, proclaimed Henry VIII. King of Ireland, and declared it high treason to impeach this title or oppose the royal authority. Murrough O'Brien renounced all idea of opposing

Henry, provided his estates were confirmed to him.

The king and council joyfully accepted his conditions. One hundred pounds was loaned O'Brien to enable him to visit London, and on Sunday, July 1, 1543, he was received by King Henry, at Greenwich, and created Earl of Thomond. Other Irish chieftains were ennobled at the same time, and all were granted residences in Dublin, so that they should be able to attend Parliament. He died in 1551, and Thomond and Desmond were again involved in a war regarding the succession; and nominal peace was not restored until 1558, when the Lord-Deputy Sussex entered Thomond at the head of a large army, and placed the rightful earl in power.

Conor O'Brien

Conor O'Brien, third Earl of Thomond, in 1570 broke out into rebellion, was defeated, and passed over into France, but was afterwards received back into favor by Elizabeth, and returned to Ireland with commendatory letters to the council. In October, 1577, after another period of civil war, he visited the Queen, and again obtained several advantages for himself and his descendants. He died in 1580, and within five years Thomond was completely settled into counties and shire ground, all old rights and customs abolished by law, circuits established, and the power of the O'Briens restricted to those enjoyed by the nobility in England.

Donough O'Brien

Donough O'Brien, fourth Earl of Thomond, the "Great Earl," son of the third Earl, was

brought up at the court of Elizabeth, and succeeded to the titles and estates on the death of his
father in 1580. In July, 1597, at the head of his
clansmen, he joined the Lord-Deputy at Boyle
for an attack on O'Donnell. In crossing the
Erne in the face of O'Donnell's troops, the Baron
of Inchiquin, the earl's relative, was killed. The
reduction of the castle of Ballyshannon was unsuccessfully attempted, and the Lord-Deputy and
O'Brien were compelled to beat an ignominious
retreat, abandoning some of their artillery and
baggage. In the following January the earl was
dispatched by the Lords-Justices to inform the
queen of the true position of affairs in Ireland,
and to be the bearer of the conditions upon which
O'Neill and O'Donnell were willing to lay down
their arms.

After O'Neill's victory at the Yellow Ford,
the flame of insurrection spread into Thomond.
The earl, in 1599, visited the domains at the head
of a considerable body of the Queen's troops,
and inflicted a terrible retaliation on his countrymen,—hanging the garrison of the castle of Dun-
beg in couples on the nearest trees, and reducing Dunmore, Derryowen, Cloon, and Lissofin.
Later in the same year he attended the Earl of
Essex in his progress through the south of Ireland,—parting from him at Dungarvan, and returning by Youghal and Cork to Limerick. In
the summer of 1600 O'Brien joined Sir George
Carew in his victorious expedition through Desmond, and was present at the reduction of Glin
Castle and other strongholds. In 1601 the earl
again visited England, and returning with reinforcements for Mountjoy, then engaged at the
siege of Kinsale.

After the surrender of Don Juan d'Aguila,

and the settlement of the country, he had leisure to look after his own affairs, and the historian of the O'Briens quotes documents to prove that he still exercised or claimed almost regal authority over the other members of his clan. In May, 1619, he was made Governor of Clare and Thomond. He died September 5, 1624, and was buried in Limerick Cathedral.

Lucius O'Brien

Sir Lucius O'Brien, baronet, descended from a younger son of the first Baron of Inchiquin, was born in the first half of the eighteenth century. On the death of his father, Sir Edward, in 1765, he entered the Irish Parliament as member for Clare. He sided with the popular party in their efforts for the advancement and independence of Ireland, and, pursuing an independent parliamentary career (which extended over the administrations of thirteen viceroys, from the Duke of Bedford to the Earl of Westmoreland, a period of thirty-six years), he left to his country and his posterity the character of a high-minded patriot and statesman, as zealous for the interests of his country as he was thoroughly acquainted with its wants, and ready to assert its rights. The appreciation of his high and independent character, his public spirit, and his illustrious lineage, by the House of Commons, was frequently testified by the deference paid to his opinions whenever questions of importance or difficulty happened to engage its attention. He was a Privy-Councillor and Clerk of the Crown and Hanaper. He died January 15, 1795.

Murrough O'Brien

Murrough O'Brien, sixth Baron and Earl of Inchiquin, known as "the Incendiary," was born about 1618. His grandfather perished at the Erne, in 1597, fighting for the English against Hugh O'Donnell. His father died when he was a minor, and Murrough did not enter into the possession of his estates until 1636. Inchiquin served for some years in the Spanish army, and, returning home in 1639, took his seat among the peers. He early attracted the notice of Strafford and was commended by Charles I. for his loyalty. In April, 1640, he was appointed Vice-President of Munster, under Sir William St. Leger, his father-in-law.

On the breaking out of the war of 1641-52, he distinguished himself against the Confederates at Rathgogan and Ballyhay, near Charleville. April 13, 1642, he defended Cork with great ability, and soon afterwards the entire civil and military administration of Munster devolved upon him. September 2, 1642, with 2,000 foot and 400 horse, he defeated Mountgarret and a superior force at the battle of Liscarroll. After the armistice of September, 1643, Inchiquin was enabled to dispatch five regiments for the service of the King. Subsequently he proceeded to Oxford to solicit the post of President of Munster; but finding that reports had been circulated to his disadvantage, and that King Charles was prejudiced against him, he returned to Ireland, "determined to assert his own importance, and prove the value of those services to which little regard had been paid."

In 1644 he appears to have put himself under

the protection of the parliament, and to have received from it the appointment he coveted. He joined Lord Broghill in the campaign of 1645, driving out the Catholic inhabitants of Cork, Youghal, and Kinsale, burning their houses and confiscating their goods. The satisfaction of the Confederates at the Papal Nuncio's entrance into Kilkenny, the autumn of the same year, was dampened by the news that Lord Inchiquin had taken Bunratty Castle from his relative, the Earl of Thomond. The Confederate Supreme Council immediately transferred Inchiquin's title to his younger brother, who still sided with them, and next summer an expedition was sent under Lord Muskerry to retake Bunratty, which was defended by MacAdam, a Parliamentary officer, and by a fleet under Admiral Penn. After a vigorous defense, MacAdam was killed and the garrison capitulated, being permitted to join Inchiquin at Cork. In 1647, at the head of 5,000 foot and 500 horse, Inchiquin successively reduced Cappoquin, Dromore, Dungarvan, Cahir, Fethard, and Cashel.

In the assault of Cashel, frightful atrocities were committed. In November he routed Taaffe's army of 8,000 men, with great slaughter, at Knocknanos, near Mallow. Upon receipt of the news of this victory, parliament voted £10,-000 for the support of the army in Ireland, and sent a present of £1,000 to Inchiquin himself. After this a misunderstanding arose between Lord Lisle, the Parliamentary Lord-Lieutenant, and Inchiquin, ending in an abortive impeachment of the latter in parliament. Inchiquin now turned again towards his Royalist friends, and commenced a correspondence with Ormond, and parliament, apprised of his designs, sent a force to blockade Cork, Kinsale, and Youghal. September 29, 1648, Ormond arrived at Cork. Inchiquin and his army received him with all honor, and the Confederation resigned its power into his hands.

On the news of the King's death, the following January, Ormond marched to Dublin and encamped at Finglas, while Inchiquin, with a body of dragoons, secured Drogheda after a short siege. On the 15th of July he invested Dundalk, and Monk, in command of the place, was forced by his soldiers to surrender. Inchiquin took no part in the unsuccessful operations for the recovery of Dublin from the Parliamentarians, but the charge that a secret understanding existed between him and Jones, Governor of Dublin, appears to be without foundation. Ormond and Inchiquin were unable to withstand the advance of Cromwell's victorious army, and December 11, 1650, accompanied by many Royalist officers, he embarked at Galway for France. Lord Inchiquin served in the French army for several years, was made Viceroy of Catalonia, and fought in the Netherlands.

In 1654 he was created Earl of Inchiquin by Prince Charles. On one occasion, within sight of Lisbon, he and his son were taken prisoners by Algerian pirates and he was not released until the English Council of State intervened on his behalf. In 1662 he served in the Portuguese army against Spain. The events of his remaining years are few and comparatively unimportant. After the Restoration, he was appointed Vice-President of Munster. He was awarded £8,000 for the losses he had suffered in the Royalist cause, and his estates in Clare, Limerick,

Tipperary, and Cork were restored to him. In his latter years he became a Catholic.

He died September 9, 1674, and was buried by his own directions in Limerick Cathedral. On the death of his descendant, James, third marquis, seventh earl, and twelfth baron, in 1855, the earldom became extinct, but the barony of Inchiquin devolved on Sir Lucius O'Brien. William Smith O'Brien, the distinguished Irish Nationalist (see Volume II.) was grandson of Sir Lucius O'Brien. Lucius W. O'Brien, fifteenth baron, is the present representative of the family.

James Butler

James Butler, first Earl of Ormond, was a minor at his father's death. He was a descendant of Sir Theobald Walter, who accompanied King Henry II. to Ireland in 1171, and, as a mark of royal favor, appointed to the high office of Chief Butler of Ireland (from which his descendants derived their family name), and had large possessions conferred upon him. James Butler married Eleanor de Bohun, granddaughter of King Edward I., was created Earl of Ormond, and had a grant made him of the annual rent of the city of Waterford. This marriage ultimately procured him still more considerable advantages,—particularly the grant of the "Regalities and Liberties of Tipperary," and the rights of a palatine in that county. As soon as he was of age (about 1327), he engaged on the side of his cousin, the Earl of Kildare, in his wars with the De Burgos and Le Poers. In 1329 and 1330 he was at war with the O'Nolans and MacGeoghegans.

He founded, in 1336, the Friary of Little Carrick, in County Waterford, and dying January 6, 1338, was buried at Gowran.

James Butler

James Butler, second Earl of Ormond, was born at Kilkenny, October 4, 1331, and was consequently but six years of age at his father's death. He was given in ward to the Earl of Desmond, and afterwards to Sir John d'Arcy, whose daughter he married during his minority. He is often spoken of as the "Noble Earl." King Edward III., his cousin, granted him an annuity of about £40, besides some additional estates. In 1359 he was Lord-Justice, with a salary of £500. He attended Lionel, Duke of Clarence, in his Irish wars, and was for a time, during the Duke's absence in England, Lord-Deputy. In 1362 he defeated MacMurrough in County Kildare, and slew 600 of his men. In 1372 he was created Constable of Dublin Castle. In 1378 he surrendered the sword of Lord-Justice to Alexander Balscot, Bishop of Ossory. The Earl died at Knocktopher, October 18, 1382, and was buried in St. Canice's Church, Kilkenny.

James Butler

James Butler, third Earl of Ormond, son of the preceding, styled "Earl of Gowran," from having built Gowran Castle. In 1391 he purchased the estate of Kilkenny Castle, thenceforth the seat of the Butlers. He filled several important offices connected with the government of Ireland; "being a mighty strong man, he is styled in some annals the head of the chivalry of Ireland, which kingdom he governed to the content of the King and his good subjects." He was not only successful in many of his incursions against the native chieftains, but checked the depredations of Scotch and Welsh pirates upon the Irish coasts. He died at Gowran, September 7, 1405.

James Butler

James Butler, fourth Earl of Ormond, known as the "White Earl," was, like many of his predecessors, a minor when his father died. He received an education in advance of most young Irish lords of his time. Before he was of age he distinguished himself in the field against the Irish, was made Lord-Deputy, and held a Parliament in Dublin about 1408. He traveled in France with Thomas of Lancaster in 1412. In 1420 he attended King Henry V. in his French wars, and ingratiated himself so much with that monarch that he returned to Ireland as Lord-Lieutenant. He headed expeditions against the native septs into Ulster and other parts of the country.

A few months after Henry V.'s death, he was replaced in the government of Ireland by Edmund Mortimer. The earl held the office of Lord-Deputy in 1425 and 1440, and was Lord-Lieutenant in 1443. A violent feud arose between the Butlers and Talbots, and members of the latter family used every endeavor, but without success, to lessen the esteem in which he was held by King Henry VI. He died at Ardee, August 23, 1452, and was buried at St. Mary's Abbey, Dublin. His first wife was a daughter of the Earl of Kildare, his second the widow of

Earl Grey. The White Earl was a deep student of history and antiquities, and an expert in the laws of arms and matters of honor. He endowed the College of Heralds with lands, and advanced the study and culture of Irish heraldry.

James Butler

James Butler, fifth Earl of Ormond, born November 24, 1420, was almost the first after the settlement of his family in Ireland that was not left a minor on the death of his father. When young he was knighted by King Henry VI. and he accompanied Richard, Duke of York, to France. In 1449 he was created Earl of Wiltshire, and was for a time Governor of Calais. In 1451 he was Lord-Deputy; and next year, upon his father's death, was appointed Lord-Lieutenant. In 1452, with other great lords, he undertook the guarding of the British seas for three years.

He was present at the battle of St. Albans; at Wakefield, in conjunction with the Earl of Pembroke, he commanded one wing of the Lancastrian army; and at Mortimer's Cross, leading a body of Welsh and Irish against the Earl of March, he was defeated with heavy loss. Shortly afterwards (March 29, 1461) he was taken prisoner at the battle of Towton in Yorkshire, and beheaded at Newcastle on the following 1st of May. He was thrice married; his third marriage, with Eleanor, sister of the Duke of Somerset, engaging him in the Lancastrian cause.

James Butler

James Butler, sixth Earl of Ormond, being present with his brother, fifth earl, at the battle of Towton, in 1461, was likewise attainted. He was afterwards, by King Edward IV., restored in blood and to most of his estates. The King used to say of him "that he was the goodliest knight he ever beheld, and the finest gentleman in Christendom; and that if good breeding, nurture, and liberal qualities were lost in the world, they might all be found in the Earl of Ormond." languages, and there was scarce a court to which He was accounted master of all the European Edward IV. did not send him as ambassador. He died in the Holy Land, on his way to Jerusalem, in 1478.

Thomas Butler

Thomas Butler, seventh Earl of Ormond, succeeded his brother in 1478. He also had been attainted by King Edward IV. and the attainder was revoked, as in the case of his predecessor. By King Henry VII. he was made a Privy-Councillor, and was in 1492 and 1497 sent on diplomatic missions to France. He was reputed one of the richest British subjects. He died in London, August 3, 1515. His daughter Margaret married Sir William Boleyn, and was mother of Anne Boleyn, who became the mother of Queen Elizabeth.

Pierce Butler

Pierce Butler, eighth Earl of Ormond, succeeded his father in 1515. He had already distinguished himself in the service of the Crown, and had been successful in suppressing the insurrections of the native Irish. In 1521 he was appointed Lord-Deputy. His marriage with a sister of the Earl of Kildare did not extinguish the feud between the Butlers and FitzGeralds. On account of the death of his friend, Richard Talbot, by James FitzGerald, he impeached the Earl of Kildare. The matter ended by FitzGerald being obliged to walk through London, candle in hand, and a halter around his neck; on the other hand, Ormond was replaced in the office of Deputy by Kildare. At one time it is stated negotiations were set on foot for the marriage of his son to his cousin, Anne Boleyn. King Henry VIII. coerced Pierce to resign his title of Earl of Ormond to Sir Thomas Boleyn, who was desirous of the honor. In its stead, the Earldom of Ossory was conferred upon him by the King, in great state, at Windsor, February 23, 1528.

After Sir T. Boleyn's death, Pierce was restored to his ancient honor of Ormond. By this deference to Henry VIII.'s wishes, he acquired large additions to his estates in various parts of Leinster. Lord Thomas FitzGerald endeavored to induce the earl to join him in insurrection,— offering to divide the Kingdom of Ireland with his son James. The earl declined in a characteristic letter, in which he wrote: "You are so liberal in parting stakes with me, that a man would weene you had no right to the game; and so importunate for my company, as if you would perswade me to hang with you for good fellowship. And think you that James is so mad as to gape for gudgeons, or so ungrateful as to sell his truth and loyalty for a piece of Ireland?" Nettled by this reply, FitzGerald, with O'Neill and other Irish chieftains, ravaged County Kilkenny, and in an engagement near Jerpoint wounded and nearly took prisoner James, the earl's son.

Ormond was foremost in suppressing the insurrection, and upon the death of Kildare and the execution of his uncles in 1537, was, as a reward, further enriched by the Crown; he then turned his arms against the Earl of Desmond, who submitted, and took an oath of loyalty. He and his countess brought workmen from Flanders, and enriched Kilkenny Castle with tapestry, Turkey carpets, and cushions. The latter part of the earl's life was spent in prayer, contemplation, and alms-giving. He died August 26, 1539, and was buried in St. Canice's Church, Kilkenny. He is described as "a man of great honor and sincerity, infinitely good-natured, plain, kind, loving, familiar, and liberal to his friends and followers; but an enemy and severe scourge to all bad people." His second son was created Viscount Mountgarret, and his natural son, Edmund, Archbishop of Cashel.

James Butler

James Butler, ninth Earl of Ormond, Earl of Ossory, succeeded on the death of his father in 1539. Seven years before, he had been Lord-Treasurer, to balance the power of the Earl of Kildare, then Lord-Deputy. In 1534 he had been entrusted with the custody of all the ports of Ireland, as Admiral of the kingdom, and was afterwards created Viscount Thurles, and specially commissioned to proceed against Irish insurgents and take them into protection where desirable. The period of the Reformation is marked by his engaging to support King Henry VIII., who granted him additional estates in various parts of the country.

In 1545 he headed a body of Irish troops in the King's service in Scotland. Upon his return, in 1546, a dispute with the Earl of Lennox necessitated reference to the King in London. October 17th he attended a feast at Ely House, Holborn. By some means the viands were poisoned. Seventeen of his servants died, and he succumbed eleven days afterwards, October 28, 1546. He was interred in London, among some of his ancestors, in the church of "St. Thomas d'Acres," but his heart, according to his desire, was deposited in St. Canice's Church, Kilkenny. He had a numerous family by his wife Joan, daughter of James, Earl of Desmond.

Thomas Butler

Thomas Butler, tenth Earl of Ormond, Earl of Ossory, surnamed the "Black Earl," born about 1532, was but fourteen at his father's death. He was brought up at the English court with Edward VI., who took delight in his company. Serving as a volunteer under the Duke of Somerset in Scotland, he distinguished himself by his bravery at the battle of Musselborough. In Queen Mary's reign he was made captain of a troop of horse, and gave distinguished proofs of fidelity and courage in the suppression of Wyatt's rebellion. In 1554 he entered into possession of his estates, and within the next three years more than once marched under the Lord-Lieutenant against the Scots in Ulster. Soon afterwards he relieved the Earl of Thomond, besieged by the native septs at Bunratty.

He stood high in the good graces of Queen Elizabeth, who made him Lord-Treasurer, and added to his estates out of the confiscated church lands. In 1564 and 1565 Munster was wasted in conflicts between him and the Earl of Desmond. Ultimately Desmond and Sir John of Desmond were sent over to London and imprisoned; whereupon several of the southern chieftains, aided by the Earl of Ormond's brothers, Sir Edmund and Sir Pierce Butler, took the field against the Government. Ormond, in England at the time, was sent over to help to quell the insurrection. He landed at Waterford, August 14, 1569, and hastened to join the Lord-Deputy at Limerick. There his two brothers submitted and were pardoned.

In consequence of the Desmond insurrection, he was, in 1578, made Governor of Munster; and in 1580, in conjunction with Lord-Justice Pelham, made an expedition into Desmond. Carrigfoyle, Askeaton, and other fortresses were taken and their garrisons put to the sword. In 1581 the Baron of Lixnaw, one of Desmond's chief followers, submitted to the Earl of Ormond, who interceded for and obtained his pardon. In 1583 he obtained supplies of men, money, and ammunition from England, and made a determined effort to capture the Earl of Desmond, to this end carrying on a war of plunder and devastation in Munster.

Within the space of a few months he cut off, of Desmond's party, "46 captains, 800 notorious traitors, and 4,000 common soldiers." Before long nearly all the great lords of the south submitted to him at Cork, and the Earl of Desmond was left a wanderer with but a few companions. It is much to Ormond's credit that he positively refused to accede to Burleigh's directions that he should disregard the protections he had accorded to the native chiefs. He wrote: "I will never use treachery to any man, for it will both touch Her Highness's honor and my own credit too much; and whosoever gave the

Queen advice thus to write, is fitter to execute such base service than I am."

The wars that desolated Munster were at length ended by the capture and death of the Earl of Desmond (November 11, 1583). In the ensuing confiscations, Ormond was given 3,000 acres in Tipperary, and a "great tract of poor land" in Kerry,—less than he considered his fair share after the part he had taken on the Queen's side in the war. In the operations against O'Neill he commanded in different parts of the country. April 10, 1600, he accompanied Sir George Carew and the Earl of Thomond to a parley near Kilkenny with Owney O'More. The parley resolved itself into a skirmish. Ormond was taken prisoner,—Sir George and Thomond escaping with difficulty.

At the instance of O'Neill, the earl was released in June, giving Owney hostages for the payment of £3,000, should he thereafter seek revenge for the treacherous injuries he had received. After Elizabeth's death, he was confirmed in his office of Lieutenant-General by King James I. He was blind the last twelve years of his life, and died at his house at Carrick, November 22, 1614, and was buried in St. Canice's Church, Kilkenny.

Carte styles him "a man of very great parts, admirable judgment, great experience, and a prodigious memory; . . . very comely and graceful . . . of a black complexion which gave occasion to the Queen (in her way of expressing kindness to such as she favored) to call him her 'black husband.'" This favor doubtless occasioned the undying hostility between him and the Earl of Leicester. He repaired and beautified Kilkenny Castle, built a hospital at Kilkenny, and castles at Holycross and elsewhere. Thrice married, he left no heir. He was a Protestant in religion.

Walter Butler

Walter Butler, eleventh Earl of Ormond, Earl of Ossory, eldest son of Sir John Butler, nephew of preceding, grandson of the ninth earl, succeeded on the tenth earl's death in 1614. He was born in 1569. His right to the estates was denied by Sir R. Preston, Baron Dingwall, afterwards Earl of Desmond, a favorite of King James I., who claimed them through his wife Elizabeth, sole daughter of the late earl. Carte cites the documents upon which these claims were founded, and then proceeds: "Nothing is clearer than that according to these feoffments all the estate of Earl Thomas (except what he had given to his daughter at her marriage) ought to have descended immediately to Sir Walter Butler, Earl of Ormond. But King James interposed so warmly in the case, and wrote such a number of pressing letters to the Deputies and Council of Ireland . . . requiring them to stand by the Earl of Desmond, that the Earl of Ormond could never get into possession. Vast sums were spent in law; but the power of the Crown still prevented a decision. At last King James took upon himself to make an award, which Walter, Earl of Ormond, conceiving to be unjust, refused to submit to, and was by the King's order taken up and committed to the Fleet prison. He remained in that prison for eight years before the death of King James, who, during that duress, seized on the liberties of the county palatine of Tipperary, and persecuted him in all the ways he could contrive, to the inconceivable detriment of the family."

Recovering his liberty in 1625, he lived for a time in London, and then removing to Ireland, died at Carrick, February 24, 1632, and was buried at St. Canice's. In his youth he had distinguished himself in the Irish wars. A devout Catholic, he was styled "Walter of the Beads and Rosaries." He married a daughter of Viscount Mountgarret, and by her had two sons and nine daughters. His second son died young and without issue. His eldest son, Thomas Butler, Viscount Thurles, father of the twelfth earl, was drowned off Skerries, near Holyhead, on a voyage to England, December 15, 1619. James Butler, twelfth Earl and first Duke of Ormond, called the "Great Duke," born in London in 1610, was one of the most prominent and active Royalists at the time of Charles I. and Charles II.

James Butler

James Butler, second Duke of Ormond, son of Thomas Butler, Earl of Ossory, born in Dublin Castle, April 29, 1665, was, with his brother and sisters, brought up by his grandfather, the "Great Duke." He was educated in France and at Oxford. When but seventeen, he married a daughter of Lord Hyde, and was left a widower at twenty. He served at the siege of Luxembourg, and in suppressing the Duke of Monmouth's rebellion. Shortly afterwards he took as his second wife a daughter of the Duke of Beaufort.

Upon his grandfather's death he succeeded to the title of duke, and was by the University of Oxford appointed Chancellor. He went over to

William of Orange upon his arrival in England, was made a Privy-Councillor, and had other honors heaped upon him. At the battle of the Boyne he commanded the Life Guards; and a few weeks afterwards entertained William at a grand banquet at Kilkenny Castle, which had been protected from plunder by General Lauzun. He afterwards attended William to Flanders. At Landen he was severely wounded, and taken prisoner, but was soon exchanged. He served again on the Continent, among other commands leading the land forces in the attack on Cadiz in 1702. He was twice Lord-Lieutenant of Ireland, and was present in the English Council Chamber at the time of Guiscard's attack on Harley.

After Marlborough's disgrace, he was appointed Commander-in-Chief, and met with a cool reception from the Dutch and Prince Eugene when he landed in Flanders in 1712; nor did the subsequent separate negotiations with the French, in which he was the instrument employed by the English Ministry, raise him in the estimation of the allies. On his return to England, he was warmly received and made Warden of the Cinque Ports and Governor of Dover, and his Duchess a Lady of the Bedchamber. Through his interest, Swift was appointed Dean of St. Patrick's. Upon George I.'s accession he was deprived of his offices, and fled to France. Before leaving he is said to have visited Lord Oxford in the Tower, and upon parting with him to have exclaimed, "Farewell! Oxford without a head." To which Oxford rejoined, "Farewell! Duke without a duchy." He was immediately impeached for: (1) correspondence with Marshal Villars in the late war; (2) having engaged not to attack the French army; (3) having endeavored to persuade the Confederate generals to raise the siege of Quesnoy.

These charges being proved, he was attainted of high treason, and his name was erased from the list of Peers and from the Order of the Garter; while the Irish House of Parliament set £10,000 upon his head, and his estate was vested in the Crown. He thenceforth lived upon an allowance of £1,500 a year from the court of Spain, and devoted the remainder of his life to the cause of the Pretender, his house at Avignon being the headquarters of Jacobite intrigue. Though of an amiable disposition, his married life was unhappy. In 1721 he is described as "short and fat in person, but yet of most graceful demeanor, and most noble aspect; remarkable for his attachment to the Church of England, and refusing large demesnes which were offered to him as the price of his conversion. . . . He loves and is beloved by the ladies; is of low stature, but well shaped, of a good mien and address, a fair complexion, and very beautiful face."

He died, after thirty years' exile, November 16, 1745. His body was conveyed secretly to England as a bale of goods, and buried in Henry VII.'s chapel, with some of his ancestors. His brother Charles, the Earl of Arran, repurchased his escheated estates from the Government, and was in truth third Duke of Ormond, but he never assumed or was aware of possessing the title, as it had not then been decided that an attainder in the English Parliament did not affect Irish titles. On his death in December, 1758, the titles of the house became dormant, until revived in 1791, by John Butler, a descendant of Walter, eleventh earl, being created seventeenth Earl of Ormond. James, nineteenth earl, was in 1825 created a

marquis, the title now borne by the Butlers.
J. E. W. T. Butler, third Marquis of Ormond, is
the present representative of the family.

Pierce Butler

Pierce Butler, Viscount Galmoy, descended
from the tenth Earl of Ormond, was born March
21, 1652.   In 1677 he took the degree of LL. D.
at Oxford.   Under James II. he was Privy-Councillor of Ireland, Lieutenant of County Kilkenny,
and Colonel of the Second Regiment of Irish
Horse.   He served with distinction at the Boyne
and Aughrim, and was one of the signers of
the Treaty of Limerick.   He might probably
have secured his old estates of 10,000 acres in
Kilkenny and 5,000 in Wexford, if he had consented to give his allegiance to William III., instead of following Sarsfield to France.   On the
establishment of the Irish troops in France he
was made Colonel of the Second Queen's Regiment of Horse.

He was at the siege of Roses in 1693, and in
1694 was Brigadier attached to the army of Germany.   He served in Italy and other parts of
the Continent from 1701 to 1703, sharing all the
fortunes of the Irish Brigade.   His son fell at
Malplaquet, 1709.   Viscount Galmoy died at
Paris, June 18, 1740.   O'Callaghan says: "The
successive claimants of the title of Galmoy were
officers in France down to the Revolution, in
whose armies, as well as in others, various gentlemen have honorably represented a name of
which the illustrious General Lafayette is related
to have said, in the war for the independence of
the United States of America, that 'whenever
he wanted anything well done, he got a Butler to
do it.' "

Richard Butler

Richard Butler, Viscount Mountgarret, descended from the eighth Earl of Ormond, was born in 1578. His first wife was Margaret, eldest daughter of Hugh O'Neill; and, taking part with his father-in-law, he particularly distinguished himself by the defense of the castles of Ballyragget and Cullahill. Nevertheless, his estates were confirmed to him both by James I. and Charles I. At the commencement of hostilities in 1641 he appeared inclined to espouse the Government side, and was appointed Governor of Kilkenny. Fearing, however, that the rights and liberties of his Catholic brethren would be still further interfered with, he wrote an explanatory letter to the Earl of Ormond, and took possession of Kilkenny in the name of the Confederates.

He endeavored to protect the lives and property of the Protestants without relaxing his efforts for the side he had espoused. Early in the war he secured all the towns and forts in Kilkenny, in Waterford, and Tipperary, and marched into Munster and took Knockordan and Mallow, and other strongholds. Unfortunately for the Confederates, Cork objected to his jurisdiction, and insisted upon the appointment of a general of its own. Thus were lost the advantages of undivided and vigorous control of the Confederate armies. April 13, 1642, he was defeated at the battle of Kilrush, near Athy, by the Earl of Ormond. Soon after, he was chosen President of the Supreme Council of Kilkenny.

In 1643 he was at the battle of Ross, and at the capture, by his son Edmund, of the Castle of Borris, in Queen's County; also at the siege of

Ballynakill, a fortress that had held out bravely
for eighteen months. Viscount Mountgarret was
outlawed by Cromwell, and excepted from pardon for life or estate. He died in 1651, and was
interred in St. Canice's Church, Kilkenny. His
son was eventually restored to his estates and
honors by Charles II. This branch of the Butlers is now represented by Henry Edmund Butler, fourteenth Viscount Mountgarret.

Maurice FitzGerald

Maurice FitzGerald, first Earl of Desmond,
was a descendant of Maurice FitzGerald, one of
the original Norman invaders of Ireland in 1169.
The first earl was called "Maurice the Great,"
and appears to have taken the place of his
elder brother, who died young. He was Lord-
Justice of Ireland, had livery of Decies and Desmond in 1312, of Kerry in 1315, and was created
Earl of Desmond August 22, 1329. He married,
at Greencastle, August 16, 1312, Margaret, fifth
daughter of Richard de Burgo (the Red Earl of
Ulster), who died in 1331; and, secondly, Ave-
line, or Ellinor, daughter of Nicholas FitzMaurice, third Lord of Kerry and Lixnaw. He took
an active part in the war against Bruce in Scotland. In contest with the O'Nolans and O'Mur-
roughs, in 1330, he first introduced the practice
of "coigne and livery," or quartering soldiers on
the inhabitants of the district they were sent to
protect.

About this time the Anglo-Normans began
to adopt Irish customs and names, and throw
off English authority. Their estrangement was
hastened by an Act of the English Parliament
under Edward III., confining offices in Ireland

to those who had estates in England, which irritated the Anglo-Norman party, and Desmond and others called a counter parliament at Kilkenny. Ufford, the Lord-Justice, marched against them, seized Desmond's estates, and threw him into prison. After Ufford's death, Desmond made his peace, attended Edward III. to the French war with twenty men-at-arms and fifty hobellars, and had his estates restored to him.

"In consequence of his having been sneeringly termed 'rhymer' by Baron Arnold le Poer, at a public assembly, this Maurice embarked in a fierce intestine strife, the nobles of Ireland banding themselves on the opposite sides. Such ravages were committed that the towns were obliged to provide garrisons for their own protection, and royal writs were issued from England, ordering the Le Poers and Geraldines to desist from levying forces for the purpose of attacking each other; but to little purpose." The first earl died in Dublin January 25, 1355, and was buried at Tralee.

Maurice FitzGerald

Maurice FitzGerald, second earl of Desmond, son of preceding. By his wife, Beatrix, daughter of the Earl of Stafford, he had but a daughter, who married Donald Oge MacCarthy Mor. He was drowned or died a natural death in 1358, and was buried in Tralee Abbey.

Nicholas FitzGerald

Nicholas FitzGerald, third Earl of Desmond, brother of preceding. Being an idiot, King Edward III. granted custody of the Desmond estates to his younger brother, Gerald. Nicholas died childless in 1367.

Gerald FitzGerald

Gerald FitzGerald, fourth Earl of Desmond, half-brother of preceding, surnamed "Gerald the Poet," succeeded to the estates and honors of the family. He married, by the King's command, Eleanor, daughter of James, second Earl of Ormond, who gave her for portion the barony of Inchiquin in Imokelly. Gerald was Lord-Justice of Ireland, 1367. In 1398 he disappeared, and is fabled to live beneath the waters of Lough Gur, near Kilmallock, on whose banks he appears once every seven years.

O'Donovan quotes the following concerning his character: "A nobleman of wonderful bounty, mirth, cheerfulness in conversation, charitable in his deeds, easy of access, a witty and ingenious composer of Irish poetry, and a learned and profound chronicler; and, in fine, one of the English nobility that had Irish learning and professors thereof in greatest reverence of all the English in Ireland." Fragments of Anglo-Norman verse attributed to him, known as "Proverbs of the Earl of Desmond," survive.

John FitzGerald

John FitzGerald, fifth Earl of Desmond, son of preceding, was drowned near Ardfinnan, on the Suir, when returning with his followers from an incursion into the Earl of Ormond's territory, March 4, 1399, and was buried at Youghal. He married, according to one account, Mary Bourke; or, according to Lodge, Joan, daughter of the Lord of Fermoy.

Thomas FitzGerald

Thomas FitzGerald, sixth Earl of Desmond, son of preceding, was deprived of his earldom in 1418, on account of his marriage with Catherine, daughter of William MacCormac of Abbeyfeale, one of his dependants. The romantic incident of his meeting Catherine as he was out hunting is told in Moore's lines, commencing: "By the Feal's wave benighted." The alliance was so unfavorably regarded by his family that he abandoned his estates and retired to France. He died at Rouen, August 10, 1420, and was buried at Paris "with great and mighty show, where the two kings of England and France were present." It is said that by his wife he left two sons,—Maurice, ancestor of the FitzGeralds of Adare and Broghill, and John Claragh, who died in 1452.

James FitzGerald

James FitzGerald, seventh Earl of Desmond, uncle of preceding, son of the fourth earl, surnamed "James the Usurper." One of the chief instruments in compelling his nephew's exile, he seized his estates, but was not generally acknowledged as earl until 1422. In the same year he was made Constable of Limerick, and two years afterwards obtained the custody of Limerick, Waterford, Cork, and Kerry. He married Mary, eldest daughter of Ulick de Burgo. He was relieved from the duty of attending Parliament in 1445. He and the Earl of Ormond were godfathers to George, afterwards Duke of Clarence. The following is a portion of a letter addressed to him as a descendant of the Geraldines in 1440, in the name of the Florentine Republic: "Magnificent lord and dearest friend: If it be true, as is publickly stated, that your progenitors were of Florentine origin, and of the right noble and antique stock of the Gherardini, still one of the highest and greatest families of our states, we have ample reason to rejoice and congratulate ourselves that our people have not only acquired possessions in Apulia, Greece, and Hungary, but that our Florentines, through you and yours, bear sway even in Ibernia, the most remote island of the world." By the Earl of Ormond he was appointed Seneschal of Imokelly, Inchiquin, and Youghal, and founded the monastery of Franciscans at Askeaton. He died in 1462, and was buried in the Friary of Youghal.

Thomas FitzGerald

Thomas FitzGerald, eighth Earl of Desmond, son of the preceding, was in 1463 appointed Lord-Deputy under the Duke of Clarence. On assuming the government he was opposed by 5,000 of the English of Meath, whom he soon reduced to obedience. On many other occasions he had to take the field both against the "King's English rebels," and the "King's Irish enemy." The Irish Parliament, in letters to the King, referred to the great services which he "at intolerable charges," and "in jeopardy of his life, rendered to the reigning monarch, as well as to his father, the right noble and famous prince of blessed memory, Richard Duke of York. They certified that he was and ever had been the King's true and faithful liegeman, governing himself always by English laws, and by those who were well-wishers to his Highness. By God's grace

and the great travail and labor of the Deputy,
the land, they wrote was in a reasonable state of
peace and tranquillity. The Parliament prayed
that it might please the King to bear in remem-
brance the great services, costs, and charges, of
the Earl Thomas, to have him in tenderness and
special favor, and to reward him according to
his wisdom and bounty."

In 1464 he founded the collegiate church of
Youghal. In 1467 he was succeeded in the government by John Tiptoft, Earl of Worcester,
"who caused him to be attainted of treason in
a parliament held at Drogheda, with the Earl
of Kildare and Edward Plunket, for alliances,
fosterage, and alterage with the Irish; for fur-
nishing them with horse and arms, and supporting them against the King's subjects; for which
he was beheaded, February 15, 1467, at Drogheda,
and was there buried in St. Peter's Church."
Lodge makes the following statement in a note:
"His tomb was removed, by order of Sir Henry
Sidney, to the Church of the Holy Trinity in
Dublin, where it seems to represent the person
of Earl Strongbow, whose monument was broken
by the fall of the roof of the church on Whit-
sun-eve, 1572." He married Ellice, daughter of
John, Lord Barry of Buttevant. Three of his
sons, James, Maurice and Thomas, became Earls
of Desmond. One account attributes his death
to the intrigues of King Edward IV.'s Queen,
Elizabeth Gray, who was jealous of Desmond's
influence over her husband.

James FitzGerald

James FitzGerald, ninth Earl of Desmond,
was born in 1459, and succeeded on his father's

execution in 1467. O'Daly says: "Now James FitzThomas, having made terms with King Edward, and received immunity for any act which he had committed to avenge his father's death, became Earl of Desmond. He was a man of singular prudence, and largely to the detriment of the Irish did he increase the territories he had acquired." He married Margaret, daughter of Thady O'Brien, Prince of Thomond. King Richard III. endeavored to attach him to his interests, and sent him a golden collar weighing 20 ounces, with the device of a white boar, pendant from a circlet of roses and suns; also a "long gown of cloth of gold, lined with satin or damask; two doublets, one of velvet, and another of crimson satin; three shirts and kerchiefs; three stomachers; three pair of hose—one of scarlet, one of violet, and the third of black; three bonnets; two hats; and two tippets of velvet."

Notwithstanding these blandishments, the Earl augmented his Irish alliances, and retained his Irish habits. He was slain at Rathkeale, December 7, 1487, "possibly at the instigation of his brother and successor," and was buried at Youghal. His sister Catherine married the MacCarthy Reagh. A book once her property (now known as the Book of Lismore), was discovered in a wall in Lismore Castle in 1811.

Maurice FitzGerald.

Maurice FitzGerald, tenth Earl of Desmond, succeeded on the death of his brother in 1487. Being lame, and usually carried in a horse-litter, he was styled "Vehiculus," and by some, on account of his bravery, "Bellicosus." He sided with the pretender, Perkin Warbeck, in the siege

of Waterford and other expeditions. Nevertheless, making submission, the King not only for-
gave, but took him into favor, August 26, 1497,
and granted him all the "customs, cockets,
poundage, and prize-wines of Limerick, Cork,
Kinsale, Baltimore, and Youghal, with other
privileges and advantages."

The condition of the inhabitants within the
Pale at this period is thus described by a contemporary writer: "What with the extortion of
coyne and livery daily, and with the wrongful
exaction of collecting money, and of carriage and
cartage daily, and what with the King's great
support yearly, and with the said tribute, and
black-rent to the King's Irish enemies, and other
infinite extortions, and daily exactions, all the
English . . . are more oppressed than any other
folks of this land."

O'Daly thus writes of Earl Maurice: "This
man was subsequently far famed for his martial
exploits. He augmented his power and possessions,—for all his sympathies were English—
and a furious scourge was he to the Irish, who
never ceased to rebel against the crown of England. The bitterest enemy of the Geraldines he
made his prisoner, to wit, MacCarthy Mor, Lord
of Muskerry; and now having passed thirty years
opulent, powerful, and dreaded, he died (in 1520)
to the sorrow of his friends and the exultation of
his enemies." He was buried at Tralee. His first
wife was daughter of Lord Fermoy; his second,
daughter of the White Knight.

James FitzGerald.

James FitzGerald, eleventh Earl of Desmond, succeeded on his father's death in 1520.

In 1529 he proferred fealty to the Emperor
Charles V., and declared himself willing to enter
into a league against England. The Emperor
commissioned his chaplain to visit Ireland. The
report of his mission to Dingle, of the resources
of the country, of the demeanor of the Earl, and
his reasons for hostility to England, are extremely interesting.

The chaplain writes: "The Earl himself is
from thirty to forty years old, and is rather above
the middle height. He keeps better justice
throughout his dominions than any other chief in
Ireland. Robbers and homicides find no mercy,
and are executed out of hand. His people are in
high order and discipline. They are armed with
short bows and swords. The Earl's guard are in
a mail from neck to heel, and carry halberds. He
has also a number of horse, some of whom know
how to break a lance. They all ride admirably,
without saddle or stirrup." He died at Dingle,
June 18, 1529, and was buried with his father at
Tralee. He had but one legitimate child, Amy,
who married (1) the ninth Earl of Ormond, (2)
Sir Francis Bryan, Lord-Justice, (3) Gerald, fifteenth Earl of Desmond.

Thomas FitzGerald.

Sir Thomas FitzGerald, twelfth Earl of Desmond, uncle of preceding, brother of the tenth
Earl, born in 1454, succeeded on his nephew's
death in 1529. He was known as "Sir Thomas
the Bald," and "Thomas the Victorious." "Far-
famed was he in feats of arms; in nine battles did
he win the palm of victory. . . . Another
subject for congratulation had this Earl—the
two Lords of Muskerry fell beneath his sword."

He took up the intrigues of his predecessor. Lodge tells us that "the King without hesitation established him in the earldom, merely endeavoring with friendly phrases to induce him to send his grandson and heir to his Majesty's court, which, with phrases equally amiable, the Earl showed the impossibility of his doing." Eventually embarrassments attendant on the question of the succession obliged him to make every profession of loyalty to the King. He died at Rathkeale in 1534, and was buried at Youghal.

James FitzGerald

James FitzGerald, thirteenth Earl of Desmond, grandson of the 12th Earl, called the "Court Page," having been hostage for his grandfather at the court of Windsor. On the earldom becoming vacant in 1534, "the King loaded him with honors, and fitted out ships to accompany him to the Irish shores, and provided him with a number of men who were ready to stand by him against those who were inclined to dispute his title to the patrimonial honors and inheritance."

His title to the Earldom was disputed by his grand-uncle, Sir John, who being supported by a large faction, was de facto the 13th Earl. This Sir John died about Christmas, 1536. The "Court Page" did not long enjoy his honors, for he was slain at Leacan Sgail in Kerry, by his cousin, Maurice an Totane, son of his late opponent, March 19, 1540. He married a daughter of his grand-uncle, Cormac Oge MacCarthy.

James FitzGerald

Sir James FitzGerald, fourteenth Earl of Desmond, son of Sir John, de facto the 13th Earl, succeeded on his cousin's death in 1540. He is called by English writers the "Traitor Earl." In 1538 he had written to the Pope, declaring that an army of 30,000 Spaniards would ensure the conquest of Ireland, proposing that Ireland be annexed to the Holy See, and offering to undertake the government as viceroy, paying a revenue to Pope Paul of 100,000 ducats. "The expedition would be costly, but the expenses would fall neither on his Holiness nor on the Emperor. Desmond, with armed privateers, would seize and deliver into the hands of the Pope the persons of a sufficient number of the heretical English, whose ransoms would defray the necessary outlay."

In July, 1539, he came out in open arms against the English power, in conjunction with O'Neill, but he was soon overcome by Viscount Thurles, who seized upon his castle at Lough Gur. Having surrendered and obtained letters from the Lord-Deputy, he sailed from Howth in 1542, went to London, made submission to King Henry VIII., was kindly received, reinstated in his ancient patrimony, and sent back with the titles of Treasurer of Ireland and President of Munster. He is afterwards said to have "lived in honour and prosperity," until he died at Askeaton, October 14, 1558. He was there buried in the Franciscan Friary. The 14th Earl was four times married—to daughters of Lord Fermoy, Lord Ely O'Carroll, 8th Earl of Ormond, and Donald MacCarthy Mor.

Gerald FitzGerald

Gerald FitzGerald, fifteenth Earl of Desmond, son of preceding by his second wife, succeeded on the death of his father in 1558. He is known to English writers as the "Rebel Earl." "Soon after his father's death," says O'Daly, "surrounded by a noble retinue of 100 youths, all of honorable birth, he proceeded to do homage to the Queen, by whom he was graciously received, and restored to all his ancestral honors by a new patent." Sir Thomas, his elder half-brother, by his father's first marriage, afterwards annulled as contracted within degrees of consanguinity, was for a short time recognized as Earl.

Gerald was, however, chosen by the septs of Desmond, and his claim was eventually allowed by the government. Thomas took no part with his brothers in the succeeding convulsions, and died at his castle of Connagh, near Youghal, January 18, 1595. Earl Gerald sat in a parliament held in Dublin in 1559. For many years he was engaged in bloody and aimless feuds with the Butlers and O'Briens. February 15, 1564, he proceeded to levy imposts on Sir Maurice FitzGerald of Decies, a relative of the Butlers. Sir Maurice applied to the latter for aid, and a battle was fought at Affane, on the Blackwater, two miles south of Cappoquin, where the Earl of Desmond was wounded and made a prisoner. While being carried on a litter from the field, one of his captors is said to have tauntingly asked: "Where now is the proud Earl of Desmond?" to which he rejoined; "Where he ought to be, still upon the necks of the Butlers." The Earl appears to have been liberated soon afterwards.

Sir Henry Sidney, in his progress through Munster in January, 1567, speaks of the Earl as "a man both devoid of judgment to govern, and will to be ruled," and describes his territories as in a wretched plight. "Like as I never was in a

more pleasant country in all my life, so never saw
I a more waste and desolate land. . . . Such
horrible and lamentable spectacles are there to
behold as the burning of villages, the ruin of
churches, the wasting of such as have been good
towns and castles." He was especially severe
against the Earl for the mismanagement of
his estates, and being likewise fearful of his
strong Catholic proclivities, seized him at Kilmallock, and carried him about in durance the remainder of his progress. The sons of the Earl
of Clanricard were also captured in Connaught,
and the Lord-Deputy returned to Dublin with
his prisoners the 16th of April. "He had caused
numberless malefactors to be executed in the
course of his visitation."

In October, Sidney proceeded to England,
bringing with him the Earl of Desmond and his
brother Sir John, Hugh O'Neill, the O'Conor
Sligo, and other chieftains. The Earl and his
brother Sir John were detained captives for six
years in the Tower of London, while their cousin,
James FitzMaurice FitzGerald assumed the leadership of the family, and carried on those hostilities against the government that will be found
detailed in his life. After their cousin's submission in 1573, they were set free and received at
court. A ship was furnished to convey them to
Dublin, where, however, the Earl was detained
under an honorable arrest, while Sir John was
permitted to return to Munster. Before long the
Earl managed to escape while out hunting, and
although large rewards were offered for his
arrest, he was soon safe among his followers in
the fastnesses of Desmond (North Munster).
During the O'Neill wars of the following months
he remained neutral.

In May, 1574, the Earl met at Waterford by appointment the Earl of Essex and the Earl of Kildare, and under the protection of a safe conduct returned with them to Dublin. There he was informed that the Queen desired his presence in London; but remembering his former captivity, he made many excuses, and Essex honorably conducted him to the frontiers of the Pale. Shortly afterwards he surrendered Castlemaine and Castlemartyr, which were occupied by English garrisons. In other respects his authority over his feudal principality was left undisturbed, and he passed for a loyal subject. In the autumn of 1575 he proffered Sir Henry Sidney his services against the northern chieftains. In 1576 he was brought into collision with the new President of Munster, Sir William Drury. He protested against the holding of courts within his palatinate; but finding Drury obdurate, and about proceeding to Tralee to hold a sessions, he made a virtue of necessity, and offered the hospitality of his castle.

On approaching Tralee, the President perceived about 800 armed men retiring into the woods. The Countess of Desmond met him outside the town and assured him that her lord had no hostile intention, but that, his visit being unexpected, the forces had assembled for a general hunting. Shortly afterwards Drury seized Sir John of Desmond in Cork, on suspicion of treasonable practices, and sent him under an escort to Dublin.

When James FitzMaurice FitzGerald landed with the Papal expedition at Smerwick, in 1579, the Earl maintained a semblance of loyalty, and even forwarded to Dublin his cousin's letters. Sir John, who appears to have been liberated, and

Sir James, hastened to meet their cousin and his allies. The Lord-Justice, who was in Cork, immediately despatched Henry Davells, Constable of Dungarvan, and Arthur Carter, Provost-Marshal of Munster, to summon the Earl of Desmond and his brothers to attack James FitzMaurice and the Spaniards. They were extremely officious and insolent to the Earl, reconnoitred the fort at Smerwick, where James FitzMaurice and the Spaniards were entrenched, and were on their way back to Cork, when they were slain by Sir John in a little inn at Tralee. "The deed was aggravated by the fact that Sir John and Davells had been intimate friends."

A few days after James FitzMaurice's death in August, 1579, the Earl met Sir William Drury at Kilmallock, and endeavored to clear himself from the charge of complicity in his cousin's proceedings. After being kept under arrest for three days, he was liberated on undertaking to send in his only son, James, as a hostage. He received a promise that his lands and tenants should be respected—an engagement violated almost as soon as made. Most of the earl's forces went over to Sir John of Desmond, who took his cousin James FitzMaurice's place—the Spanish officers materially assisting in disciplining these irregular levies. Sir William Drury, on the other hand, collected a considerable army, chiefly composed of Catholic Irish. In an engagement that ensued between a portion of these forces and those under Sir John and Sir James, at Springfield, in the south of County Tipperary, the latter were successful. Shortly afterwards, in September, Sir William Drury sickened of the fatigues of the campaign, and died at Waterford, whereupon the command of the royal forces devolved upon Sir Nicholas Malby, who was reinforced by 600 Devonshiremen, landed at Waterford. A fleet also hovered off the coast under the command of Sir John Perrot.

Leaving 300 foot and 50 horse at Kilmallock, Malby early in October marched with some 600 of his army to Limerick; then turning south, he encountered and gave battle to Sir John and Sir James with vastly superior forces, two miles from Croom. For a time victory seemed undecided. Malby's lines were twice broken; but ultimately the Geraldines were routed with the loss of Thomas FitzGerald, the Earl's cousin, and some 260 men. The Earl of Desmond and FitzMaurice, Lord of Lixnaw, watched the progress of this engagement from the top of Tory Hill, little more than a mile distant, and late in the evening sent to congratulate Malby on his victory. This message was treated with contempt—there being little doubt that the earl would in any case have congratulated the winning side—and Malby proceeded to lay waste Desmond's territory in the neighborhood. Askeaton, Rathkeale, and Adare, were given to the flames.

October 30, the Earl of Ormond, acting under Malby, demanded that Desmond should give up the Papal Nuncio (Dr. Saunders), and surrender for the Queen's service the castles of Carrigfoyle and Askeaton. Desmond hesitated; November 2, a proclamation was issued declaring him a traitor unless he submitted within twenty days, and the next day the Queen's troops marched into the earl's palatinate of Kerry, and the Earl of Ormond was constituted governor of all Munster. The reluctant Earl of Desmond was forced to choose a side, and he took the field with his brothers about Christmas, 1579.

The war in which he now found himself involved continued the four remaining years of his life. It had already been carried on by his cousin, James FitzMaurice and his brothers for nearly six years. For ten years the country was desolated by contentions of the most sanguinary and merciless character. The conclusion of the war found Munster well-nigh depopulated, and the whole of Desmond parcelled out among new proprietors. The war had its origin in the effort of Elizabeth to impose English habits and laws, and English religion upon the people of Munster; in the rapacity of adventurers thirsting for the confiscation of Irish estates; and in the almost inevitable contest between Elizabeth and her Catholic subjects. The points at issue were clearly put by the Earl of Desmond himself: "It is so that I and my brother are entered into the defence of the Catholic faith, and the overthrow of our country by Englishmen, which had overthrown the Holy Church, and go about to overrun our country, and make it their own, and to make us their bondmen."

The earl was, however, unprepared to conduct a successful insurrection; no important engagement occurred; and his exploits were never more "than an occasional skirmish or plundering excursion; and he gradually sank into a fugitive, and finally into a mere criminal fleeing from justice. . . . The interest or the existence of the mass of the people was wholly disregarded. On the one hand, they were excited by the promises of Spanish invasions, and succor which never arrived (in sufficient force to effect anything); on the other, they were trampled down and deci-

mated by way of precaution; and thus, from year
to year, the plundering and killing went on, until
there was nothing left to plunder, and very few
to kill." On more than one occasion the earl
nobly refused terms for himself which would in-
volve the surrender of Dr. Saunders, the Papal
Legate.

In January, 1580, two Italian vessels with
powder arrived at Dingle, bringing news that
he might soon expect other forces from abroad.
As spring opened Pelham and Ormond "passed
through the rebel counties in two companies, con-
suming with fire all habitations, and executing
the people wherever they found them. James
FitzMaurice's widow and her two little girls were
discovered by the way, concealed in a cave. They
are heard of no more, and were probably slain
with the rest. The Irish annalists say that the
bands of Pelham and Ormond killed the blind and
the aged, women and children, sick and idiots,
sparing none. Pelham's own words too closely
confirm the charge."

In August, 1580, Sir James of Desmond was
captured and taken to Cork. There he was
hanged and quartered, and his head spiked over
one of the city gates. In September, 700 Spaniards and Italians were landed from four vessels
in Smerwick harbor. They conveyed arms for
5,000 men, together with large sums of money
and promises of further aid. The fort, at Smerwick, garrisoned by James FitzMaurice and his
party the previous year, was again occupied, repaired and strengthened. The earl hastened to
meet his foreign auxiliaries, and some weeks were
spent in desultory excursions in the neighborhood. October 31, Lord Grey, burning to retrieve his recent defeat in Glenmalure, encamped

with a strong force under experienced officers
some eight miles from Smerwick. Five days afterwards Admiral Winter arrived with his fleet from
Kinsale. Heavy guns were landed, trenches opposite the fort were opened on the 7th, and on
the 10th the Spaniards surrendered—unconditionally, according to English dispatches: Irish
authorities state that the lives and liberties of the
soldiers were guaranteed.

After surrendering, the English commander
asked who they were, and for what purpose they
had landed in Ireland; to which they replied in
effect that they had been brought over to Ireland
"upon fair speeches and great promises, which
they had found vain and false." Next morning
the officers were, by Lord Grey's orders, reserved
for ransom, while the soldiers were slaughtered in
cold blood, and a few women and a priest among
them were hanged. The bodies, 600 in all, were
stripped and laid out upon the sands—"as gallant and goodly personages," said Grey, "as ever
were beheld."

Sir Walter Raleigh was one of the officers
commanding the party who carried the Deputy's
barbarous orders into execution. The war in
Munster now assumed, if possible, a more savage
character, and untold atrocities were committed
on both sides. A large though diminishing number of followers still surrounded the earl and his
countess. About July, 1581, while encamped at
Aghadoe, Killarney, he was taken unawares by
Captain Zouch, many of his men were slain, and
he escaped with difficulty. In September he penetrated as far as Cashel, and carried off to Aherlow large spoils of cattle and other property. In
the course of the next winter Dr. Saunders, the
Papal Legate, died of cold and exposure. In

August, 1581, one year after his brother's death, Sir John of Desmond was intercepted (a spy having given information as to his whereabouts) at Castlelyons by Captain Zouch with a strong party, was wounded by a spear thrust, and expired before his enemies had carried him a mile. His body was thrown across his own steed, and conveyed to Cork, where it was hanged in chains —his head being cut off for exposure on Dublin Castle.

The unhappy earl now remained alone in arms. While the government offered terms to such minor persons as would submit, he was excluded from mercy. The large rewards offered for his capture appeared to attach the peasantry of Desmond only the more to the faith and fortunes of their old lord. Hunted from place to place, he occasionally dealt heavy blows at his adversaries. The Glen of Aherlow was his favorite retreat, at other times he frequented the woods in the southwest of Limerick, or the fastnesses of Kerry. He passed Christmas of this year at Kilquane, near Kilmallock. There he was surprised by a party of soldiers led by a spy, John Welch; the earl's retreat was surrounded, and he and the countess only saved themselves by plunging into a river hard by, and hiding in the water under an overhanging bank until the enemy had retired. April 28, 1583, he wrote to Queen Elizabeth, offering to come to terms—"So as my country, castles, possessions, and lands, with my son, might be put and left in the hands and quiet possession of my council and followers, and also my religion and conscience not barred."

About June, Lady Desmond, the companion hitherto of all her husband's wanderings, left him, probably by his own desire. Free from the incumbrance of her presence, the aged earl wandered from glen to glen, and mountain to mountain, attended only by a priest and three or four faithful followers who would not leave him. "Where they did dress their meat," says Hooker, "thence they would remove to eat it in another place, and from thence go into another place to lie. In the nights they would watch; in the forenoon they would be upon the hills and mountains to descry the country, and in the afternoon they would sleep."

On the 9th of November he left the woods near Castleisland and went westward towards Tralee. Some of his kerns carried off some cows and horses for his use from Maurice MacOwen, who immediately despatched messengers to Lieutenant Stanley at Dingle, and to his brothers-in-law, Owen and Donnell Moriarty. The two latter followed in the track of the prey, with a band of eighteen kerns. At Castlemaine they obtained the assistance of a few soldiers. From Tralee they traced them to Glanageenty. When dusk fell they saw a fire in the glen beneath them. At dawn (November 11, 1583), the Moriartys with Daniel O'Kelly, one of the soldiers, took the lead of the band up the glen, and rushed with a loud shout to the cabin where the earl's party had lain. All escaped except a venerable looking man, a woman, and a boy. O'Kelly, who entered first, aimed a blow with his sword and almost severed the arm of the old man, who cried: "I am the Earl of Desmond: spare my life." O'Kelly immediately cut off his head, which was forwarded to London and impaled on the bridge.

His body, after being concealed for some time by the peasantry, was ultimately interred in the little chapel of Kilnamanagh, near Castleisland. The spot where the earl was killed is still pointed out as Bothar-an-Iarla, and the trunk of an old tree under which his body was thrown, remained in 1850. So ended the Desmond war, which it took the English power ten years to suppress, though hardly one-half of Ireland had been engaged in it. Had the whole island heartily united against the English there would have been a different issue to the war. The victory was terribly purchased.

The entire province of Munster was utterly depopulated. Hecatombs of helpless creatures, the aged, the sick, and the blind, the young mother, and the babe at the breast, had fallen under the English sword. And though the authentic details of the struggle have been forgotten, the memory of a vague horror remains imprinted in the national traditions. The whole of Desmond, extending over nearly four modern counties, or 800,000 acres, was confiscated to the Crown, and the greater part divided among English settlers. The countess appears to have been made an allowance by the government. This was afterwards disallowed, and she was permitted to live in Dublin Castle. In March, 1587, she repaired to Elizabeth, who gave her a pension of £200 to be paid in Ireland, with 100 marks for her two daughters.

The earl left no issue by his first wife, daughter of the 11th Earl, widow of James, Earl of Ormond. She died in 1564, and was buried at Askeaton. By his second wife, daughter of Lord Dunboyne (who remarried Sir Donough O'Conor Sligo, and died in 1636), he left two sons and five daughters. One of these sons, James, 16th Earl, born in England in 1571, is commonly spoken of as the "Queen's Earl." He was educated in the religion of the Established Church and for a while, for political reasons, patronized by the government, and sent over to Ireland, but was soon recalled to London, where he died in great poverty in 1601.

James FitzMaurice FitzGerald

James FitzMaurice FitzGerald, cousin of the 15th Earl of Desmond, commonly called Fitz-Maurice, was born early in the 16th century. His early life abroad is thus referred to in the Desmond pedigree: "In his lifetime, being a great traveler in France, Spain, the Low Countries, Germany, and Turkey, and a renowned Irish warrior, had letters of recommendation from the King of France to the Emperor, and from the Emperor to the King of Poland, where he was honorably entertained, and promoted for his fighting against the Turks. In that war he behaved himself so bravely that he won great applause and honor both for himself, his king, and his country."

On the imprisonment of Gerald, 15th Earl of Desmond, and his brother, in the Tower of London, in 1567, the leadership of the family fell by their desire to James FitzMaurice. He resisted the pretensions of Sir Thomas FitzGerald of Desmond to his brother's earldom. Sir Thomas was supported by the Butlers and by FitzMaurice of Kerry. The chieftains of the South and the government were also engaged in hostilities. Old title deeds were raked up, and a number of farms and castles belonging to the Desmonds, Mac-Carthys, and Butlers were occupied by English adventurers. At this juncture Sidney set out on

a military expedition into Munster, and the Earl
of Ormond was sent over to bring his seditious
brothers to order.

March 2, 1570, FitzMaurice invested, plundered, and burned Kilmallock; and in 1571 Sir
John Perrot took the field in Munster. Fitz-
Maurice, however, in the wilds of Aherlow was
able to set Perrot and his troops at defiance. At
the same time a desultory warfare was waged by
the Irish chiefs in Connaught and Ulster. In
1572 the Earl of Clanricard having been taken
prisoner by Sir Edward Fitton, his sons renewed
the war; multitudes of the Irish rallied to their
standard, and among the rest FitzMaurice. In
May he went into Ulster, collected 1,500 Scots,
and came down upon the country bordering the
Shannon. His first step was to burn Athlone.
Thence he moved down to Portumna, where he
was joined by the De Burgos, and crossed the
river into Limerick. Sir John Perrot came up
with him between Limerick and Kilmallock, and
cut his forces in two. Perrot again surprised
FitzMaurice at Ardagh, and killed thirty of his
Scots; a month later the Butlers destroyed a hundred more.

FitzMaurice having encountered innumerable perils, forced his way South, only to find that
Castlemaine, the last of his strongholds, had been
compelled to surrender. He sustained himself in
the woods until the following February (1573),
when he sent in hostages and proffered his submission to the president. This was gladly received; and he was still powerful enough to ensure his life being preserved. The ruined church
of Kilmallock was selected for the ceremony of
reconciliation.

FitzMaurice after this appears to have taken up his residence in France, and before long was engaged in plots for the subversion of Elizabeth's power in Ireland. Having made application unsuccessfully both to Henry III. of France and Philip II. of Spain, to furnish him with means for an expedition against the English power in Ireland, he proceeded to Rome, where he was favorably received by Gregory XIII. in 1578. His solicitations were warmly seconded by the Bishop of Killaloe, and Dr. Saunders, an English ecclesiastic. The Pope granted a bull encouraging the Irish to fight for their autonomy and in defence of their religion, and an expedition was fitted out under the command of Stukely, an adventurer—formerly high in the confidence of Sidney in Ireland.

Stukely acted as admiral of the expedition, while Hercules Pisano, an experienced sailor, had the military command. The soldiers numbered about 800. The squadron sailed from Civita Vecchia. Touching at Lisbon, he was easily persuaded to join Sebastian, King of Portugal, in an expedition to Morocco, upon the promise of after assistance in the Irish project. At the battle of Alcansar, Stukely, Sebastian, and the greater part of his troops were killed. Meanwhile Fitz-Maurice, traveling by land to Spain, embarked for Ireland with about eighty persons in three small vessels. Off the Land's End they took a couple of small vessels, and on July 17, 1579, landed at Dingle, and crossed over to Smerwick.

FitzMaurice sent a long explanatory letter to the Earl of Desmond, who immediately forwarded it to the government with assurances of his loyalty. He was, however, joined by the earl's

brothers, Sir John and Sir James FitzGerald of
Desmond, and by some 200 of the O'Flahertys,
who came from Galway in their galleys. Eight
days after landing, their vessels were captured
by English crusiers, the O'Flahertys returned
home, and to avoid starvation the Spaniards left
their fort and marched inland under the three
Desmonds.

On August 17, they separated into small
parties. Sir John retired to the fastness of Lyna-
more; Sir James to that of Glenflesk; while Fitz-
Maurice, accompanied by a few horsemen and
kerns, proceeded towards Tipperary, to rally the
disaffected in Connaught and the North. In the
district of Clanwilliam their horses gave out, and
they seized some from the plough. These horses
belonged to William Burke, of Castleconnell,
whose sons, Theobald and Ulick, pursued the
party, and came up with them a few miles east of
Limerick, near the present Barrington's bridge,
August 18, 1579. FitzMaurice remonstrated with
his assailants, but was fired at and mortally
wounded. Even after this he rushed into the
thick of the melee that ensued, with one blow
cleft the head of Theobald Burke, and with another that of his brother. FitzMaurice expired
in a few hours, the rites of religion being admin-
istered to him by Dr. Allan, who was in his company.

FitzMaurice left two sons, one of whom was
shortly afterwards slain in the Irish wars, and
the other is said to have perished by shipwreck
on the Irish coast in one of the vessels of the
Spanish armada. His widow and younger children died shortly afterwards at the hands of the
Anglo-Irish soldiers who were ravaging Desmond.

James FitzGerald

James FitzGerald, "Sugan Earl" of Desmond, was a nephew of the 15th Earl of Desmond. In 1598, exasperated at seeing his ancestral territories in the hands of the English settlers, and at the efforts made to extirpate Catholicism, he joined Hugh O'Neill in his war, and by him was created an earl. Hence "Sugan Earl" ("earl of straw"), not appointed by regular authority. He soon became a distinguished commander in Munster against the Queen. The plot for his capture, formed by Sir George Carew, may be here summarized. Dermot O'Conor Don, a valiant man, had, with a body of 1,500 kerns and gallowglasses, entered his service. O'Conor's wife was a sister of the 16th Earl of Desmond, and with a view to promote his interests, she met the advances of Carew, and his advocate, Miler Magrath, Anglican Archbishop of Cashel, and persuaded O'Conor to betray his chief for the sum of £1,000.

Carew furnished O'Conor with a forged letter as if from the Sugan Earl to Carew, offering to betray O'Conor. This letter was to serve as a pretext with his followers for his treachery. Matters being arranged, O'Conor asked the Sugan Earl to an interview at Connello, on the borders of Limerick, June 18, 1600. After some controversy, O'Conor produced the forged letter, made the earl a prisoner in the name of O'Neill, and carried him off to his fortress of Castleishin, in the great wood and fastnesses of Connello, in the present County Limerick. The ruins of the castle still remain. The earl's followers, with Pierce Lacy and others, immediately assembled, took the castle June 26, and liberated him.

At the siege of Glin Castle, by Carew, in July, the earl, with 3,000 men, watched the proceedings from a distance without being able to interfere. Afterwards, while on his way to the Castle of Aherlow, he was attacked by a strong body of troops from Kilmallock, and after a skirmish, was defeated and driven to seek refuge elsewhere. Even at this low ebb in his fortunes, so strong was his hold on the affections of the people, that the plan of bringing over the "Queen's Earl" completely failed in its object. The successes of Carew, however, left him a hunted fugitive flying from forest to forest, on the Galtee mountains, and in Aherlow glen—now sheltered by a faithful harper, Dermond O'Dogan, now escaping by changing clothes with a follower, who allowed himself to be taken in his place. He was upheld through all by the hopes of Spanish succor. Carew made two attempts to have him assassinated; both of which resulted in the death of those who had undertaken the task. All efforts to suborn his immediate followers proved unavailing.

At length his relative, the White Knight, agreed for the sum of £1,000 to discover his retreat, and betray him. He came upon him concealed in a cave on the Galtees, May 29, 1601, and affected his capture—although the earl appealed to his honor as a gentleman, and to the ties of relationship between them. He was first imprisoned in the White Knight's castle of Kilvenay, and afterwards removed in fetters to Cork. Carew was careful to preserve him alive, lest the English adventurers might possibly be balked of the plunder of his estates by their reverting to an heir, for the confiscation of whose property no legal pretext could be found. June

22, he wrote an appeal to the Queen to spare his life, but nobly refused to have any share in betraying O'Neill to the government—which, it was hinted, would ensure his restoration to favor.

He was sent to the Tower of London, August 13, 1601. Sir George Carew, in sending him to London, wrote of him as being "a man the most generally beloved by all sorts (as well in this town as in the country), that in my life I have ever known;" and calls him a "dull spirited traitor," for not being willing to entrap his associates. His mind soon succumbed under the confinement of the Tower. His death took place about 1608, and he was interred in the chapel of the Tower.

The Sugan Earl is designated in state documents "James McThomas," any acknowledgment of his Desmond title being avoided. The Desmond pedigree states: "He ever proved himself an honorable, truthful, and humane man." Cox says he was one of the handsomest men of his time. Though thrice married, he left no descendants.

Maurice FitzGerald

Maurice FitzGerald, second Baron Offaly, grandson of Maurice FitzGerald (the famous ancestor of the Earls of Desmond and Kildare and one of the most prominent of the Norman invaders who came to Ireland in the time of King Henry II.), must have been very young at his father's death, as it was not until 1216 that he was put in possession of Maynooth and the other paternal estates, by a mandatory letter of King Henry III. In 1215 he introduced into Ireland the order of the Franciscans, and in 1216 the Domini-

cans. He was appointed Lord-Justice both in
1229 and 1245. In 1232 he built the Franciscan
Abbey of Youghal. In 1234, at a conference on
the Curragh between Richard, Earl Marshal, the
Baron of Offaly, and others, the former was
treacherously slain; whereupon FitzGerald proceeded to London, and took an oath before
Henry III. that he was innocent of all participation in the deed.

In 1234 the English King issued a writ directing FitzGerald to proclaim free trade between Ireland and England. In 1236 the latter
founded the Dominican Abbey at Sligo as the
abode of a community of monks to say prayers
for the repose of the soul of Earl Marshal, and
the same year he built the Castle of Armagh, and
in 1242 that of Sligo. In 1235 he marched at the
head of a large force into Connaught, and reduced the province to submission. In 1245 he
and Felim O'Conor, of Connaught, were admon-
ished for tardiness in joining the English King in
an expedition into Wales. After this, among
other rights, the Irish Barons claimed exemption
from attending the sovereign beyond the realm.
In 1246 FitzGerald subdued Tirconnell, and in
1248 marched into Tyrone, and forced O'Neill
to give hostages; but in 1257 he was defeated by
Godfrey O'Donnell at the Rosses, near Sligo.
Soon after this he retired to the Franciscan
monastery at Youghal, assumed the habit of the
order, and died the same year. He had married
a daughter of John de Cogan.

Maurice FitzGerald

Maurice FitzGerald, third Baron Offaly, succeeded his father in 1257. Terrible feuds raged

in his time between the Geraldines and De
Burghs. In 1272 he was made Lord-Justice. He
more than once invaded Thomond, in 1277, taking prisoner and executing O'Brien Roe, prince
of that district; on his return, with part of his
forces, he was surrounded in a pass of the Slieve
Bloom mountains, and his men were reduced to
eat horse flesh, and ultimately compelled to give
hostages, and grant to the Irish the Castle of
Roscommon. A poem celebrating the efforts
made to defend Ross against rival factions, by
walling it in 1265, is given by Crocker in his
"Popular Songs of Ireland." The Baron of Offaly
died at Ross in 1277.

Gerald FitzGerald

Sir Gerald FitzGerald, fourth Baron Offaly,
succeeded his father in 1277. He completed the
Grey Abbey at Kildare, and founded the Franciscan Abbey at Clane. He carried on wars with
the O'Conors. In a battle with the O'Briens in
1287, many Anglo-Norman knights were slain,
and he received a wound from which he shortly
afterwards died at Rathmore. He was buried
at Kildare. Maurice FitzGerald, fifth Baron Offaly succeeded. He married Agnes de Valence,
great granddaughter of Eve and Strongbow.

John FitzGerald

John FitzGerald was the first Earl of Kildare. On the death of the fifth Baron Offaly, who
left no children, John, descended from the third
son of the second baron, was the only surviving
male descendant of the first baron. The story of
an ape saving a member of the family from a

burning castle, is told of the first Earl of Kildare, as well as of one of the Desmonds. When Swift was writing Gulliver's Travels, he had quarrelled with the then Earl of Kildare, and hence introduced the incident of Gulliver being carried off and fed by the Brobdingnagian ape. Whatever may be the truth of the story, the ape was adopted as the FitzGerald crest.

In 1293, in consequence of a dispute between him and William de Vesci, Lord of Kildare, they were both summoned to appear before King Edward I. After mutual recrimination, FitzGerald challenged De Vesci to single combat. When the day came, De Vesci fled to France, and the King declared FitzGerald innocent and added: "Albeit Albert de Vesci conveyed his person into France, yet he left his lands behind him in Ireland," and he granted them to FitzGerald. Having consistently opposed the "Irish enemy," assisted on three occasions against the Scotch, and in 1315 opposed Edward Bruce at Ardscull, in Kildare, he was, May 14, 1316, created Earl of Kildare, and granted the castle and town of that name. He died at Maynooth or at Laraghbryan, September 10, 1316, and was buried in the Grey Abbey, at Kildare.

Thomas FitzGerald

Thomas FitzGerald, second Earl of Kildare, succeeded his father in 1316. In 1317 he took the field at the head of an army of 30,000 men against Edward Bruce, who was slain the following year near Dundalk. FitzGerald held the office of Lord-Justice more than once. During his lifetime Ireland continued to be torn by contending factions. The earl introduced into his territories the Irish

exaction of "bonaght," or "coigne and livery"—
money and food for man and horse without payment, as did the Earls of Ormond and Desmond
into their palatinates. He died at Maynooth,
April 9, 1328, and was buried in the Grey Abbey
at Kildare. Richard, third Earl of Kildare, born
in 1317, died at Rathangan, in 1329, and was
buried beside his father.

Maurice FitzGerald

Maurice FitzGerald, fourth Earl of Kildare,
brother of preceding. In 1345 he was imprisoned
in Dublin Castle by the English King's order, but
was released the next year on the recognizances
of twenty-four lords and gentlemen. In 1347 he
attended King Edward III. to Calais with thirty
men-at-arms and forty hobellers, and for his
bravery was knighted by the King. In 1378 we
find him granted £10 from the Exchequer as
compensation for his loss of six men, four coats
of mail, and other armour, "in a certain great
hosting." He died August 25, 1390, and was
buried in Christ Church, Dublin.

Gerald FitzGerald

Gerald FitzGerald, fifth Earl of Kildare, succeeded his father. In 1398 he was taken prisoner
by Calvagh O'Conor Faly, and was not released
until he had paid heavy ransom. In 1407 he defeated O'Carrol at Kilkenny, slaying him and
800 of his men. In 1408 he was sent prisoner to
Dublin Castle, and all his goods plundered by the
servants of the Lord-Lieutenant, for disrespect to
the latter's authority. He was afterwards liberated on paying a fine of 300 marks. He died in

1410, and was buried in the Grey Abbey at Kildare. He acted as Lord-Deputy in 1405. His son John, sixth Earl of Kildare, enlarged the Castles of Maynooth and Kilkea. He died in 1427.

Thomas FitzGerald

Thomas FitzGerald, seventh Earl of Kildare, succeeded his father in 1427. He more than once acted as Lord-Deputy to the Duke of York, who as far as possible divided his favors between the FitzGeralds and the Butlers. When the Duke fell at the battle of Wakefield, several members of both these powerful families were slain under his banners. As deputy the Earl of Kildare held several parliaments, at Naas, Drogheda, and elsewhere; he also acted as Lord-Chancellor. In 1467 he and his brother-in-law, the Earl of Desmond, were attainted "for alliance, fosterage, and alterage with the King's Irish enemies." Desmond was beheaded, but Kildare pleaded his own cause before the King, had the attainder reversed, and the same year he was appointed Lord-Justice. He established the "Brothers of St. George," the only standing army of the Pale, consisting of 120 mounted archers, 40 horsemen, and 40 pages; the archers received sixpence a day, the horsemen fivepence. The object of the fraternity was to resist the "Irish enemies and English rebels." The earl died March 25, 1477, and was buried beside his father.

Gerald FitzGerald

Gerald FitzGerald, eighth Earl of Kildare, called the "Great Earl," succeeded his father in 1477. He was appointed Lord-Deputy to the young Duke of York; but was shortly dismissed, and Lord Grey appointed in his place, on the plea that an Englishman was more suited to the office. This roused the indignation of the lords of the Pale, who, declaring that Lord Grey's patent was informal, opened a parliament of their own, under the presidency of Kildare. On appeal, King Edward IV., believing it his best policy to govern Ireland through the Geraldine faction, recalled Lord Grey and appointed the earl. Kildare displayed great vigor in the government, and continued in his post undisturbed by the accession of King Richard III. On the accession of King Henry VII. it was a matter of surprise that the King for a time permitted the earl, a known Yorkist, to continue in office.

The earl was summoned to London, but made many excuses for non-compliance, with which Henry had to content himself at the time. Kildare's adhesion to the cause of the impostor, Simnel, afforded clear evidence of his insincerity, and Henry, still unable to dispense with his services, sent over Sir Richard Edgecomb to exact the most binding oaths possible from him and the other men of mark who had espoused Simnel's cause and invaded England. FitzGerald continued to exhibit ability in the government. Lodge mentions that he received a present from Germany of six muskets, then a great novelty, with which he armed his guard at Thomascourt. After some time Kildare found it necessary to go over to London to answer complaints of the Archbishop of Armagh. The decision was to his favor, and he and his friends were entertained at a banquet, where it is said they were deliberately humiliated, by Simnel (whom they had once crowned), being set to attend on them.

When the adventurer Warbeck appeared in Ireland, King Henry prudently displaced the earl, and for a time the Butlers, of Ormond, regained their supremacy. Both Kildare and Ormond joined Lord-Deputy Poynings in a raid on the O'Hanlon's territory in Ulster. Eventually the enemies of Kildare triumphed, and he was thrown into the Tower of London, where he remained two years. During his imprisonment, November 22, 1494, his countess, Alison, died of grief, and was buried at Kilcullen. When brought to trial in 1496, and asked whether he was provided with counsel, Kildare replied: "Yea, the ablest in the realm; your Highness (the King) I take for my counsel against these false knaves." Accused by the Archbishop of Cashel of burning down his cathedral, he answered: "I would not have done it if I had not been told that my Lord Archbishop was inside." This frankness delighted the King, and we are told that when some one exclaimed, "All Ireland cannot govern this earl," Henry VII. rejoined, "Then let this earl govern all Ireland."

He had been sent to England almost a convicted traitor, and returned Lord-Deputy. Soon afterwards he showed his zeal by expeditions against the O'Briens in Thomond and the O'Neills in the north. In 1499 he entered Connaught and established castles at Athleague, Roscommon, Tulsk, and Castlerea. Many useful enactments were passed at a parliament held by him at Castledermot in 1499. Next year he marched against malcontents in the North, and also against Cork, the mayor of which city he hanged. Some years later a powerful confederacy under Lord Clanricard was formed in Connaught, and a large army assembled. Kildare marched against them, and August 19, 1504, a battle was fought at Knocktuagh ("Hill of Axes"), now Knockdoe, seven miles from Galway.

Clanricard was routed with a stated loss of 4,000 to 9,000 men, and Galway and Athenry were taken. O'Brien fell, and two sons and a daughter of Clanricard were taken prisoners. The battle is thus described by the Four Masters: "Far away the troops were heard, the violent onset of the martial chiefs, the vehement efforts of the champions, the charge of the royal heroes, the noise of the lords, the clamour of the troops when endangered, the shouts and exultations of the youths, the sound made by the falling of brave men, and the triumphing of nobles over plebeians." Kildare's power was firmly established by this victory, and he was created a Knight of the Garter by the King.

In 1513, in an expedition against the O'Carrolls, he was wounded by the enemy while watering his horse in the river Greese at Kilkea. He was conveyed by slow stages to Kildare, where, after lingering a few days, he died, September 3, and was buried in his chapel of St. Mary in Christ Church. He it was that first introduced artillery into Ireland. The door was until lately shown in St. Patrick's through a hole in which the Earl of Ormond and he shook hands after an encounter between their followers in the church. Some of the coins issued in Ireland in his time bear his arms.

He was thrice married. Holinshed says: "He was a mighty man of stature, full of honor and courage, who had been Lord-Deputy and Lord-Justice of Ireland three and thirty years. Kildare was in government mild, to his enemies stern. He was open and plain, hardly able to rule

himself, when he was moved; in anger not so
sharp as short, being easily displeased and sooner
appeased.   .   .   .   Notwithstanding his simplicity in peace, he was of that valor and policy in
war, as his name bred a greater terror to the
Irish than other men's armies."

Gerald FitzGerald

Gerald FitzGerald, ninth Earl of Kildare, son
of the preceding, was born in 1487. He is said
to have been one of the handsomest men of his
time. The Irish annalists call him "Geroit Oge,"
or "Garrett MacAlison," after his mother. In
1496 he was detained by King Henry VII. at his
court as a hostage for his father's fidelity. In
1503, when but sixteen, he married Elizabeth
Zouche, and was soon after permitted to return
to Ireland. Next year he was appointed Lord
High Treasurer.

In August, 1504, he commanded the reserve
at the battle of Knockdoe, where his rashness
and impetuosity were the cause of some loss. On
the death of his father in 1513 he succeeded to
the title and was by the council chosen Lord-
Justice. Henry VIII. soon afterwards appointed
him Lord-Deputy. Some of the Irish chiefs at
the end of 1513, having ravaged parts of the Pale,
the earl, early in the following year, defeated
O'More and his followers in Leix, and then,
marching North, took the Castle of Cavan, killed
Chief O'Reilly, drove his followers into the bogs,
and returned to Dublin laden with booty. This
energetic action was so highly approved by the
King that he granted the earl the customs of the
ports in County Down,—rights repurchased by
the Crown from the seventeenth earl in 1662.

In 1516 the earl invaded Imayle, and sent the head of Shane O'Toole as a present to the Mayor of Dublin. He then marched into Ely O'Carroll, in conjunction with his brother-in-law, the Earl of Ormond, and James, son of the Earl of Desmond. They captured and razed the Castle of Lemyvannan, took Clonmel, and in December he returned to Dublin "laden with booty, hostages and honor." In March, 1517, he called a parliament in Dublin, and then invaded Ulster, stormed the Castle of Dundrum, marched into Tyrone, and took Dungannon, "and so reduced Ireland to a quiet condition." October 6 of the same year his Countess died at Lucan and was buried at Kilcullen.

Next year, 1518, his enemies having accused him of maladministration, he appointed a deputy and sailed for England. He was removed from the government, and the Earl of Surrey appointed in his stead. He appears to have accompanied the King to France in June, 1520, and was present at "the Field of the Cloth of Gold," where he was distinguished by his bearing and retinue. On this occasion he met the King's first cousin, Lady Elizabeth Grey, whom he married a few months afterwards, and thereby gained considerable influence at court.

Kildare was permitted to return to Ireland in January, 1523. About this time he founded the College of Maynooth, which flourished until suppressed in 1538. He signalized his return to Ireland by an expedition into Leix in company with the Mayor of Dublin. Having burnt several villages, they were caught in an ambuscade, and after considerable loss retreated with some difficulty to Dublin. In consequence of disputes and misunderstandings between the Earl of Kildare and the Earl of Ormond, who was now Lord-Deputy, they appealed to the King, accusing each other of malpractices and treasons. Arbitrators were appointed, who ordered that both the earls should abstain from making war without the King's assent; that they should cease levying "coigne and livery"; that the two earls should persuade their kinsmen to submit to the laws, and that they should be bound by a bond of 1,000 marks each to keep the peace for one year.

Before long, however, their mutual hatreds blazed forth again in consequence of the death of James Talbot, one of Ormond's followers, by the retainers of Kildare. Again the earls appealed to the King, and again commissioners were sent over, who conducted an inquiry at Christ Church, Dublin, in June, 1524. Their decision was in the main in favor of Kildare, and an indenture was drawn up, by which the earls agreed to forgive each other, to be friends, and to make common cause for the future. Soon afterwards, Kildare was reappointed Lord-Deputy. He took the oaths at Thomascourt, his nephew, Con B. O'Neill, carrying the sword of state before him.

He then entered into an indenture with the King not to grant pardons without the consent of the council, to cause the Irish in his territories to wear English dress, to shave their upper beards, and not to levy "coigne and livery" except when on the King's business, and then only to a specified amount.

Next year, 1525, Kildare and Ormond were again at daggers drawn. They appealed to the King concerning a disputed sum of £800 in account between them, accusing each other as before, of many enormities and malfeasances.

About the same time Kildare, in accordance with a royal mandate, assembled a large force, and marched into Munster to arrest the Earl of Desmond, making a show of great eagerness, but sending private instructions to the earl how to keep out of the way. He next turned North, and by diplomacy and force pacified the O'Neills and O'Donnells.

In 1526 he was ordered to England to meet the charges of the Earl of Ormond, of having secretly assisted the Desmonds, and having slain many good subjects because they were adherents of the Butlers. On arrival in London, he was for a time committed to the Tower, and was retained in England for four years, and when he was brought before the council a violent altercation ensued between him and Cardinal Wolsey, which is reported at full length by Holinshed.

Wolsey is said to have obtained an order for his immediate execution, which his well-wisher, the Constable of the Tower, frustrated by exercising a right (still inherent in the office) of demanding a personal interview with the King. Liberated on bail for a time, Kildare was recommitted on the discovery of his intriguing with the Irish princes to induce them to commit assaults on the Pale, so as to make his return appear necessary.

Liberated again, he was one of the peers who in 1530 signed the letter to the Pope relative to the divorce of Queen Catharine. The same year, to the joy of his retainers, he was permitted to return to Ireland with Skeffington, the new Lord-Deputy. On his arrival he marched against the O'Tooles to punish them for ravages on his tenantry in his absence, and then accompanied the Deputy against the O'Donnells. The friendship of the Deputy and earl did not last long, and they sent letters and messages to the King accusing each other. The Deputy, as might be expected was supported by the Butlers. Nevertheless, the earl appears to have cleared himself, and to have been appointed to succeed Skeffington as Deputy to the Duke of Richmond.

Landing at Dublin in this capacity, in August 1532, Kildare was received with great acclamations. But lengthened peace appeared impossible. He insulted the late Deputy, wasted the territories of the Butlers, was accused of forming alliances with the native chiefs, and in 1533 the council reported to the King that such was the animosity between the Earls of Kildare and Ormond that peace was out of the question as long as either of them was Deputy. At this period, Kildare had partially lost the use of his limbs and his speech, in consequence of a gunshot wound received in an attack upon the O'Carrolls at Birr. He was again summoned to court, and in February, 1534, at a council at Drogheda, in an affecting speech, he nominated his son Thomas, Lord Offaly, as Vice-Deputy, and then, embracing him and the lords of the council, set sail for England.

On his arrival in London he was arraigned on several charges, and was committed to the Tower, where he died of grief, December 12, 1534, on hearing of his son's insurrection, and perusing the excommunication launched against him. He was buried in St. Peter's Church in the Tower. He is described as valiant and wellspoken, "nothing inferior to his father in marshal prowess," hospitable and religious, beloved by his friends and dependants. He strengthened and kept in repair several castles,—Rathangan,

Rheban, Kildare, Woodstock, Athy, Kilkea, Castledermot, and Carlow.   His likeness, painted by Holbein in 1530, is still preserved at Carton, while a book containing his rent-roll, and lists of his horses, plate, and furniture, is in the British Museum.

From it we learn that his library consisted of thirty-one Latin, thirty-seven French, twenty-two English, and eighteen Irish books.   Lord Thomas, called "Silken Thomas," born in England in 1613, was the tenth Earl of Kildare.   He fought the English forces successfully for a long time, but eventually surrendered on promise of pardon, but was, with his five uncles, executed at Tyburn in 1537.

Gerald FitzGerald

Gerald FitzGerald, eleventh Earl of Kildare, half-brother of the tenth earl, was born February 25, 1525, and was consequently but ten years old at the time of Lord Thomas' surrender.   He was then lying ill of the smallpox at Donore, in Kildare, and, being the only hope of the family, he was carefully conveyed in a large basket, by Thomas Leverous, a priest and foster-brother of his father, into Offaly, to his sister, Lady Mary O'Conor, and, when recovered, was removed into Thomond, to the care of his cousin, James Delahide.

The Irish Council spared no efforts to induce the O'Briens to surrender him; but, after using all their diplomacy, they had to confess to the Lord Chamberlain, Thomas Cromwell: "And as to O'Brien, notwithstanding his letters and promises of subjection and obedience to the King's Highness, we could neither get him to condescend to any conformity according the same, ney yet to deliver the Earl of Kildare's plate and goods." After six months' rest in Thomond, Delahide and Leverous conveyed Gerald to his aunt, Lady Eleanor MacCarthy, at Kilbriton, in Cork. Her son, the MacCarthy Reagh, was tributary to the Earl of Desmond, and the Government endeavored to induce the earl to compel the lad's surrender.

Royal Commissioners were appointed, and a "most gracious pardon" offered to the lad himself if he would but come in. Remembering the fate of Lord Thomas and his uncles, and the known anxiety of the King for the extinction of the Geraldines, he wisely declined putting himself into the English power. It appeared desirable that he should seek some safer asylum, and accordingly his aunt, Lady Eleanor, urged by O'Neill and Desmond, consented to a long-talked-of marriage with Manus O'Donnell of Tirconnell, so as to be enabled to offer him an asylum in the North. The marriage took place, and all the plottings and plans of the Government for securing Gerald's person were completely frustrated.

In September, 1539, Cromwell was informed by an Irish correspondent: "I assure your Lordship that this English Pale, except the towns, and a very few of the possessioners, are too affectionate to the Geraldines, that for kindred marriage, fostering, and adhering as followers, they desire more to see a Geraldine reign and triumph than to see God come among them; and if they might see this young Gerald's banner displayed, if they should lose half their substance, they would rejoice more at the same, than otherwise to gain great goods." Later on, in the beginning of 1540, the Council informed the King that "the detestable traitors, young Gerald, O'Neill, O'Donnell, the pretended Earl of Desmond, O'Brien, O'Connor, and O'Mulmoy, continued to destroy the property of his Majesty's subjects, to subdue the whole land to the supremacy of the Pope, and to elevate the Geraldines."

In March, 1540, Lady Eleanor O'Donnell, suspecting that her husband harbored intentions of surrendering the young earl, determined to send him away. "She engaged a merchant vessel of St. Malo, which happened to be in Donegal Bay, to convey a small party to the coast of Brittany. She then gave 140 gold Portugueses to Gerald, and he departed with his tutor Leverous, and Robert Walsh, a faithful servant of his father. He is described as having been dressed in a saffron-colored shirt like one of the natives. The vessel immediately set sail, and arrived safely at St. Malo, where Gerald was hospitably received by the Governor. Gerald once in safety, Lady Eleanor reproached O'Donnell for his intended treachery, told him no further inducement existed for her tolerating his company, "and trussing up bag and baggage, returned to her country."

After Gerald's departure, the Irish league fell to pieces and O'Donnell, O'Neill, Desmond, and the other Irish princes submitted, and were ultimately pardoned and received into royal favor. The attention young Gerald met with on the Continent, and the reports sent abroad that he was the rightful heir to the Irish Crown, created much manœuvering and correspondence at the court of King Henry VIII. Francis I., King of France, placed him with the young Dauphin for a time; he was next sent privately into Flanders, then part of the dominions of the Emperor Charles V., the English ambassador keeping a careful watch on his movements. From Charles V. he was passed on to Cardinal Pole at Rome, who settled upon him an annuity of 300 crowns, treated him with affection, and had him educated and trained as a prince of high expectations.

In 1544, when his education had been completed, he visited the Knights of Malta (to which body two of his uncles had belonged), and gathered laurels in an expedition to the coast of Africa. In 1545 he was appointed master of the horse to Cosmo de Medici, with a salary of 300 ducats per annum, besides other handsome allowances. In June of the same year Lady Eleanor O'Donnell was pardoned for her part in his escape. After the death of Henry VIII., in 1547, Gerald visited London, together with some foreign ambassadors, accompanied by his old friend, Thomas Leverous. At a masque given by Edward VI., he fell in love with Mabel Brown, a lady of the court, whom he shortly afterwards married.

He was received into favor and restored to his Irish estates by patent of April 25, 1552. His faithful adherent, Leverous, was appointed Bishop of Kildare and Dean of St. Patrick's, preferments of which he was deprived in 1559, on refusing to adopt the reformed tenets. He afterwards kept a school at Adare, and died about 1577, in the eightieth year of his age, at Naas, where he was buried in the parish church of St. David. Reinstated in all his father's possessions and titles, the young earl returned to Ireland in November, 1554, and was received with an outburst of delight by the dependents of the Geraldines. If we except one recall to London in

1560, in consequence of reported machinations between him and the Earl of Desmond, he appears to have been regarded as a loyal and trusted servant of the Crown, and as such often accompanied the Deputy in his expeditions against seditious Irish chieftains.

He is praised by some contemporary writers for having "presented the Government many times with a number of principal outlaws' heads." In 1562 he accompanied Shane O'Neill on his visit to Queen Elizabeth. August 25, 1580, he formed one of the party that accompanied the Lord-Deputy, Lord Grey, and was defeated in Glenmalure by the O'Byrnes. Later on, however, the Government had occasion to suspect his loyalty, and he and his family were for some time confined successively in Dublin Castle and the Tower of London.

He was eventually liberated, and died in London, November 16, 1585; his remains were brought over and interred at Kildare. His wife survived him until August 25, 1610. "He was of low stature and slender figure, and was reputed to have been the best horseman of his day. With many good qualities,—honorable, courteous, valiant, affable, and having all the qualifications belonging to a gentleman—he was passionate and covetous. He conformed to the Protestant religion in the beginning of the reign of Queen Elizabeth."

Henry FitzGerald

Henry FitzGerald, twelfth Earl of Kildare, second son of preceding, was born in 1562. He was called "Henry na Tuagh"—"of the battle-axes." Espousing the Anglo-Irish side in the wars with Hugh O'Neill, he was wounded in

a skirmish on the Blackwater, in July, 1597.
Brought to Drogheda, he died there September
30, from the effects of the wound and through
grief for the death of his two foster-brothers,
O'Conors, who had been slain by his side. He
was buried in St. Bridget's Cathedral, Kildare.
His wife was Lady Frances Howard, daughter
of the Earl of Nottingham. His brother William, thirteenth Earl of Kildare, died at sea in
1599.

Gerald FitzGerald

Gerald FitzGerald, fourteenth Earl of Kildare, grandson of the ninth earl, succeeded on
the death of his cousin in 1599. He was well
affected towards the Crown, and occupied several
positions of trust. He died February 11, 1612,
and his obsequies were solemnized at Maynooth,
but his remains were not buried at Kildare
until November. He married Elizabeth Nugent,
daughter of Lord Delvin. His son Gerald, fifteenth Earl of Kildare, born shortly before his
father's death, died at the age of nine.

George FitzGerald

George FitzGerald, sixteenth Earl of Kildare, great-grandson of the ninth earl, born January, 1612, was known as the "Fairy Earl," apparently for no other reason that that his portrait,
still extant, was painted on a small scale. Given
in charge to the Earl of Cork, he, when but
eighteen, married the earl's daughter, Lady Joan
Boyle. The Castle of Maynooth, which had
fallen into decay on the death of the fourteenth
Earl of Kildare, was restored and improved for
him by his guardian.

In 1638 he was committed to prison for refusing to submit the title-deeds of his estates to the Earl of Strafford. He took the Anglo-Irish side in the war of 1641-52, and suffered much in estate, Maynooth Castle being pillaged and dismantled by the Confederates. After Cromwell's landing in 1649, his regiment was with many others disbanded. He died in 1660, and was buried at Kildare. Wentworth FitzGerald, seventeenth Earl of Kildare, son of preceding, born in 1634, died in 1664, and was buried in Christ Church, Dublin.

John FitzGerald

John FitzGerald, eighteenth Earl of Kildare, son of the seventeenth earl, was born in 1661, died in 1707, and was buried in Westminster Abbey. In 1683 the degree of D. C. L. was conferred upon him by the University of Oxford. In 1689 his estates, of the annual value of £6,800 in Ireland, and £200 in England, were sequestered by James' Irish Parliament. He sold the family lands of Adare and Croom to pay off incumbrances on his other property.

Robert FitzGerald

Robert FitzGerald, nineteenth Earl of Kildare, grandson of the sixteenth earl, was born in 1675. He died February 20, 1744, and was interred in Christ Church. Finding Maynooth Castle too much dilapidated to be restored, he purchased Carton, the present seat of the family. He is said to have been "extremely formal and delicate, insomuch that when he was married to Lady Mary O'Brien, one of the most shining

beauties then in the world, he would not take off his wedding gloves to embrace her."

James FitzGerald

James FitzGerald, twentieth Earl of Kildare, and first Duke of Leinster, son of preceding, was born May 29, 1722. He laid the foundations of Leinster House, Dublin, saying, when told that it was in an unfashionable part of the town, "they will follow me wherever I go." In consequence of a spirited remonstrance to the King relative to the disposition of the large unappropriated surplus of Irish revenue, he became one of the most popular men in Ireland,—a medal being struck in his honor. He was created a marquis in 1761, and Duke of Leinster in 1766.

He died in Leinster House, November 19, 1773, and was buried in Christ Church. In 1746 he married Lady Emily Mary Lennox, daughter of the Duke of Richmond, sister of Lady Holland, Lady Louisa Conolly, and Lady Sarah Napier. They had nine sons and ten daughters. Among the sons was Lord Edward FitzGerald, who became commander-in-chief of the United Irishmen, and died in prison in 1798 (see Volume II.). She survived the duke many years, and married William Ogilvy, by whom she had two daughters. She died March 27, 1814.

William R. FitzGerald

William Robert FitzGerald, second Duke of Leinster, the second son of the preceding, was born March 2, 1749. Upon the death of his elder brother, in 1765, he became Earl of Offaly, and when his father was created duke, in 1766, he was made Marquis of Kildare. In 1767 he became member of Parliament for Dublin, and continued to be a member of the Irish House of Commons until his father's death, in 1773. He held many important offices connected with the State, was one of the generals of the Volunteers, and on the institution of the Order of St. Patrick, in 1783, was the first of the original knights.

Upon the Union, he received £28,800 compensation for the disfranchisement of Kildare and Athy. He died October 20, 1804, leaving a family of five sons and eight daughters. Barrington says: "His disposition and address combined almost every quality which could endear him to the Nation; . . . he always intended right. . . . Something approaching to regal honors attended his investiture" (as a General of the Volunteers).

Augustus F. FitzGerald

Augustus Frederick FitzGerald, third Duke of Leinster, Grand Master of the Freemasons of Ireland, eldest son of the second duke, was born August 21, 1791. When quite a boy he succeeded his father as Duke of Leinster. He was educated at Eton and at Oxford. In politics he was a Whig, and supported in the House of Lords the cause of Queen Caroline, Catholic emancipation, the Reform Bill, and other measures of a liberal tendency. Most of his life was passed in Ireland, attending to the duties connected with his estates and his position in the country. He was a man of great refinement and amiability of character. He died October 10, 1874, and was succeeded by his son. Maurice FitzGerald, sixth Duke of Leinster, born in 1887, "the Premier Duke, Marquis, and Earl of Ireland," is the present representative of the House of Kildare.

Robert FitzGerald

Robert FitzGerald, second son of the sixteenth Earl of Kildare, and father of the nineteenth earl, born in August, 1637, was an active promoter of the restoration of Charles II. He received estates, and many offices of trust and emolument were conferred upon him. Opposing James II.'s Irish policy, he was deprived of his lands and was for a time confined in Trinity College with about fifty other persons of distinction. When the news of the battle of the Boyne arrived, he was released, and exerted himself to preserve Dublin from pillage before its surrender to William III., exhibiting the greatest nerve and executive capacity.

July 6, when William entered Dublin in state, it was FitzGerald that presented him with the keys of the castle and city. The King returned them, saying, "Sir, they are in good hands; you deserve them well and may keep them." He was shortly afterwards restored to all his estates and offices of trust, and reappointed on the Privy-Council. He died January 31, 1699. He was the author of a work extolling the benefits of salt water sweetened (London, 1683), and of "A Full and True Account of the Late Revolution in Dublin" (London, 1690).

Elizabeth FitzGerald

Lady Elizabeth FitzGerald, generally known as "The Fair Geraldine," daughter of the ninth earl by his second wife, Lady Elizabeth Grey, was born about 1528, and was still an infant when she was taken by her mother to England. She was brought up at Hunsden, with the Princesses Mary and Elizabeth. When about thirteen she was there seen by the Earl of Surrey, who has immortalized her in several sonnets. "There is no reason to suppose that the friendship which existed between them in the following years was anything but platonic." There is an apocryphal story that Surrey, at a tournament at Florence, defied all the world to show such beauty as hers, and that he visited the celebrated alchemist, Cornelius Agrippa, who revealed to him in a magic mirror the object of his affections. Scott, in his "Lay of the Last Minstrel," recounts the tale in five spirited stanzas.

In 1543, when but fifteen, "The Fair Geraldine" married Sir Anthony Brown, K. G. After his death, in 1548, she became the third wife of the Earl of Lincoln, who died in 1583, without issue by her. She died in March, 1589, and was interred beside the earl, her husband, under a fine monument in St. George's Chapel at Windsor. A fac-simile of a letter written by her, and a photograph from her portrait preserved in the Duke of Bedford's gallery (a copy of which is at Carton) are given in the Kilkenny Archæological Journal for 1873.

John F. FitzGerald

John FitzEdmund FitzGerald, seneschal of Imokelly, in County Cork, was one of the distinguished FitzGeralds of the sixteenth century,— "the chief man of service among the rebels." In 1569 Sir H. Sidney captured his castle of Ballymartar; and eventually, with FitzMaurice, he

had to submit to Sir John Perrot among the ruins
of the church of Kilmallock, which they had destroyed a short time before.   When FitzMaurice
proceeded to France to seek assistance against
England, the seneschal was discovered to be in
communication with him; and in November,
1579, he threw aside the mask of loyalty and
invaded the country of the Butlers, burning Ne-
nagh and some other of Ormond's towns.

Soon after, we are told, "Sir Walter Rawley
returning from Dublin, had a hard escape from
the seneschal, who set on him with fourteen horse
and sixty foot. . . . The seneschal of Imokelly
killed thirty-six of Pers's soldiers, and ten of Sir
W. Morgan's, as they had been to get a prey."
Next year he burned down numerous towns in
the Decies, and carried off 7,000 head of cattle,
reaping all the corn and conveying it into hiding
places in the woods.   In September, 1582, he was
in the field at the head of 200 horse and 2,000
foot; but his fortunes, like those of his friend,
the Earl of Desmond, were soon on the wane.
Shortly before the earl was slain, the seneschal,
much to the satisfaction of Queen Elizabeth, submitted unconditionally; and Ormond, respecting
the character of his former antagonist, successfully exerted himself to save his life.   In 1585 he
was committed to Dublin Castle, where he appears to have ended his troubled career early in
1589.   He should not be confounded with his
namesake and cousin, Sir John FitzEdmund
FitzGerald.

John F. FitzGerald

Sir John FitzEdmund FitzGerald, seneschal
of Imokelly, cousin of preceding, was born about

1528. He remained with the Government all through the Desmond war, although often sorely tempted to join the earl, who was a relative of his. In July, 1572, he was recommended to the Queen by Sir Henry Sidney as deserving of reward for his sufferings in her service, and was granted an immediate sum of 100 marks and an annuity of 100 more out of the Munster forfeitures. When Parliament met for the arrangement of the forfeitures of the Desmond estates, he produced a deed which the deceasel earl had made of his property to him before the war. The dates of the document were proved to be erroneous, and his character for loyalty was compromised by this attempt to aid the family of his kinsman, and "cheat the greedy undertakers out of their prey."

Nevertheless, he continued to show himself "the best subject the Queen had in Munster." In March, 1601, when Mountjoy sojourned at his house in Cloyne, he was knighted. He was a friend of Sir George Carew, and in his old age was in the enjoyment of as much leisure and dignity as official favor could procure for him. He died January 15, 1612, and was buried in Cloyne Cathedral, where his monument may still be seen.

Edward FitzGerald

Edward FitzGerald, a leader in the insurrection of 1798, was a country gentleman of ample means, who was born at Newpark, County Wexford, about 1770. He was in Wexford jail on suspicion at the breaking out of the insurrection in 1798, was released by the populace, and during the occupation of the town commanded in some of the engagements that took place in different parts of the country, showing far more ability than the Commander-in-chief, Bagenal B. Harvey. Dr. Madden says: "With regard to the prisoners that fell into his hands at Gorey, he behaved in the most humane manner possible; amid the threats and shouts of the people for vengeance on those who had recently slain or butchered their nearest relatives, . . . he said to the people: 'You cannot bring the dead to life by imitating the brutality of your enemies. It is for us to follow them, and come face to face with them.'"

He particularly distinguished himself at the battle of Arklow, where he commanded the Shelmalier gunsmen. He afterwards joined in the expedition against Hacketstown; and surrendered upon terms to General Wilford, in July. With Garrett Byrne and others he was detained in custody in Dublin until the next year, when he was allowed to remove to England. He was rearrested, March 25, 1800, imprisoned for a short time, and then permitted to emigrate to Hamburg, where he died in 1807. He is described as a handsome, finely formed man.

Richard De Burgh

Richard De Burgh, Lord of Connaught, was the son of William Fitzadelm De Burgh, one of the original Anglo-Normans who came to Ireland under King Henry II. The name is variously spelled De Burgh, De Burgo, De Burgho, Burke, or Bourke. In 1204 he succeeded to large estates in the province of Connaught, which were confirmed to him by King John for a fine of 300 marks, and by Henry III. for a fine of 3,000 marks. In 1225, after Cathal O'Conor's death, the whole of Connaught, with the exception of five cantreds for the support of Athlone garrison, was made over to him for 500 marks a year. But the O'Conors clung to their patrimony, and upon one occasion Felim O'Conor was even deputed by Henry III. to act against De Burgh and check his rising power. De Burgh exercised almost regal sway, and at his castle at Galway (built in 1232), and in that at Loughrea (built in 1236), he was attended by a train of knights, barons, and gentlemen.

He was for some time Lord-Deputy of Ireland. He died on his passage to France, January, 1243, whither he was proceeding, attended by his barons and knights, to meet the King of England at Bordeaux. His wife was Una, daughter of Hugh O'Conor, Prince of Connaught.

Walter De Burgh

Walter De Burgh, first Earl of Ulster, son of preceding, married Maud, daughter and heiress of Hugh de Lacy, Earl of Ulster. At her father's decease, about 1243, he became, in her right, Earl of Ulster. He was eminent for power and enterprise, and the active part which he took in the events of that troubled period of Irish history. The contest with the O'Conors, bequeathed by his father, was continued by Walter. He died in 1271, at his castle in Galway.

Richard De Burgh

Richard De Burgh, second Earl of Ulster, son of preceding, commonly called, from his complexion, the "Red Earl," was educated at the court of Henry III. For his successes against the Scots he was made general over the Irish forces in Ireland, Great Britain, and France. He was considered the most powerful subject of his time in Ireland. Besides carrying on hostilities with the native chieftains, he besieged Thomas de Verdon in Athlone, and advanced with a great army to Trim. Three times he assisted the English kings in their descents upon Scotland.

He founded monasteries or castles at Loughrea, Ballymote, Corran, Sligo, Castleconnel in Limerick, and Greencastle in Down. So high was his position that his name was placed before that of the Lord-Lieutenant in all public documents. In 1326 he sumptuously entertained the Anglo-Norman knights of the Pale assembled at Kilkenny, previous to shutting himself up in the monastery at Athassel, where he died the same year.

William De Burgh

William De Burgh, third Earl of Ulster, was born in 1312, and succeeded his grandfather in 1326. "He was slain June 6, 1333, by Robert FitzRichard Mandeville (who gave him the first wound), and others, his servants, near to the Fords, in going towards Carrickfergus, in the 21st year of his age, at the instigation, it was said, of Gyle de Burgh, wife of Sir Richard Mandeville, in revenge for his having imprisoned her brother Walter and others." Three hundred of Sir Richard Mandeville's followers were put to death for this crime.

De Burgh married Maud, great-granddaughter of Henry III. His estates were seized by his relatives, a branch of the De Burghs, who abandoned the Norman name, and adopted that of MacWilliam, assumed Irish dress and customs, and ruled over Connaught conjointly. Through his daughter, who married Lionel, Duke of Clarence, third son of King Edward III., the titles of Ulster and Connaught were added to those of the royal family.

Elizabeth De Burgh

Lady Elizabeth De Burgh, only child and heiress of preceding, born in 1332, married, in 1352, Lionel, son of Edward III., who became in her right fourth Earl of Ulster and Lord of Connaught. Her daughter Philippa, wife of Edmund Mortimer, was ancestor of Edward IV. and subsequent British sovereigns.

Ulick De Burgh

Ulick De Burgh, first Earl of Clanricard, was a descendant of the second son of Richard De Burgh, Lord of Connaught. He fortified Roscommon, Galway, Loughrea, Leitrim, and several other towns. He was, according to Lodge, called by the native Irish "Negan," or the beheader, having made a mound of the heads of men slain in battle, which he covered with earth." In 1538 he covenanted to furnish King Henry VIII. with men and supplies, and, surrendering his large estates into the King's hands, received them back with the title of Earl of Clanricard in 1543. He died October 19, 1544, and was succeeded by his son Richard.

Richard De Burgh

Richard De Burgh, second Earl of Clanricard, succeeded upon his father's death in 1544. He was known among the native Irish as "Sassanagh," on account of being a firm adherent to the English rule. In 1548 he captured Cormac Roe O'Conor, of Offaly, and sent him to Dublin, where he was executed. He was constantly engaged in harassing and sanguinary feuds with other branches of the De Burghs. In 1553, with Sir Richard Bingham, he routed the Scots on the Moy. He was thrice married: (1) to Margaret, daughter of Murrough, first Earl of Thomond; (2) Catherine, daughter of Donough, second Earl of Thomond; (3) Honora, daughter of O'Brien of Duharras. He died July 24, 1582, and was succeeded by his son. The last years of his life were disturbed by dissensions of his sons.

Richard De Burgh

Richard De Burgh, fourth Earl of Clanricard and Earl of St. Alban's, son of the third earl, succeeded in 1601, upon his father's death. In 1599 he was made Governor of Connaught by the Earl of Essex; and he greatly distinguished himself on the English side at the siege and battle of Kinsale in 1601, when he was knighted on the field. King James I. appointed him Governor of Connaught and one of the privy council. In 1624 he was raised to an English peerage as Baron Somerhill, and four years afterwards was advanced to the Earldom of St. Alban's. He married Frances, the widow of Sir Philip Sidney and the Earl of Essex, by whom he had an only son, who succeeded him. He died November 12, 1635.

Ulich De Burgh

Ulich De Burgh, fifth Earl and Marquis of Clanricard, son of preceding, was born in 1604. He attended Charles I. on his campaign in Scotland in 1640, and continued on the Royalist side in the war of 1641-52. Although his name appears prominently in "Clarendon's History," his role was rather that of a negotiator than a warrior. In 1644 he was created a marquis and appointed commander-in-chief in Connaught. He supported the Marquis of Ormond in the matter of the cessation of hostilities; and when Ormond retired to France, accepted the Lord-Lieutenancy of Ireland. "He was a prime mover in the negotiations with the Duke of Lorraine, for making over to him some of the strong places of the island in return for a sum of money, but ultimately was obliged to repudiate the arrangement."

In 1652, wearied with Irish affairs, by the consent of Prince Charles and with the leave of the Puritan General Ludlow, he retired to his estate in Kent. He died in 1657, worn out by the fatigues and troubles to which he had been exposed. He was buried with his father at Tunbridge. He was a zealous Catholic. Both Clarendon and Carte speak in the highest terms of his character. The latter writes: "He had a greatness of mind, a nobleness of sentiments, and an integrity of heart, that were not to be corrupted by any temptation, or biased by any selfish, mean, or unworthy views; compassionate in his temper, sincere in his professions, true and constant in his friendships, and delicate (if possible to an excess) in the point of honor; no man ever loved his country or his friend better than he did, being ready on all occasions to sacrifice himself for either."

John De Burgh

John De Burgh, ninth Earl of Clanricard, commanded a regiment of foot in the service of King James II., and was taken prisoner at the battle of Aughrim. He was outlawed and attainted, and died in 1722. On the accession of Queen Anne the attainder was removed and the estates restored to his children. This branch of the De Burghs is now represented by Hubert, second Marquis and fifteenth Earl of Clanricard.

Grace O'Malley

BY S. M. O'MALLEY

Grace O'Malley flourished in the 16th century. In the history of Ireland and the consequent delineations of the lives of Irish men and women, there is not a character in all the chroniclings that receives the conflicting attentions bestowed upon the personalities of "Grainne O'Malley." A few historians are desirous of placing her character in the evilest construction, and others are determined to glorify her appearance and attributes to angelic perfection.

To conceive the proper setting for this strong and magnetic woman, one must picture the time in which she reigned and place well in mind the men and women who were her contemporaries. Her name "Grainne" does not signify

a virtue in the accepted meaning, but translated
reads "The Ugly," and is supposed to refer to
her terrible temper. The majority of writers
compared indicate that she was tall and robust,
masculine in appearance, and so prominent and
dominant in her character that the West of Ireland is filled with traditions of her prowess, her
temper, her wild escapades, and the singularly
just and impartial decisions she made when, in
her capacity of warrior chieftainess, she was
called to decide disputes or annihilate an enemy.
Outside of tradition there is very little authentic
history of this Queen of Ireland, many writers
falling into vague or mythical compositions from
which it is difficult to extract the radiant jewel
of Truth.

In the year 1877 there were old people living
in Ireland "who," as one author quaintly records,
"had talked with people who knew this fiery and
heroic queen"; therefore, traditionary history
may be considered fairly authentic. Beyond all
other attributes she was a Queen of the sea without parallel in mediæval or modern times. A
pirate she was, no doubt, but when we consider
the seafaring side of Sir Walter Raleigh or his
half-brother, Sir Humphrey Gilbert, and Sir
Francis Drake, who were her contemporaries,
we must consider their adventures on the sea in
no other light than that of piracy.

Therefore we can suppose that the expeditions by sea of the doughty Queen were undertaken in the same maritime spirit which actuated her wealthier contemporaries. Her mother
was an O'Malley as well as her father, but her
dark complexion indicated the presence of Spanish blood, for in these days the Western Irish
had large tradings with the commercial and wine

trading Spanish. Her father, Owen O'Malley, known as Dhubdara,—"Of the Black Oak,"— was Lord of O'Malley's Land, or "Ui-ni-haille" (pronounced "hoole"), comprising the Baronies of Murisk and Borriholle, along the seacoast. He was also Lord of Arran. In these days Arran was inhabited by a singularly wild race known as the most intrepid mariners along the Irish coast.

At her father's death, she began to take the part that has made her famous. The laws of Ireland at that date denied to women the right to inherit property, and any leadership was rigidly forbidden them. But Grainne, by right of might, put aside her younger brother and soon evidenced herself along the shores of Connemara (bays of the sea), her chief harbor being on Clare Island in Newport Bay. Here was her stronghold. Carrigahowly Castle, built to the water's edge, where, tradition says of her, she slept with a rope fastened to her own ship, and running through a hole in the castle wall to the watchful chieftainess' couch, where it was fastened to her wrist, so that the enemy could not find her unaware at any hour.

It may be said of her truthfully that, while England's Queen controlled the British nation with a well organized code of laws, "Grana Wail," as Irish balladists love to sing of her, was, by the sheer force of her indomitable will, holding in subjection the fiercest and most lawless body of men in Ireland, the so-called pirates of the Atlantic coast.

Her first husband was an O'Flaherty, whose warlike deeds earned him the cognomen of "Au Chogaidh,"—i. e., "Of the Wars." So much was the name of O'Flaherty feared it is said that when the Anglo-Normans took possession of Galway, they inserted in their rosary the following special clause: "From the ferocious O'Flahertys, good Lord, deliver us."

At her husband's death, according to law, she could not control his property, and by her marriage she had lost prestige with her own family; therefore she gave as an excuse to Queen Elizabeth, for her piratical expeditions, that she was very poor; or, in other words, piracy was her commerce. For a second husband she took Sir Richard Bourke, Lord of the Mayo Sept of the great Norman-Irish Clan. The Irish have a peculiar tendency to create names descriptive of some particular personality; therefore he was called "Richard in Iron," because of the plate armor he was encased in. The Irish Queen visited England some time after this marriage, and presented her son Theobald, whom Queen Elizabeth created Viscount Mayo, the first of the lords of that name.

Illustrative of her just impulses and the wild and warlike way in which she arrived at the desired conclusions, is related in the following story: Returning from England to Connaught, a storm blew her vessel into Howth harbor, and landing, Grace craved the hospitality of Howth Castle, but in vain, for all the doors were locked and her summons remained unanswered. Seeing a child walking in the grounds, and being told he was heir of Howth, she kidnaped him and carried him to Connaught. As a ransom she demanded that the doors of the castle should never be closed at meal time, a command that was literally obeyed.

Grace, too, gave a great impetus to education and religion in building and endowing monasteries, especially one on Clare Island, and in this, tradition says, she was buried.

All in all, tradition and authentic history sifted, and facts preserved, we see only a woman to admire—a strong and fierce personality, forced into questionable positions by the weakness of others, and holding in obedience to her orderly rule some of the most unruly and ferocious warriors of that day. Always mindfully inclined to justice and religion, and living, as she demanded of others, a life of strenuous endeavor, she is a woman to worship, as many of her followers did,—a mighty mantle of protection to the poorer and weaker creatures of her clan.

Michael Murphy

Michael Murphy, R. C. clergyman, who took an active part in the insurrection of 1798 in County Wexford, was born at Kilnew, in that county, and was educated at a hedge-school at Oulart. Having been ordained at Ferns in 1785, he proceeded to Bordeaux, and pursued his studies at the Irish College. After his return he became parish priest of Ballycanew. Dr. Madden says he was driven into joining the insurrection by his chapel being wrecked by the yeomen. He shared the fortunes of Dr. John Murphy's brigade until his heroic death at the battle of Arklow, June 9, 1798.

John Murphy

John Murphy, D. D., R. C. clergyman, acted as one of the leaders of the Wexford insurgents in 1798. He was born at Tincurry, County Wex-

ford, studied at Seville, took orders, and returned
to Ireland in 1785, and became parish priest of
Boulavogue. In November, 1797, he joined
eighteen Catholic clergymen in endeavoring to
avert the proclamation of martial law in their
parishes. He is said to have been driven into
insurrection by the oppressive conduct of the
soldiers and yeomanry, and by the wreck of his
chapel. On the 25th of May he took the field at
the head of a large body of pikemen, defeated a
party of troops at Oulart, next day took Camo-
lin and Enniscorthy, and encamped on Vinegar
Hill. After the defeats at Arklow and Vinegar
Hill, he joined the column that passed through
Scollagh Gap, crossed the Barrow, and was defeated at Kilcomney. Dr. Murphy found his
way to Taghmon, where he was recognized and
arrested. He was executed, June 26, 1798.

Edward Duffy

Edward Duffy, a Fenian leader, was born in
County Mayo, in 1840. In 1863 he gave up a situation and devoted himself to spreading Fenian
principles in Connaught. He was arrested in
November, 1865, in company with James Stephens, at Fairfield House, Sandymount, and was
sentenced to a term of imprisonment, but was
liberated on bail in January, 1866, in consequence
of ill health. He again applied himself to the
organization, was rearrested, and tried again in
May, 1867, and sentenced to fifteen years' penal
servitude. He died in Millbank prison, January
17, 1868. A portion of his speech delivered in the
dock before conviction has been inscribed on his
tomb in Glasnevin.

Esmonde Kyan

Esmonde Kyan, leader in the insurrection of 1798, was a gentleman of some property, who resided at Monamolin, near Oulart. At the breaking out of hostilities in County Wexford, he threw himself heartily into the struggle. Courageous to desperation, his arm was shattered at the battle of Arklow, while leading his division against the Royalist artillery. Confined in Wexford by this wound, he did all he could to prevent the massacre of Royalists on the bridge. He subsequently joined the patriot force that, after the fall of Wexford, endeavored to penetrate the County of Carlow, and for a time held out with Holt, Myles Byrne, and Dwyer in the glens of Wicklow.

Returning to his home secretly to visit his relatives, he was arrested, and executed in July, 1798. Few particulars are preserved of his life. He was uniformly spoken of by his associates in terms of the highest respect, as a man of talents and nobility of character. Myles Byrne writes: "He was, of all the chiefs of our little Irish army, the one who merited most good terms from the English. Throughout the war he had shown the greatest humanity, and made unceasing exertions to save the lives of prisoners, even of those whose hands were steeped in the blood of the inhabitants of County Wexford."

Henry Munro

Henry Munro, United Irishman, was born in Lisburn, about 1768. At the termination of his apprenticeship he entered into the linen business, and shortly afterwards married. He is described as of fair complexion, with intelligent features and large blue eyes; of middle size, and remarkable for strength and agility. He was, says Dr. Madden, scrupulously honorable in his dealings, truthful and faithful. A liberal Presbyterian, he was the ardent advocate of Catholic Emancipation, and to forward this object he joined the United Irishmen in 1795. He had been a Volunteer, and always had a taste for military studies; yet we are told that leadership in the ensuing insurrection was rather pressed upon him. At the breaking out of the insurrection in 1798, Munro occupied Ballynahinch, in Down. The disposition of his forces was made with great care.

There on the 13th of June he was attacked by General Nugent with about 1,600 men and eight pieces of artillery, and what has been since known as the battle of Ballynahinch was fought. The insurgents defended themselves for a time with stubborn pertinacity. Exposed to the crossfire of musketry in the market square, raked by artillery, their ammunition exhausted, they still pressed boldly on the Royalists with pike and bayonet. But in the end they were overpowered. Munro escaped, alone and unattended, to the mountains, but was eventually captured, tried by court-martial, and executed at Lisburn, opposite his own house. He displayed wonderful fortitude at the foot of the gallows, gave directions concerning an unsettled account with a neighbor, and after uttering the words, "Tell my country I deserved better of it," gave the signal for his own execution. His widow survived until 1840.

William Archer Butler

William Archer Butler, professor of moral philosophy in the University of Dublin, was born at Annerville, near Clonmel, in 1814, or perhaps a year or two earlier. At the age of nine he was sent to the endowed school at Clonmel, whose able master, the Rev. Dr. Bell, sent many eminent scholars into the world. Two years after this Butler entered Trinity College, Dublin, and in 1832 obtained a scholarship.

While still in his undergraduate course he contributed largely to the periodical literature of the day. The Dublin University Magazine was just then launched, and among its ablest contributors was Butler. His poetical pieces attracted notice, and helped to give that periodical the high reputation for poetry which it has ever since retained. His refined taste in criticism and his elegance of diction made him an able and popular reviewer, and some of his essays on history and philosophy still rank high in the estimation of scholars. In November, 1835, Butler obtained the first ethical moderatorship at his degree examination,—a prize then for the first time instituted. Just at the time his scholarship ended Dr. Lloyd, the provost of Trinity College, estimating the abilities of Butler, succeeded in founding a professorship of moral philosophy, and he who was the first to gain an ethical moderatorship in the college was also the first to fill the professor's chair. The young professor was now upon a field worthy of his endowments. His lectures were as remarkable for their eloquence as for their profound philosophy. The living of Clondehorka in County Donegal was presented to him with the chair of moral philosophy. This prefer-

ment he held till 1842, discharging with zeal and
faithfulness the duties of his office, in a wild and
poor district. In the last-mentioned year he was
re-elected to the professorship, and promoted to
the rectory of Raymoghy in the diocese of
Raphoe, where he spent a large portion of the
rest of his life in parochial ministrations, and in
literary, religious and philosophic study.

During the year 1845 the religious controversy engaged his attention, the result of which
was his "Letters on Mr. Newman's Theory of
Development," pronounced by eminent Protestant divines to be "models and masterpieces of
polemical composition." In 1848 he was employed on a work on Faith, and, in collecting materials for it, he was engaged during the short
period of his life that remained. On Trinity Sunday, 1848, he preached with his usual power the
ordination sermon for the Anglican Bishop of
Derry at Dunboe. On his return home the following Friday, he was seized with fever. The
progress of the malady was rapid and fatal, and
he died on the 5th of July.

"As a poet he was tender, imaginative, refined, and classical, and won the commendation
of so severe a judge as Professor Wilson. As a
preacher his eloquence was of the highest order,
—passionate without rant, affluent in all the
grace of figure and illustration, yet comprehen-
sible to the most ordinary intelligence. As an
ethical philosopher, he attained to a deservedly
high repute, considering the few years he was
permitted to devote to so arduous a study; and
the lectures which he delivered and the essays
which he has left are characterized as well by
the soundness of their views and brilliancy of
their rhetoric as by the elegance and classicality

of a style which is nevertheless eminently practical and often thoroughly simple." The work on which his reputation is based is the "Lectures on the History of Ancient Philosophy," two volumes, 1856; second edition, 1875.

Henry Cooke

Henry Cooke was born at Grillagh, near Maghera, County Londonderry, May 11, 1788. He was the youngest of four children. At fourteen he entered the University of Glasgow; completed his undergraduate career in 1805; passed through the ordinary course of theological training, and in November, 1808, was ordained to the pastoral care of the congregation of Duneane, near Randalstown. His ministerial income amounted at first to about £25 a year. After two years he removed to the care of another congregation at Donegore, near Templepatrick, and about the same time married Miss Ellen Mann. In 1815 he obtained leave of absence, and resumed his studies at Glasgow for eighteen months.

In 1817 he entered Trinity College, Dublin, and attended medical classes at the Royal College of Surgeons. Upon Sundays he occupied the pulpits of Presbyterian congregations in Dublin and other parts of Leinster. September 8, 1818, found him installed pastor of Killyleagh, on the banks of Strangford Lough. In 1829, chiefly through his efforts, matters were brought to a point with the Presbyterian ministers who held Unitarian views, and his wishes were gratified in their withdrawing from the general Presbyterian body, and forming the Remonstrant Synod of Ulster. In 1829 the degree of D. D.

was conferred on him by the board of Jefferson College, in the United States. He opposed the new system of Irish National Education; also Daniel O'Connell's Irish policy. In 1837 the degree of LL.D. was conferred upon him by Dublin University. In 1841 O'Connell went to Belfast in promotion of the Repeal movement, which was responded to by the holding of a large anti-Repeal meeting headed by a number of peers, officeholders, and magistrates, all obnoxious to national sympathies. Cooke made a speech on this occasion, and a testimonial of £2,000 was presented to him for his exertions in opposition to O'Connell.

For seven years his spare hours were devoted to the preparation of an "Analytical Concordance of Scripture." When the manuscript was complete, he took it to London to arrange for a publisher. The hotel at which he stopped was burned, and the work which had cost him so many years' toil was reduced to ashes. In the midst of other avocations, he managed to edit a new edition of "Brown's Family Bible." In the Theological College endowed in Belfast by the government, Cooke was appointed president, an office which he held until his death. In 1849 he was appointed the Dean of Residence for the Presbyterian students of Belfast. For many years he was the leading preacher and champion of the orthodox party of his church in Ireland.

It is stated that three-fourths of the new Presbyterian churches in Ireland, besides many in England and Scotland, were opened by him; so that a considerable portion of his time was taken up in traveling. He died December 13, 1868. A public funeral and the erection of a statue testified the esteem in which he was held

in Belfast. The Athenæum thus writes: "His oratory was powerful and effective; . . . great powers of sarcasm, a store of anecdote, which he could draw upon at will, a vivid imagination, words of all kinds at his command, and a fine elocution. . . ." His portrait is prefixed to his biography by J. S. Porter, London, 1871.

Adam Clarke

Adam Clarke, Methodist Minister, particularly distinguished as a biblical commentator, was born in County Londonderry in 1760 or 1762. At the age of fourteen he was placed in the establishment of a linen manufacturer, but finding this employment not suited to his tastes, he returned home after a short time. On the invitation of John Wesley, he became a pupil in a school at Kingswood, near Bristol. There he devoted his time unreservedly to preparing himself for the ministry. In 1782 he was ordained by Wesley, and for twenty years he labored principally in Great Britain, in furtherance of the religious missions of the Wesleyan Church. As an intelligent and powerful preacher, he was remarkably popular during the whole of his ministerial career. By diligent application, without neglecting the duties of his ministry, he acquired a practical knowledge of not only Greek and Latin, but also of Hebrew, Chaldee, Syriac, Persic, Ethiopic, Coptic, and the Arabic languages.

In 1802 he published a "Bibliographical Dictionary," in six volumes. This work increased his already great reputation. For a short time he was librarian of the Surrey Institution. He was elected a member of the Society of Antiquaries and of the Royal Irish Academy; and

the University of St. Andrews conferred on him
the degrees of M. A. and LL. D. By the Commissioners of Public Records Dr. Clarke was engaged to prepare a new edition of "Rymer's
Fœdera," of which, however, only three volumes
were published. To one great work he devoted
the best energies of his life,—"The Holy Bible,
with a Commentary and Critical Notes." The
first volume appeared in 1810; the eighth and
last in 1826,—"a monument of learning and industry." Some critics, however, believe he was
too fond of innovations, and that many of his
comments are exceptionable. He was the author
of several other works, among which are: "The
Succession of Sacred Literature," 1807; "Memoirs of the Wesley Family," 1823; and "The
Eucharist." He also edited Harmer's Observations, Butterworth's Concordance, Sturne's Reflections, and Fleury's Manners of the Ancient
Israelites. In 1831 Dr. Clarke established several schools in his native province of Ulster. He
accumulated a valuable library, including many
manuscripts and a small museum of curiosities.
He died of cholera, during a passing visit to Bays-
water, August 26, 1832. He is described as five
feet nine inches in height, of a large frame, his
limbs straight and well proportioned, and his
person unbowed the last hours of his life.

James Duchal

James Duchal, D. D., a Presbyterian divine,
was born at or near Antrim, in 1697. He studied
at the University of Glasgow, where he took the
degree of M. A., and became pastor of a small
congregation in Cambridge. In 1730 he accepted
an invitation to settle in Antrim. After he had

served there for ten years, his friend Abernethy, then minister of the dissenting congregation in Wood Street, Dublin, died, and Duchal was induced to become his successor. Duchal was a voluminous writer; in addition to several theological works issued during his ministrations, in the decline of life he wrote more than 700 sermons, from which a selection was made after his death, and published in three volumes. He died in 1761.

Francis Hutcheson

Francis Hutcheson, "the reviver of speculative philosophy in Scotland," was born August 8, 1694, at Downpatrick, where his father, John Hutcheson, was a minister. He studied theology and followed his father's profession of Presbyterian divine. His "Inquiry into the Original of Our Ideas on Beauty and Virtue," a work which made his name widely known, introduced him to the notice of such men as Archbishop King, Dr. Synge (Bishop of Elphin), and Viscount Molesworth. In 1728 he published his essay on "The Passions and Affections," in consequence of which he was the following year promoted to the Chair of Moral Philosophy in Glasgow. His next works were text-books for the use of his classes. He died at Glasgow in 1747. His "System of Moral Philosophy," the work on which his fame as an ethical writer depends, did not appear until 1755. It was edited by his son, with a memoir by Dr. Leechman prefixed.

John George Beresford

John George Beresford, Anglican Archbishop of Armagh, son of the first Marquis of

Waterford, was born at Tyrone House, Dublin, November 22, 1773. Educated at Eton and Oxford, he entered the Church, where his preferment was rapid,—Bishop of Cork and Ross, 1805; transferred to Raphoe, 1807; Clogher, 1819; to the archbishopric of Dublin, 1820, and to Armagh in 1822, "being the first Irishman that was raised to the primacy of Ireland for 120 years." Although his published works were confined to four sermons, he was considered a distinguished prelate. In 1851 he was appointed chancellor of the University of Dublin. He restored the Cathedral of Armagh, and Trinity College is indebted to him for the erection of the beautiful campanile in the Library Square. He died July 19, 1862, and was succeeded in the primacy by his cousin, Marcus G. Beresford, Bishop of Kilmore.

Nicholas Barnewall

Nicholas Barnewall, Viscount Kingsland, was born April 15, 1668. The family had been ennobled by King Charles I., September 12, 1645, for loyalty to his cause. Before Nicholas was of age he married a daughter of George, Count Hamilton, by his wife, Frances Jennings, afterwards married to the Earl of Tirconnel. In 1688 he entered King James' Irish army as captain in the Earl of Limerick's Dragoons. After the defeat of the Boyne he was moved to Limerick, and being in that city at the time of its surrender, was included in the articles, and secured his estates. In the first Irish Parliament of William III. he took the oath of allegiance, but upon declining to subscribe the declaration according to the English act, as contrary to his conscience, he was obliged to withdraw with the other Catholic Lords. In February, 1703, he joined with many Irish Catholics in an unavailing petition against the infraction of the Treaty of Limerick. He died June 14, 1725, and was buried at Lusk.

Alexander Henry

Alexander Henry, merchant, was born in the North of Ireland in June, 1766. His father died when he was two years old and his care and education devolved upon an elder brother, who directed his studies with a view of training him for one of the professions. But preferring a mercantile life, young Henry chose America as the most promising field, and arrived at Philadelphia in 1738 with a stock of dry goods (which he disposed of) and letters of introduction which aided him in securing a clerkship at a salary of $250 per annum. His industry so attracted the attention of his employers that within two months a branch house was opened, of which Henry was made superintendent. Going into the commission business a few years later on his own account, he became very successful, and in 1807, having accumulated a comfortable fortune, he retired.

For a period of nearly fifty years Henry was a liberal patron of the public institutions of Philadelphia. In 1817 he was one of the founders and first president of the Philadelphia Sunday and Adult School, which was merged into the American Sunday School Union in 1824, Henry continuing its president until his death. He was also president of the Board of Education of the Presbyterian Church, president of the House of Refuge, and of the Magdalen Society. He died at Philadelphia, August 13, 1847. His nephew, Alexander Henry, was a prominent merchant of Manchester, England. His son, Thomas C. Henry, born in 1790, studied theology at Princeton College and became pastor of the Second Presbyterian Church at Charleston, S. C., where he died October 24, 1827. He was the author of "Inquiry into the Consistency of Popular Amusements with a Profession of Christianity," 1825; "Letters to an Anxious Inquirer," 1828; and "Moral Etchings from the Religious World," 1828. His grandson was mayor of Philadelphia in 1864.

Thomas Blood

Thomas Blood, a daring adventurer, commonly called Colonel Blood, was born in Ireland, about 1628, served for a time as lieutenant in the parliamentary army. After the restoration of Charles II., he became the leader of some discontented parliamentary officers in a conspiracy to surprise Dublin Castle and seize the Duke of Ormond, who was then Lord-Lieutenant of Ireland. Just before carrying out the bold plan, the plot was discovered, but Blood managed to make his escape, cleverly concealing his identity under various disguises.

After various adventures in Ireland and on the continent, he finally settled in England, passing as a physician under an assumed name. He fought with the Scottish Covenanters in 1666 and afterwards passed himself off as a Quaker. He now entered upon a daring scheme to capture his old enemy, the Duke of Ormond. With five accomplices or confederates, he seized that nobleman in his coach one night in 1670, in the very heart of London, and carried him off. The populace, however, was aroused and the duke rescued, but Blood escaped.

His next design was to steal the crown jewels. Disguised as a clergyman, he made the acquaintance of the keeper of the crown and jewels at the Tower of London, where they were carefully guarded. When, by repeated visits, he gained the keeper's confidence, he appeared one day with two associates, under the plea of wishing to see the royal crown. On being admitted, they threw a cloak over the head of the keeper, gagged him and carried away the crown; but they were, however, captured and brought to trial. King Charles attended the examination, and Blood, by craft, flattery and threats of vengeance by his associates, so worked on the fears and vanity of the King that the latter not only pardoned Blood, but granted him a handsome yearly pension; and he was "generally received in such royal favor that the whole affair became a public scandal." For a time actually a favorite at court, Blood finally fell into disgrace and died in obscurity at Westminster, August 24, 1680.

Gustavus Hamilton

Gustavus Hamilton, Viscount Boyne, was born in 1639, and obtained a commission in the army towards the end of Charles II.'s reign. At the commencement of the war of 1689-91, the Protestants of Coleraine entrusted him with the defense of their town. He was ultimately forced to evacuate it and fall back on Enniskillen, and organized those regiments of horse and foot afterwards known as the Enniskilleners,—the forerunners of the present Inniskilling regiments. He defeated Lord Galmoy in his attack on Crom Castle, and in the spring of 1689 was successful in several engagements with the Catholic forces. In July his army is said to have numbered seventeen troops of light horse, thirty companies of foot, and a few very ill-armed troops of heavy dragoons. Later on, at the head of his Enniskilleners, he defeated General MacCarthy at Newtownbutler.

He commanded a regiment at the battle of the Boyne, and took a prominent part in the after operations of the war, heading the troops in the successful attack on Athlone in 1691, and being afterwards made governor of the town. When peace was concluded he received an ample share of the forfeited estates, and was made privy-councillor and brigadier-general. For his bravery afterwards at the siege of Vigo, he was presented with a service of plate by Queen Anne, and George I. raised him to the peerage as Viscount Boyne. He died September 16, 1723.

Henry Johnson

Sir Henry Johnson, baronet, G. C. B., general, was born in Dublin in 1748, entered the army in 1761, and rose through the several grades—captain, 1763; lieutenant-colonel, 1778; colonel, 1782; major-general, 1793; general, 1808. He commanded a battalion of Irish light infantry in the American Revolutionary war, and was severely wounded; and while in command at Stony Point was surprised by General Wayne on the night of July 15, 1779, and made prisoner with his whole force. In 1782 he married an American lady, and returned to England after the surrender of Yorktown. During the insurrection of 1798 in Ireland, he commanded a division of the army in County Wexford, and on the 5th of June defended New Ross.

It was attacked early in the morning of that day by an overwhelming body of insurgents under Bagenal Harvey, who were at first successful, driving most of General Johnson's troops out of the town, but, not following up their success, were in the afternoon obliged to retreat. Musgrave places the insurgents' loss at 2,500, while Johnson's casualties numbered altogether only 227. In the engagement General Johnson displayed uncommon bravery, and had two horses shot under him. He received a baronetcy in 1818, and died March 18, 1835, being succeeded in the baronetcy by his son, a distinguished officer in the Peninsular War, who survived until June 27, 1860.

Edward Blakeney

Sir Edward Blakeney, soldier, G. C. B., son of the member of Parliament for Athenry before the Legislative Union, was born in 1778. He entered the army when but sixteen, as cornet in a dragoon regiment, and saw much active service in Holland, Nova Scotia, the West Indies, at Copenhagen, and elsewhere. During the Peninsular War, he took part in the battle of Busaco, in the sieges of Ciudad Rodrigo and Badajoz, and in the battles of Albuera, Vittoria, and the Pyrenees. In 1814 he was employed in the expedition against New Orleans. He acted as commander-in-chief in Ireland from 1832 to 1855, during which time he was a privy-councillor. He was appointed governor of Chelsea Hospital in

1856, and became a field marshal in 1862. He died August 2, 1868.

William Francis Butler

Sir William Francis Butler, soldier, was born in Suirville, County Tipperary, October 31, 1838. His early education was received at the Jesuit College, Tullabeg, Kings County, and afterwards in Dublin. After a course of study at the Royal Military College, Sandhurst, he entered the 69th regiment, September 17, 1858, as ensign, served in the East and in Canada, and in November, 1863, was promoted lieutenant. After serving on the Canadian frontier survey and in the Red River expedition under Colonel Wolseley, he acted as Special Commissioner to the Indian tribes of the Saskatchewan River, 1870-71, and was made a captain in 1872. He next proceeded to Ashanti with Sir Garnet Wolseley, where he was employed as a Special Commissioner in collecting the West Akim native forces for service. For his tact in this mission he was several times mentioned in despatches and was thanked by the House of Lords through the Duke of Cambridge, and Butler was promoted major, April 1, 1874, and made a C. B.

In 1875 he was sent to Natal as a special service officer, and on his arrival proceeded to Bloemfontein on a confidential mission at a time when the Zulus were restless and the Boers uneasy. He assisted Sir George Colley to draft a bill for the better government of the natives, and was largely responsible in smoothing subsequent difficulties with the Zulus. Returning to England for a post in the army, he again sailed for South Africa in 1879, served in the Zulu war as assistant - adjutant and quartermaster - general, and for his services was given the brevet of lieutenant-colonel, April 21, 1880. He returned to England in the latter year, and in 1882 went to Egypt with the expedition sent against Arabi Pasha. He was present at the battles of El Magfar, Tel-el-Mahuta, Kassassin, and Tel-el-Kebir, where his brilliant service was brought to the notice of the government by Lord Wolseley, and he was promoted colonel, November 18, 1882, and aide-de-camp to Queen Victoria. In the advance to the relief of General Gordon at Khartum, Colonel Butler was assigned the task of organizing a boat service which would surmount the difficulties of transportation over the Nile cataracts.

In a short space of time and in the face of many difficulties he had 400 Canadian pattern boats despatched to Egypt, together with a band of Indians who had worked the boat service on the Red River. In command of this service he gained world-wide renown by the ingenuity and resource with which he passed hundreds of boats over the cataracts. Later he commanded the advance guard of the river column and discovered the enemy in position on the ridges of Kirbekan. General Earle, in command of the British forces, proposed a frontal attack, but Colonel Butler, having reconnoitred the enemy's position very closely, and believing the ground too broken to allow a direct assault, an attack on the left flank was made at his instigation, which resulted in the victory of Kirbekan.

On his return from Egypt, in 1893, he was given command of the Second Brigade at Aldershot as a major-general. The grant of a Distinguished Service Reward was made to him in

1898, and after a period in command of the south-eastern district, he was sent to South Africa, with the rank of lieutenant-general, to take up the reins of military government after the death of General Goodenough. In 1899 he was placed in charge of the Cape, with the temporary powers of high commissioner. He had formed strong opinions of the character of the military preparations being made by the Boers, but his estimate of their strength did not find acceptance in South Africa or in England. He sided with the Afrikander party, having convinced himself that the English population of the Transvaal had little cause for grievance. When a petition for intervention was placed before him by the Uitlanders, he rejected it and expressed his disapproval of any agitation. At Grahamstown he delivered a speech in which he said: "South Africa does not need surgical operations; it needs, peace, progress, and development." Considering this utterance a political mistake, he was superseded in the military command in South Africa, and in 1900 was placed in command at Aldershot.

After he had placed the garrison in a sound condition, he returned to the Western district, and was placed on the retired list, October 31, 1905. After his retirement General Butler enjoyed the quiet life in his native county of Tipperary, where he won the esteem of all classes. He devoted himself to religious and educational matters, and in 1907 was appointed a member of the Board of National Education. His political views were strongly Nationalist, and he was an active member of the Catholic Truth Society, under whose auspices he delivered several striking addresses.

He took a deep interest in the preservation

of the Irish language and believed strongly in the
necessity of a great upbuilding of national character and self-reliance among his fellow-countrymen. He lived to see his views take deep root.
He married Elizabeth Thompson, the painter of
"The Roll Call" and other battle scenes. General Butler won considerable reputation as a lit-
terateur, and his publications include: "The
Great Lone Land," 1872; "The Campaign of the
Cataracts," 1887; "Charles George Gordon,"
1889; "Life of Sir George Pomeroy Colley,"
1889; and "Sir Charles Napier," 1890. He died
at his residence in County Tipperary, June 7,
1910.

John C. Douglas

John C. Douglas, M. D., a distinguished ob-
stetrician, was born at Lurgan, June 14, 1778.
Having passed through the College of Surgeons
in 1800, he acted for a time as surgeon to a militia
regiment, in 1803 took the degree of M. D. at St.
Andrew's, and in 1808 commenced practice in
Dublin, where he soon attained a prominent position. The Journal of Medical Science declares
that his published treatises, "along with Dr.
Clarke's reports and papers, laid the foundation
of the high repute of Dublin as a school of obstetrics." He received important foreign ac-
knowledgments of his worth, was for a time
President of the King and Queen's College of
Physicians in Ireland, and in 1832 was elected
an honorary fellow. He died of apoplexy, November 20, 1850.

Richard Helsham

Richard Helsham, M. D., an eminent Dublin
physician, Professor of Physic and Natural Phi-

losophy in the University of Dublin in the first half of the 18th century. He became a Fellow of Trinity College, Dublin, in 1704, a Senior Fellow in 1714; he resigned in 1730, and was appointed Regius Professor of Physic in 1733. His course of "Lectures on Natural Philosophy" was much esteemed, and have been more than once reprinted. He was Swift's intimate friend and medical adviser. In a letter of July 12, 1735, Swift writes of him as "the most eminent physician of this city and kingdom." He died August 1, 1738.

William Henry Harvey

William Henry Harvey, M. D., botanist, was born at Limerick, February 5, 1811. His attention was turned to flowers when quite a child, and he early developed a passionate love for the study of nature. He was educated at a Ballitore school, and his youth was passed in business pursuits in Limerick. From 1835 to 1841 he held the position of Colonial Treasurer at the Cape of Good Hope, where he had ample opportunities of studying the flora of South Africa, and he soon acquired a European reputation as a careful and laborious student. Shortly after his return he was appointed Professor of Botany in the University of Dublin. He devoted himself specially to algae, and in pursuit of this department of botany visited the United States, and in 1853 undertook a voyage round the world for the purpose of collecting specimens.

His "Seaside Book," his "Thesaurus Capensis," "Flora Capensis" and "Phycologia Britannica," embellished with illustrations from his pencil, are among the best known of his numer-

ous works. The "Smithsonian Contributions to
Knowledge" contain some elaborate treatises by
him on American algae. He belonged to many
of the learned societies of Europe. Originally
a member of the Society of Friends, he joined
the Established Church. He was the intimate
friend of Dr. Hooker. Dr. Harvey died of con-
sumption, May 15, 1866, at Torquay, where he
was buried by his special desire. He was eminently remarkable for the spirituality and amiability of his disposition. Besides his botanical
works he was the author of some poems published in his youth, and of "Charles and Josiah,
or Friendly Conversations Between a Church-
man and a Quaker," published in Dublin in 1862.

Patrick Browne

Patrick Browne, M. D., naturalist and author, was born at Woodstock, County Mayo, in
1720. While young he was sent to the West
India Islands, but on account of ill-health, returned to Europe. He resided some years at
Paris, and applied himself to the study of medicine, graduating as M. D. at Leyden, Holland,
where he became acquainted with Linnaeus and
other eminent naturalists.

After two years' practice of his profession
in London, he returned to the West Indies and
made a collection of the fauna and flora of the
islands. In 1755 he published in London a new
map of Jamaica and the following year he
brought out his "Civil and Natural History of
Jamaica." He made in all six visits to the West
Indies. The latter part of his life was passed
in Mayo, where he died, August 29, 1790, and

was buried at Crossboyne. In 1774 appeared his "Catalogues of the Birds and Fishes of Ireland."

William H. Fitton

William Henry Fitton, M. D., F. R. S., an eminent geologist, was born in Dublin, January, 1780. At Trinity College he acquired his degree of B. A. in 1799. During a residence in Edinburgh he formed the acquaintance of Sydney Smith, Jeffrey, Lord Brougham and other eminent men, and in 1809 he removed to London. In 1811 he began to write geological articles, the first being on the geological structure of the neighborhood of Dublin. In 1812 he settled as a physician at Northampton, occasionally contributing articles to the Edinburgh Review on his favorite study. As an original observer, he worked hard from 1824 to 1836, developing the true order of the secondary strata of England and France. He was President of the Geological Society, and a Fellow of the Royal and other scientific societies. He died in London, May 13, 1861.

William Brouncker

William Brouncker, Viscount Castlelyons, mathematician, was born at Castlelyons, County Cork, in 1620. His father was President of Munster, and was made a viscount in 1645. For his adherence to the Stuarts he was, at the restoration, appointed Chancellor to the Queen, Lord of the Admiralty, and Master of St. Catherine's Hospital, in London. He was the first President of the Royal Society, an office which he retained for fifteen years. Among other mathematical works, he published "Continued Fractions" and "The Quadrature of a Portion of the Equilateral Hyperbola." In 1653 he published a translation of Descartes' "Music Compendium," enriched with observations which show that he was deeply skilled in the theory of music. He died at Westminster, April 5, 1684.

Edward Hincks

Edward Hincks, D. D., philologist, was born in Cork, August, 1792. His father, T. D. Hincks (born in 1767, died in 1857), a Presbyterian minister, was a well-known orientalist. After a careful training under his father, Edward entered Trinity College, Dublin, became scholar in 1810, and obtained a fellowship in 1813, having as an opponent the Rev. Thomas R. Robinson. He retired on the College living of Ardtrea in 1819, and in 1826 exchanged it for that of Killileagh, which he held until his death. The fact of his not having received any other promotion, notwithstanding his European reputation and high personal character, has been ascribed to the earnestness with which he advocated a reform in the Irish Established Church, and a larger and more liberal system of education. He was an excellent Oriental scholar, and published a Hebrew grammar. But it was in the field of Egyptian and Assyrian translation that his reputation chiefly rests. Layard remarks: "It is to Dr. Hincks we owe the determination of the numerals, the name of Sennacherib on the monuments of Kouyunjik and of Nebuchadnezzar on the bricks of Babylon—three very important and valuable discoveries."

He threw a flood of light on the grammar

of the language, on cuneiform writings generally, and in various ways did much to smooth the path for subsequent investigators. His views have not all met with acceptance; but concerning the value of his researches and the soundness of his judgment, there is no difference of opinion. Most of his investigations were published in the "Transactions of the Royal Irish Academy." In 1854 he published a "Report to the Trustees of the British Museum respecting certain Cylinders and Terra-cotta Tablets, with Cuneiform Inscriptions," and in 1863 a "Letter on the Polyphony of the Assyrio-Babylonian Cuneiform writing." He died December 3, 1866. His brother, Francis Hincks, C. B., "may be said to have secured for Canada the independence she possesses."

Patrick Kennedy

Patrick Kennedy was born in County Wexford early in 1801. In 1823, although a Catholic, he came to Dublin as assistant at the Protestant Training School, Kildare Place. After a few years he established the small circulating library and bookshop in Anglesea Street where he spent the remainder of his life. He was a man of ability, and contributed interesting articles to the pages of the University Magazine. The best of these, "Legends of the Irish Celts," "Tales of the Duffrey" and "Banks of the Boro," were afterwards published separately. In the graphic delineation of Irish rural life, as he experienced it when a boy in County Wexford, he has seldom been surpassed. His works are singularly pure, and he curtailed his prospects in trade by declining to lend or deal in books that he considered of an objectionable tendency. For many years the committees of the Hibernian Temperance Association and kindred bodies were held at his house. Kennedy was widely known and respected by the literary people of Dublin. He died March 28, 1873, and was buried at Glasnevin.

John Keegan

John Keegan, the author of several poems of great beauty, was born in 1809, on the banks of the Nore, in Queens County. He received a hedge-school education, and was all through life essentially a man of the people. In a short notice in the Irishman of October, 1876, it is remarked: "All the different phases of Irish passion—the fierce outbursts of anger—the muttered tone of contempt—all the deep and heart-rending sorrow of the people—John Keegan was master of all! Not a side of the Irish character was there that he did not probe and understand. From the sweet mood of love murmured in the eventide over the milk-pail, to the violent words of animosity at the faction fight, there was not a page of the Irish character that escaped the keen eye of Keegan." Several of his poems will be found in Hays' "Ballads of Ireland": "Caoch the Piper" and ".The Dark Girl at the Holy Well" are among the best. Keegan died in 1849.

Richard Cox

Sir Richard Cox was born at Bandon, County Cork, March 25, 1650. His grandfather, Michael Cox, was one of the many English adventurers who went to Ireland in the reign of

James I. After being called to the bar, Richard was made recorder of Kinsale by Sir Richard Southwell in 1685. The troubles which followed in Ireland upon the accession of James II alarmed Cox, and he removed with his family to Bristol. Here he wrote "Hibernia Anglicana." Upon the arrival of the Prince of Orange in England, Cox, who had published a pamphlet in favor of the Revolution, was made under secretary of state, and shortly after went to Ireland as secretary. He was afterwards made recorder of Waterford, and then a justice of the common pleas, in September, 1690; and in a few months after he was appointed military governor of Cork. In 1692 he was knighted by Lord Sidney, and in the following year he was elected a member of the philosophical society, and also one of the commissioners of forfeited estates in Ireland.

In 1700 he was promoted to the chief justiceship of the common pleas, and to a seat in the privy council. In 1703 he was appointed Lord Chancellor of Ireland. In 1705 Cox with Lord Cutts, was appointed lord justice during the absence of the Duke of Ormond in England. The duke was recalled in 1707, and the Earl of Pembroke was appointed his successor. Cox soon found himself obliged to resign the seals, and meet the active enmity of those to whom his politics had made him obnoxious. He died May 3, 1733, leaving a son and a daughter. His writings and actions were void of any broad-minded views, and it is said he availed himself of his position to imprison illegally for one year in Newgate, Hugh MacCurtin, an Irish historiographer, for having published a treatise in 1717 exposing the unfounded statements which were promulgated in his "Hibernia Anglicana" relative to the laws and customs of the Irish previous to the English invasion.

Edward King

Edward King, Viscount Kingsborough, author of "The Antiquities of Mexico," was born in County Cork in 1795. With the exception of a parliamentary career of six years, which he voluntarily abandoned, his life was devoted to the study of Mexican antiquities. This passion was acquired when a student at Oxford, where a Mexican MS. in the Bodleian Library fired his imagination. His magnificent work, replete with illustrations, was given to the world in 1831, in seven volumes, imperial folio, price £210. Two additional volumes appeared after his death. The book cost him upwards of £32,000, and his life; for, oppressed with debt, he was arrested at the suit of a paper manufacturer, and lodged in the debtors' prison, Dublin, where he died of typhoid fever, February 27, 1837.

Had he lived he would within a year have become Earl of Kingston, with a fortune of £40,-000 a year. William H. Prescott, the historian of Mexico, says: "The drift of Lord Kingsborough's speculations is to establish the colonization of Mexico by the Israelites. To this the whole battery of his logic and learning is directed. For this, hieroglyphics are unriddled, manuscripts compared, monuments delineated. . . . By this munificent undertaking, which no government, probably, would have, and few individuals could have, executed, he has entitled himself to the lasting gratitude of every friend of science."

William Haliday

William Haliday, a promising Irish scholar, the son of a Dublin tradesman, was born about 1788. He studied Irish diligently, and produced a grammar in his nineteenth year. He was one of the founders of the Gaelic Society, and projected a translation of Keating's "History of Ireland" with the Irish text and memoir of the author, only one volume of which (Dublin, 1811) had appeared at the time of his death. Edward O'Reilly, in the preface of his "Irish Dictionary" (1821), acknowledges in warm terms his obligations to him. The inscription on his tomb in Dundrum churchyard, County Dublin, was written by his friend, Dr. Lanigan. He is thus spoken of in the "Transactions of the Royal Irish Academy," Volume XV: "Had this young gentleman lived he would most probably have achieved more for the ancient literature of Ireland than any other individual of his time. His early display of talents, and deep knowledge of the Greek, Latin, and some of the Oriental languages, joined with unwearied antiquarian research and an enthusiastic zeal for devoting his talents to the service of his country, would have rendered him one of its brightest literary ornaments." He died October 26, 1812.

Peter Finnerty

Peter Finnerty, one of the ablest reporters of his time, was born at Loughrea, in 1766. At an early age he sought his fortune in Dublin, and became a printer. In 1797 he was printer and editor of The Press, the organ of the United

Irishmen, to which both Curran and Moore are said to have contributed. December 22, 1797, he was tried for a libel on the government concerning the trial and execution of Orr, and, refusing to disclose the name of the author, was sentenced to stand in the pillory, pay a fine, and suffer imprisonment for two years. Arthur O'Connor, Lord Edward FitzGerald, and others of his party, attended him at the pillory in Green Street.

At the expiration of the sentence he removed to London, and procured an engagement as a reporter on the Morning Chronicle. He sailed as an army reporter with the Walcheren expedition in 1809. Two years afterwards he was committed to Lincoln jail for eighteen months, for a libel on Lord Castlereagh. In the course of his defense on his trial, he made a false quantity in a Latin quotation, and was set right by Lord Ellenborough, whereupon he rejoined: "Pronounce it as you like, my lord; isn't the English of it the same?" He memorialized the House of Commons against the treatment he received, and in the several discussions on the subject he was highly spoken of by Brougham, Romilly, Burdett and Whitbread. He died at Westminster, May 11, 1822.

Dorothea Jordan

Dorothea Jordan, a distinguished actress, was born near Waterford, in 1762. Her maiden name was Bland. When but sixteen she went on the stage, appearing in Dublin in Daly's company under the assumed name of Miss Francis, so as not to hurt the susceptibilities of her father's relatives. The charms of her manner, her graceful figure, her talents, and her voice, captivated the public, and it was not long before she came to be acknowledged one of the foremost British actresses. She appeared in London in October, 1785, as Mrs. Johnson. Hazlitt, in his criticisms of the stage, writes: "Her face, her tones, her manner were irresistible; her smile had the effect of sunshine, and her laugh did one good to hear it; her voice was eloquence itself— it seemed as if her heart was always at her mouth. She was all gaiety, openness, and good nature; she rioted in her fine animal spirits, and gave more pleasure than any other actress, because she had the greatest spirit of enjoyment in herself."

In 1790 she formed a liaison with the Duke of Clarence (afterwards King William IV.), and for twenty years, it is said, they lived peacefully together. About 1811, "partly in consequence of her extravagance," a separation took place, and an annuity of £4,400 was secured to her upon certain conditions. In August, 1815, she was obliged to fly to France from her creditors, and at Versailles, under the name of Johnson, in the greatest privacy, she awaited in vain some settlement of her affairs. She died at St. Cloud, July 3, 1816. Sir Jonah Barrington bears testimony to Mrs. Jordan's disposition and accomplishments. She had nine children by the Duke of Clarence; these were granted the titles and precedency of the younger issue of a marquis. The sons were well provided for in the army, the navy, or the established church; the eldest was created Viscount FitzClarence, and eventually Earl of Munster, while the daughters made brilliant marriages. Aubrey FitzClarence succeeded his brother as fourth Earl of Munster in 1902.

Thomas Sheridan

Thomas Sheridan, son of Thomas Sheridan,
D. D., was born in Quilca, County Cavan, in 1721.
He was educated under his father, and next at
Westminster School, where he became a king's
scholar; but not being able to go to Oxford or
Cambridge, he returned to Dublin, where he
entered Trinity College, and took his degree in
1739. After this he went on the stage, and as a
tragedian is said to have possessed considerable
merit. He next undertook the management of
the Dublin Theatre; but his attempts at reformation occasioned violent outrages, in which the
playhouse was destroyed, and Sheridan was
obliged to remove to England. At length peace
was restored and he resumed his management
when another opposition arose in the erection of
a rival theatre.

Sheridan now began his career as a teacher
of oratory, which art he considered as the funda-
mental principle of education. Accordingly he
delivered lectures on elocution in England, Ireland and Scotland, but as the novelty wore away
his popularity declined. He, however, received
a pension from the king, and published several
works on his favorite subject.

After the retirement of Garrick from the
stage, Sheridan was appointed (through the influence of his distinguished son, Richard Brins-
ley Sheridan) manager of Drury Lane Theatre.
He soon disagreed with the proprietors, and
again became a lecturer. He also resumed his
literary pursuits, and printed a "Dictionary of
the English.Language," and "The Life of Swift."
He died at Margate, August 14, 1788. His wife,
Frances, the daughter of Dr. Philip Chamber-

laine, of Dublin, wrote a novel, and a romance in the eastern style, also two comedies. His daughters, Alicia and Elizabeth, became successful writers.

Anthony Malone

Anthony Malone, politician, was born in Ireland December 5, 1700. In his twentieth year he entered Oxford University, pursued his legal studies at the Middle Temple, and in May, 1726, was admitted to the Irish bar. The following year he was elected to represent West Meath, a seat he held without interruption until 1760. In 1740 he was appointed prime-sergeant, a position from which he was dismissed in 1754 for joining in the assertion of the right of Parliament to dispose of unappropriated taxes. In 1757, under the Duke of Bedford's government, he was made Chancellor of the Exchequer. From this office he was also removed, for maintaining the right of the Irish House of Commons to originate the supplies. Soon afterwards, however, he was placed on the privy-council, and granted a patent of precedence at the bar. In 1771 he voted against Lord Townshend's government.

"To a commanding person, fine voice, an impressive yet conciliatory manner, temper rarely to be ruffled by an opponent, were added powers of argument and persuasion so effective that it was once proposed to transfer him from the Irish to the English House of Commons, in order to oppose Sir Robert Walpole." Grattan declared, "Malone was a man of the finest intellect that any country ever produced." He died May 8, 1776. His nephew, afterwards Lord Sunderlin, inherited most of his estates.

Roger Boyle

Roger Boyle, Earl of Orrery, fifth son of
Richard, Earl of Cork, was born in Ireland, April
25, 1721, and at the age of seven was created
Lord Broghill. Having graduated at Trinity
College, Dublin, he went abroad, and on his
return married the daughter of the Earl of Suffolk. During the Irish war of 1641-52 he commanded a troop of horse in the forces raised by
his father; but when the royal cause was ruined
and the king executed, he retired to his seat in
Somersetshire, where he lived privately till 1649.
Being, however, much affected by the state of
affairs, he resolved to go abroad, and accordingly applied for leave, on the plea that this measure was necessary to his health. The committee
of state soon penetrated into his real design
(which was that of joining the exiled Prince
Charles), and therefore resolved to shut him up
in the Tower of London.

Cromwell, being at this time nominated to
the command in Ireland, diverted his colleagues
from this resolution; and by his persuasion Lord
Broghill was induced to accept a commission
under him, to act against the Irish Confederates
only. His conduct in Ireland gave Cromwell
such satisfaction that, when the latter became
Lord Protector, he made Boyle one of his privy
council. After the Restoration of Charles II.
(which Boyle promoted) he was created Earl of
Orrery, and constituted one of the lords justices
of Ireland. He died October 16, 1679, leaving
two sons and five daughters. He wrote "Par-
thenissa, a Romance"; a "Treatise on the Art of
War," several poems and plays and other works,

and, long after his death his "State Letters" were published in one volume folio.

Robert Stewart

Robert Stewart, Viscount Castlereagh, second Marquis of Londonderry, was born, probably, at Mount Stewart, in County Down, June 18, 1769. His father, Robert Stewart, represented County Down in two parliaments, was elevated to the peerage as Baron Stewart, in 1789, advanced to be Viscount Castlereagh in 1795, Earl of Londonderry in 1796, and Marquis of Londonderry in 1816. Robert Stewart, the subject of this sketch, received his early education at the Royal School of Armagh, and at seventeen entered St. John's College, Cambridge. In 1790 he was put in nomination by his father for a vacancy in the representation of Down, and was elected, after a struggle of two months' duration, and an outlay of £60,000. In 1794 he married the youngest daughter of the Earl of Buckingham. In the House of Commons he at first sided with the popular party, and advocated among other liberal measures, that which gave Catholics the ballot in 1793. Gradually, however, his views underwent a complete change, and from an ultra Liberal he became a most strenuous supporter of the British influence in Ireland.

On the advancement of his father in the peerage in October, 1795, he succeeded to the courtesy title of Viscount Castlereagh. In 1797 he was appointed keeper of the privy seal. In 1799 he was made Chief Secretary of Ireland. Both Castlereagh and Cornwallis threw themselves with the utmost energy into Pitt's project

of a legislative union between Ireland and Great
Britain. January 23, 1799, after a debate lasting
twenty-one hours, the address in which the project was proposed was carried by a majority of
one (106 to 105), but the next night the union
paragraph was expunged, 109 to 104, and great
rejoicing ensued throughout Ireland. The measure was abandoned for that session. Castlereagh
and his colleagues now bent their energies to
bring about the union by every means within
their power. Ireland was overawed with the
presence of a large army. Bribery was openly
resorted to, and promises of place and peerages,
or elevations in the peerage, were freely made.
The wavering members were brought over by
declarations that the government would never
lose sight of the measure until it was carried.
Opponents were dismissed, officers in the army
who held seats in parliament and were likely to
vote against the measure were refused permission to return home. After another year of unwearied labor on the part of the chief secretary
the preliminary motion in favor of the union was
carried in the House of Commons, about 1 o'clock
on the morning of February 6, 1800, by a vote of
158 to 115.

It is pleasant to note that, in spite of threats,
arguments and lavish promises of place and titles, so many members of the Irish House stood
out to the last against those who sought the extinction of the autonomy of their country. The
act of union came into operation January 1, 1801.
Castlereagh and Cornwallis experienced almost
as much difficulty in redeeming their promises
as to the granting of peerages as they had in
passing the measure. The English cabinet stood
aghast at the list presented, and it was only by

threatening to resign office that the chief secretary and lord lieutenant were able to secure the fulfilment of their pledges. To save appearances, Pitt resigned, and with him Castlereagh and Cornwallis. In order not to further embarrass the government, Castlereagh refrained from seeking immediate advancement for himself in recognition of his services in bringing about the union. He represented County Down in the United Parliament, where he was regarded by the great majority of his fellow-countrymen and the English Liberals with feelings of the deepest hatred.

In July, 1802, he was appointed president of the board of control, and in 1805 was transferred to the head of the war department. He lost his position on the death of Pitt in January, 1806, but was reinstated on the return of the Tories to power in April, 1807, and remained in office until September, 1809.

Alison thus eulogizes his administration: "If Lord Castlereagh had not broken through the usual routine of military promotion, and given Wellington the command in Portugal . . . the campaign of Torres Vedras would have never encouraged the Russians to resist French invasion, and furnished a model on which their system of defense was to be framed. If he had not, in the same year, strenuously combatted the recommendation of the Bullion Committee . . . national bankruptcy would have prostrated Great Britain at the very crisis of the war. If he had not withstood the loud clamor against the Peninsular war, if he had failed in feeding Wellington with adequate supplies, the battle of Vittoria would never have caused Joseph's crown to drop from his head, or brought Austria at the decisive moment into the field, after the armistice of Pleswitz."

On April 4, 1809, in consequence of disagreements between Castlereagh and Canning, as to the conduct of the Peninsular war, it was resolved at a private meeting of the cabinet that Castlereagh should be called upon to resign. This resolution was not communicated to him until the 7th of September. The result was a duel between Castlereagh and Canning, in which the latter was wounded, and the resignation of both. On Lord Wellesley's resignation in February, 1812, he was appointed Secretary of Foreign Affairs, a post he held until his death. In December, 1813, he was appointed minister plenipotentiary with the allied sovereigns; and although not actually a member of the Chatillion Congress of the following February, exercised, through his brother, a preponderating influence upon its proceedings. For these services he was decorated with the order of the Garter.

During the Hundred Days he was indefatigable in his exertions to keep together the Grand Alliance and prepare the means of resisting Napoleon, and after the battle of Waterloo he went to Paris to conduct the negotiations then pending for the settlement of the affairs of Europe. After these events his attention was mainly directed to home politics, and the course he took was one of uncompromising opposition to all measures of reform.

In 1821, on the death of his father, he became Marquis of Londonderry. The nature of the duties in connection with the congresses of Troppau, Laybach and Verona, which assembled between 1820 and 1822, pressed heavily upon his mind, and, August 12, 1822, he committed suicide at his seat in Kent, England. No words can express the varied feelings of grief, horror, and delight that pervaded the country at the news of his death. While the coffin was being removed from his residence to Westminster Abbey the people vented their joy at his death in shouts of exultation. The feelings of the masses in Ireland were not more regardful of his memory.

Barrington says: "In private life, his honorable conduct, gentlemanly habits, and engaging demeanor were exemplary. Of his public life, the commencement was patriotic, the progress was corrupt, and the termination criminal. His first public essay was a motion to reform the Irish Parliament, and his last was to corrupt and annihilate it by bribing 154 of its members. It is impossible to deny a fact so notorious. History, tradition, or the fictions of romance contain no instance of a minister in Ireland who so fearlessly deviated from all the principles which ought to characterize the servant of a constitutional monarch, or the citizen of a free country." Castlereagh was succeeded by his brother Charles. The "Memoirs and Correspondence," edited by the latter, appeared in twelve volumes between 1848 and 1853.

Francis Kirwan

Francis Kirwan, R. C. Bishop of Killala, was born in Galway in 1589, and received the rudiments of education from his uncle, Rev. Arthur Lynch, a Catholic clergyman, who from time to time had endured the most trying persecutions on account of his faith. Francis subsequently studied at Lisbon, and was ordained in 1614. Proceeding to France the year following, to pursue his studies, he taught philosophy at Dieppe for some time. In 1620, returning to Ireland, he was commissioned by Archbishop Conroy as vicar general of his province of Taum, and in this capacity labored untiringly in the wilds and islands of the West of Ireland until the archbishop's death in 1629, after which he proceeded to France.

At Paris, May 7, 1645, Kirwan was consecrated Bishop of Killala, when he returned to his native city for a time, but after its fall in 1651 had to lie concealed from the fury of the Parliamentary troops in the neighborhood for many months. He underwent the greatest sufferings and privations—during eight entire months being able but thrice to leave his hiding place in a miserable garret infested by mice. He was afterwards imprisoned in Galway, where, forgetful of his own sufferings, he strove to alleviate those of his fellow-prisoners. In August, 1655, the bishop was banished to France, and, at Nantes, was for some years sheltered in the house of a friend. His death took place at Rennes, August 27, 1661. His "Life," written by his nephew, John Lynch, the Archdeacon of Taum, was republished, with a translation and notes by Rev. C. P. Meehan, in 1848.

Oliver Plunket

Oliver Plunket, R. C. Archbishop of Armagh, was born in Loughcrew, County Meath, in 1629. He was descended from an old Anglo-Norman family, and was related to Dr. Plunket, Bishop of Ardagh, and Peter Talbot, Archbishop of Dublin. In 1645 he was sent to Rome under the care of Father Scarampo, Papal Legate, to complete his education, and next year entered the Irish College, where he remained eight years. In 1654 he was ordained for the Irish ministry, but the state of the country rendered his return impossible, and he continued to reside in Rome, where he spent altogether some twenty-five years —from 1645 to 1669. In 1857 he was appointed professor in the College of the Propaganda, where he lectured for about twelve years.

In 1668 he was appointed agent of the Irish clergy in Rome. About this time he composed his Irish poem, "O Tara of the Kings." July 9, 1669, he was nominated Archbishop of Armagh. When leaving Rome he presented a small estate to the Irish College, besides many books and pictures. He was consecrated in November at Ghent, it being supposed that his consecration there would be less likely to bring him into trouble with the government in Ireland than if done in Rome. While in London, on his way, he was secretly lodged for ten days in the royal palace, by Father Howard, Grand Almoner.

During the ten years of his episcopate he was unceasing in his endeavors to re-establish and strengthen the fabric of his church, torn and shattered by the events of previous years. He presided at synods, held confirmations, established colleges and schools—traveling incessantly, not only in Ireland, but the Hebrides. Writing December 15, 1673, he said he had confirmed 48,655 in the previous four years. He bore persecution and poverty with unflinching fortitude. At times he had to preach and administer the sacraments in forests or on remote hillsides, and to hide himself in garrets and miserable cabins. In 1674 the clergy were everywhere obliged to fly to the woods and mountains to seek refuge, and he wrote that in the city of Cashel there was not a single Catholic who could give lodging for one night, and that there was but one parish priest in the whole city.

The archbishop's correspondence with Rome continued even in the worst times of persecution, and is said to have cost him £25 a year—half the revenue of his see. In July, 1679, he was arrested in Dundalk, and committed to New-gate prison, Dublin. He was charged with having compassed the invasion of Ireland by foreign powers; with having obtained money from the Irish clergy to maintain a French army of 70,000 men, and with having conspired to take all the forts and harbors in Ireland.

In October, 1680, the archbishop was removed to England, and on May 3, 1681, was arraigned at the King's Bench, when he pleaded not guilty. Five weeks were allowed him to procure witnesses, and on the 8th of June he was again brought up. His messengers had long been detained at Holyhead by stress of weather, and had not had time to gather in Ireland the scattered witnesses necessary to disprove the assertions of his adversaries. The trial proceeded notwithstanding; the jury after a quarter of an hour's consideration returned a verdict of guilty, and he was sentenced to be hanged, drawn and quartered. He bore himself with great dignity throughout the trial, and on its conclusion again maintained his innocence, and simply asked that a servant and some friends might be permitted to visit him.

He was brought to Tyburn, July 1, 1681. After making a long and dignified speech, pointing the absurdity of the charges brought against him, he resigned himself to the executioner. Wood says in his "Athenæ Oxonienses" that

Archbishop Plunket's remains rested in the churchyard of St. Giles-in-the-Fields until 1683, when they were removed to Landsprug, in Germany. His head is preserved in a shrine in the convent of St. Catherine at Drogheda. Subsequent events proved his entire innocence of the charges brought against him.

Michael Moor

Michael Moor, D. D., provost of Trinity College, was born in Dublin in 1640. He was educated in France; for some years taught philosophy and rhetoric in the college at Grassin, and upon his return home was ordained priest by Luke Wadding (not the Franciscan), who was R. C. Bishop of Ferns, in 1684. For some time Father Moor had, as vicar general, charge of the whole diocese of Dublin. During James II.'s personal government of Ireland he was, in opposition to the Jesuits, and although a Catholic, made provost of Trinity College. He did much to mitigate the sufferings of the Protestant prisoners, and it was largely owing to his exertions that the valuable collections in the library were preserved from injury during the military occupation of the college.

In preaching before the king he upon one occasion took the text: "If the blind lead the blind, both shall fall into the ditch." This so incensed James (who having a confessor with weak eyes, considered the discourse levelled against himself) that he deprived Moor of his preferments, and obliged him to retire to France, from which, on James' return, he removed to Rome, where he enjoyed the favor of Innocent XII, and Clement XI. After the death of James II. he returned to

France, and, according to Harris' Ware, was made Rector of the University of Paris, in which he established an Irish College. To it he bequeathed his choice library, which, however, was found greatly thinned at his death, owing to the depredations of a secretary he had employed when afflicted in his latter days with blindness. He died in Paris, August 22, 1726, and was buried in the chapel of the Irish College. Harris' Ware gives a list of his theological works, which are all in Latin.

James A. Goold

James Alipius Goold, R. C. Bishop, was born in Cork, November 4, 1812. He studied for the priesthood at Rome, and after being ordained was induced to enter the Australian mission and arrived at Sydney, N. S. W., in 1838. He was for some years assistant to Archbishop Polding and subsequently became Dean of Campbelltown. In 1847 he was appointed bishop of the newly-constituted see of Melbourne, and consecrated at Sydney in August, 1848, by Archbishop Polding. The discovery of gold in Victoria caused a rapid increase of population and by his energetic labors churches, schools and convents were erected to meet the demands of the Catholic emigration. On his recommendation the Pope created Sandhurst and Ballarat into separate bishoprics in 1874, and in the same year he was made the first Archbishop of Melbourne and Metropolitan of the province of Victoria. He died June 11, 1886.

John Miley

John Miley, D. D., a distinguished Catholic divine, was born in County Kildare about the

year 1800. He received his education at Maynooth and at Rome. After his ordination he was
appointed a curate in the metropolitan parish,
Dublin, by Archbishop Murray. He became
Rector of the Irish College, Paris, in 1849; and
in 1859 was appointed parish priest of Bray. He
was the friend of O'Connell, whom he attended
in his last moments, and whose funeral panegyric
he pronounced in Dublin. Dr. Miley was an accomplished preacher, and was the author of several works, among which may be noted "Rome
Under Paganism and the Popes" (1848); "History of the Papal States" (1850), and "Temporal
Sovereignty of the Popes." He died at Bray,
April 18, 1861.

Patrick Leahy

Patrick Leahy, R. C. Archbishop of Cashel,
was born near Thurles about 1807. Entering
Maynooth, he distinguished himself, and at the
end of his course was appointed Professor in St.
Patrick's College at Thurles. He soon became
president of that institution, and in 1850 occupied
the important post of Secretary to the synod of
Thurles. Not long afterwards he was appointed
vice rector of the Catholic University. On the
death of Archbishop Slattery he was in 1857 consecrated Archbishop of Cashel. One of his first
acts was the enforcement of the Sunday closing
of public houses, and he made strenuous efforts
to put down the practice of faction-fighting. The
fine cathedral in Thurles is an enduring monument of his zeal and energy. He had special gifts
which fitted him to make a profound impression
as an ecclesiastical orator; such as wide and varied learning, a profound mastery of theology, a

comprehensive grasp of intellect, an unfailing store of language, powerful voice and an imposing presence, and to these were added the apostolic zeal and tender piety which distinguished him from his youth. He died January 26, 1875.

William Bathe

William Bathe, educator and author, was born in Dublin about 1564. He studied at Oxford, but being converted to Catholicity he retired to the continent and joined the Society of Jesus at Tournay in 1596. Traveling in Italy and Spain, he was ultimately appointed professor of languages at the Irish College in Salamanca. He was the author of "An Introduction to the Art of Music," London, 1584; "Mysteries of the Faith," and other works on the study of Latin. He died at Madrid, June 17, 1614.

John McMullen

John McMullen, R. C. Bishop, was born in Ballinahinch, County Down, January 8, 1832, son of James and Alice McMullen. In 1833 the family emigrated to Canada, settling first in Halifax, Quebec, and afterwards in the Province of Ontario. In 1837 they removed to Ogdensburg, N. Y., and finally, in 1843, settled in Chicago, Ill. John was early destined for the church, and after graduating at the University of St. Mary of the Lake in 1853, he completed his studies at the Urban College in Rome, where he was ordained priest June 20, 1858, and received the degree of D. D.

Returning to Chicago, he was attached to several churches until 1861, when he was ap-

pointed President of the University of St. Mary
of the Lake by Bishop Duggan. He subsequently became pastor at Wilmington, Ill., but shortly
after the installation of Bishop Foley he returned to Chicago and became pastor of the Cathedral of the Holy Name and vicar general of
the diocese in 1877. He was chosen Bishop of
the new see of Davenport, Iowa, by Pope Leo
XIII., and was consecrated in the Cathedral of
the Holy Name by Archbishop Feehan, July 25,
1881. Here he remained the rest of his life. He
died at Davenport, Iowa, July 4, 1883. His "Life
and Writings," by the Rev. James J. McGovern,
D. D., was published in 1888.

Paul Cullen

Paul Cullen, cardinal, Archbishop of Dublin,
was born near Ballytore, County Kildare, April
29, 1803. His early education was received at
the Shackleton School in Ballytore, where Edmund Burke had formerly been a pupil, and in
Carlow College, under Dr. Doyle, afterwards
Bishop of Kildare and Leighlin. In 1820 he entered the Urban College of the Propaganda in
Rome. His college course was brilliant and in
a public disputation before Pope Leo XIII. and
his court, September 11, 1828, Cullen undertook
to defend all theology in 244 theses. At the close
of the proceedings the doctor's cap was conferred
on him by the Pope. After his ordination as
priest, in 1829, he was appointed vice rector, and
afterwards rector of the Irish College in Rome.
From May, 1848, to January, 1849, he was
rector of the College of the Propaganda. During
the Roman Revolution an order was issued by
the Revolutionary Triumvirate commanding the

students of the Propaganda to leave the college
within a few hours. As a number of the students
were American citizens, Dr. Cullen immediately
applied to Lewis Cass, United States Minister at
Rome, for intervention. Cass promptly demanded protection to the college, which was at once
granted, and also resulted in a new order being
issued by the Triumvirs forbidding interference
with the institution. Thus Dr. Cullen managed
to save the famous college by placing it under
American protection. On the death of Dr. Crol-
ly, Archbishop of Armagh, in 1849, he was appointed to fill the vacancy in the primatical see,
and was consecrated in Rome by Cardinal Cas-
trocane, February 24, 1850.

Soon after his return to Ireland, as Apostolic
Delegate, he convened the synod of Thurles, in
August, 1850, being the first national assemblage
held in Ireland since the so-called reformation,
in which the establishment of a Catholic university was recommended. May 1, 1852, Archbishop Cullen was transferred to the See of Dublin, and in 1867 he was created a Cardinal Priest,
with the title of San Pietro in Montorio, being
the first Irishman to attain that great dignity.
In September, 1875, he presided at the synod of
Maynooth.

In the course of his long episcopate he paid
frequent visits to Rome, where he was always a
welcome visitor to Pope Pius IX. He died in
Dublin, October 24, 1878, and was interred in
the high altar in the chapel of Clonliffe College.
Archbishop Cullen was a noted theologian, and
one of the foremost ecclesiastics of his time. He
erected many churches, convents and asylums—
the diocesan College of Clonliffe and the Mater
Misericordite Hospital are monuments of his

zeal and energy. He took especial interest in all matters relating to Irish education. His opposition to revolutionary doctrines was outspoken.

Bernard O'Reilly

Bernard O'Reilly, R. C. bishop, was born in County Longford, in March, 1803. Evincing a desire to devote himself to the missions of America, he went to Montreal in 1825, and prepared for the priesthood in the Sulpician Seminary. On the completion of his studies there he entered St. Mary's College, Baltimore, Md., and was ordained priest in the city of New York, October 13, 1831, by Bishop Kenrick, of Philadelphia. His first mission duty was in New York and Brooklyn. During the ravages of cholera in the latter city in 1832 he was twice stricken with the malady while ministering to the sufferers. In December, 1832, he was appointed pastor of St. Patrick's Church in Rochester, N. Y., where he remained until 1847, when he was made vicar general of the diocese of Buffalo by Bishop Timon.

Shortly after his removal to Buffalo the hospital there under the charge of the Sisters of Charity was attacked by John C. Lord, D. D., a Presbyterian clergyman, which resulted in an extended controversy between the latter and Father O'Reilly in the public press. The discussion ended, with his adversary completely silenced, when Father O'Reilly published three able articles, including "The Catholic Church the Church of Christ." At the Council of Baltimore in 1849 he was nominated Bishop of Hartford, Conn., and was consecrated in St. Patrick's

Church, Rochester, by Bishop Timon, to succeed
Dr. Tyler, deceased.

He introduced the Sisters of Mercy into the
diocese, and erected St. Joseph's Church in Providence, R. I., in 1854. In 1855 St. Francis Xavier's
Convent was threatened by a mob, but through
the great courage of the bishop in facing the dis-
turbers the institution was saved from harm.
"The Sisters are in their home," he said. "They
shall not leave it even for an hour. I shall protect them while I have life, and, if needs be,
register their safety with my blood." He went
to Europe in 1855 to secure teachers for his diocesan schools, and pay a visit to his parents in
Ireland. Embarking for this country in the ill-
fated steamship Pacific, January 23, 1856, he nor
the vessel was ever seen again.

Francis Xavier Gartland

Francis Xavier Gartland, R. C. bishop, was
born in Dublin in 1805. Coming with his parents
to the United States he was left an orphan at
an early age. Having passed through the theological course in Mount St. Mary's College, Emmitsburg, Md., he was ordained priest by Bishop
Conwell, of Philadelphia, in 1832, and appointed
assistant to Rev. John Hughes (afterwards archbishop) in St. John's Church, in the latter city.
On the appointment of Dr. Hughes to the coad-
jutorship of New York, Father Gartland succeeded him as pastor, and in 1845 was made
vicar general of the Philadelphia diocese by
Bishop Kenrick. On the erection of the See of
Savannah, Ga., in 1850, he was appointed first
bishop and was consecrated September 10, 1850.
Archbishop Eccleston was the consecrating

prelate, assisted by Bishops Kenrick and O'Connor.

Bishop Gartland at once proceeded to his new field of activity, began the work of organization, and made a personal visitation of the diocese, which then embraced the state of Georgia and a part of Florida. In 1851 he visited Europe to secure assistants and co-laborers. On his return he established a house of Sisters of Mercy at Augusta, founded an orphan asylum at Savannah and built schools in various other places. While laboring among the sick, during an epidemic of yellow fever in Savannah, in 1854, he contracted the disease and died there September 20, 1854.

John Barry

John Barry, R. C. bishop, was born in County Wexford, in 1799. He came to America before the completion of his theological studies and finished his course at the seminary in Charleston, S. C., under Bishop England. He was ordained priest at the Cathedral of St. Finbar, September 24, 1825. He was made pastor of the Church of the Holy Trinity at Augusta, Ga., in 1826; vicar general of the diocese of Charleston and superior of the theological seminary in 1844, and on the death of Bishop Gartland, he was appointed administrator of the See of Savannah. In 1857 he was appointed bishop and consecrated in the Baltimore Cathedral, August 2, 1857.

Dr. Barry was distinguished for his charities and great labors for the sick and poor. In 1832, during the cholera epidemic in Georgia, he cared for the sick in his own house, and in 1853, when yellow fever broke out in Savannah, he exerted himself assiduously toward assisting the sick and dying. He went to Europe to recuperate his failing health, but died at Paris, November 19, 1859. Bishop Barry established the first Catholic day school in the State of Georgia.

Patrick Kelly

Patrick Kelly, R. C. bishop, was born in Kilkenny, April 16, 1799. He was for many years professor and afterwards President of St. John's Seminary, Birchfield, Kilkenny. He had studied in the Irish College at Lisbon, Portugal, and was ordained priest in 1802. On the erection of the See of Richmond, Va., July 11, 1820, Father Kelly was selected as its first bishop. He was consecrated in Kilkenny, August 24, 1820, by Archbishop Troy, of Dublin, assisted by Bishops Murray and Marum. He arrived in Norfolk, Va., which city he selected as his residence, January 19, 1821.

He found the diocese without any facilities for a Catholic education, and with but seven churches, one of which was in Norfolk. He opened a school, which he himself conducted, and in addition to his teaching and episcopal function performed the duties of a mission priest. In consequence of Bishop Kelly's failing health he was transferred to the See of Waterford and Lismore, and in July 1822, he returned to Ireland. Here he ministered for seven years and died at Waterford, October 8, 1829.

William Clancy

William Clancy, R. C. bishop, was born in Cork in 1802. He studied in Carlow College for six years, and in 1829 was appointed to the chair of theology in the same institution. He was made coadjutor to Bishop England, of Charleston, S. C., in 1835, and consecrated in the Cathedral of Carlow, February 1, 1835, by Bishop Nolan, of Kildare, with the title of Bishop of Omense. He reached Charleston in November, 1835, and for two years assisted Bishop England in his arduous duties. In 1837 he was transferred to British Guiana as vicar apostolic, where he remained about ten years. He returned to Ireland in 1847, where he died June 19, of that year.

Richard Luke Concanen

Richard Luke Concanen, R. C. bishop, was born in County Roscommon about 1740. At an early age he went to Lorraine and entered the Dominican Convent of the Holy Cross, and from there proceeded to Rome, where he completed his theological studies. He was ordained priest in 1770, and appointed to a professorship in the Dominican Convent of St. Clement's; subsequently theologian of the Casanatensian Library, prior of the Convent of St. Clement's in 1781, and acted as agent for the Irish bishops at Rome. In 1798 he was obliged to decline the bishopric of Kilmacduagh, Ireland, owing to poor health. He was afterwards appointed first Bishop of New York, and was consecrated in Rome April 24, 1808.

He had previously taken a deep interest in the Dominican missions in America, and had contributed towards the support of the Convent of St. Rose, in Kentucky, of which he continued to be a personal contributor as long as he lived. Before leaving Rome he was commissioned by the

Pope to carry the pallium to Archbishop Carroll, along with the bulls erecting Baltimore into an archiepiscopal see. Owing to the French operations in southern Europe he made an unsuccessful effort to depart for America at Leghorn. After a few months' stay there and at Locanda, he returned to Rome, where he remained until 1810. He then made another attempt to reach New York by way of Naples, but was arrested by order of Napoleon's brother-in-law, Murat (as he was about to embark on a vessel bound for Salem, Mass.), on the pretext that he was a British subject. He was imprisoned there in the Convent of St. Dominic, where he died of fever, June 19, 1810.

John Connolly

John Connolly, R. C. bishop, was born in Drogheda in 1750. He studied theology in Drogheda and at Liege, Belgium, and joined the Dominicans. He subsequently went to Rome and after his ordination, in 1787, was elected prior of the Convent of St. Clement's and agent of the Irish bishops. He was appointed Bishop of New York by Pope Pius VII. in 1814, and was consecrated in Rome in November of that year. After visiting the diocese of Liege in Belgium, and his native country, he embarked at Dublin and reached New York late in the year 1815.

On taking possession of his diocese, which embraced the State of New York and part of New Jersey, Bishop Connolly found only four priests to assist him in his numerous duties. He erected a church at Utica, and at Rochester, N. Y.; built an orphan asylum in New York City, and introduced the Sisters of Charity into the diocese.

During an epidemic of yellow fever in New York in 1822 and 1823 his strength was greatly exhausted and he died in New York City, February 6, 1825.

Henry Conwell

Henry Conwell, R. C. bishop, was born in County Derry, Ireland, about 1745. He studied in the Irish College at Paris, was ordained priest in 1776, and labored in his native country for over forty years, at the end of which time he was vicar general of the See of Armagh. He was consecrated Bishop of Philadelphia in London, England, September 24, 1820. On arriving in this country the spirit of dissension which had begun in his diocese long before, he found, was still rife, and in 1821 was compelled to leave St. Mary's Church (the bishop's cathedral) and retire to St. Joseph's Chapel, near by. The trustees of the Cathedral Church refused to recognize him as bishop and they installed a refractory priest as their pastor. The schism continued, and after every effort to establish peace had been made, he went to Rome in 1828 to lay the matter before the Holy See.

On arriving in Rome he was advised to remain in Europe, but the aged bishop suddenly left the city and went to Paris, where the papal nuncio also advised him not to return to Philadelphia. Shortly afterwards, however, he returned to this country, and at the Council of Baltimore was prevailed upon to accept a coadjutor. Dr. Francis P. Kenrick was appointed to the place, and thereafter Bishop Conwell lived in retirement. He became blind in the latter years of his life and died in Philadelphia, April 22, 1842, at the age of ninety-four.

Andrew Byrne

Andrew Byrne, R. C. bishop, was born in Navan, County Meath, December 5, 1802. While a student in the College of Navan, he volunteered to accompany Bishop England to South Carolina, who was seeking recruits in Ireland for the American mission. He arrived in this country in 1820, and, pursuing his studies under the direction of Bishop England, he was ordained priest by that prelate November 11, 1827. Serving as a missionary priest in North and South Carolina for many years, in which he was compelled to endure long and fatiguing journeys to the scattered Catholic families, Father Byrne's health became much impaired and he returned to Charleston in 1830.

He was made vicar general of the diocese and in 1833 accompanied Bishop England to the Council of Baltimore as theologian. In 1836, removing to New York, he was for some time assistant pastor at the Cathedral and afterwards pastor of St. James' Church. In 1841 Archbishop Hughes sent Father Byrne on a mission to Ireland for the purpose of securing a community of Christian Brothers to teach in the parochial schools of New York. Owing to the heavy demand and scarcity of teachers at the time his endeavors proved unsuccessful. After his return to this country he was made pastor of the Church of the Nativity in New York City, and March 19, 1841, established the Church of St. Andrew in the same city.

During the various pastoral duties which Father Byrne filled both in Charleston and New York, he was noted for his devotion to duty and earnest labors. In 1844 he was appointed first

Bishop of Little Rock, which embraced the State of Arkansas and the Cherokee and Choctaw Nations, in the Indian Territory. He was consecrated in the Cathedral of New York by Archbishop Hughes, March 10, 1844. Proceeding to his diocese his missionary duties were even more arduous than his former labor as a young priest in the Carolinas. While on his visitations he was on many occasions compelled to travel a distance of one thousand miles from one mission to another. He twice visited Ireland to obtain recruits for his diocese and induce the tide of European emigration to the Southwest.

In 1845 he opened an academy in Little Rock in charge of the Sisters of Mercy, and the next year attended the Council of Baltimore. In 1856 he was present at the first Provincial Council of New Orleans. The growth of the Church in the Southwest during his episcopate made wonderful strides. His zeal was unceasing and his labors widespread. In 1843 only four churches had been established in his vast diocese. In 1862 there were seventeen churches, with fifty stations, four religious institutions and twelve schools, with a Catholic population increased from 5,000 to over 50,000. He died in Helena, Ark., June 10, 1862.

Patrick Dillon

BY WILLIAM HOYNES.

Patrick Dillon, C. S. C., educator, was born January 1, 1832, in County Galway, Ireland. His parents were noted for piety, industry and integrity. They were in easy circumstances and well educated. At an early age Patrick was entered as a pupil in the local parish school. His

studies tended to the classics as a preparation
for the priesthood. Actuated by an outraged
sense of patriotism at the conditions obtaining
under British rule in Ireland, the Dillon family
immigrated to the United States and settled in
Illinois while Patrick was still in his infancy.
Sharing the patriotic aspirations of his parents,
he found his new environments agreeable in a
land of freedom, and resumed his studies without unnecessary delay in St. Mary's College,
Chicago.

In 1856 he determined to complete his theological studies at the University of Notre Dame,
located at Notre Dame, in the State of Indiana,
some eighty-six miles east of Chicago. To this
end he became a member of the Congregation of
Holy Cross, under whose auspices the university
is conducted. While prosecuting his ecclesiastical studies at Notre Dame, he served inciden-
tally in the capacity of steward, doing so with
such signal ability as to attract the attention and
win the appreciation of all concerned. In 1858
he finished most creditably his sacerdotal studies
and was ordained priest. His conspicuous ability in administrative lines marked him as a suit-
able candidate for the vice-presidency of the university, to which position he was chosen the
same year. He held this office by annual reap-
pointment until 1865, when he was chosen president, succeeding the Very Rev. Edward Sorin,
its founder and first president. His strong common sense and practical knowledge of affairs
united to make his administration exceptionally
successful. The number of students increased
apace, and a new college building strikingly
artistic, commodious, and attractive, was erected
under his management. He provided also for

broadening the scope and raising the standard of studies. Moreover, he added to the curriculum a commercial department and more clearly marked out and defined the scientific course.

In 1866, however, his health became seriously impaired through overwork. He was thus constrained to seek rest and relinquish his office, in which he was succeeded by the Very Rev. William Corby, famous as chaplain of Meagher's Irish Brigade in the Civil War. The same year he accompanied Father Sorin as a delegate to the general chapter of the Congregation, then held at the branch college in Neuilly, adjacent to Paris, France. In the course of the deliberations of this body, Father Sorin was elected Superior General of the Congregation, and Father Dillon was chosen Assistant Superior General. He remained in France until 1868, when his health appeared to be much improved. About this time he was invited by the Bishop of Chicago to assume the pastorate of St. Patrick's Church. Finding that he could be spared from Notre Dame, and cherishing the hope that closer proximity to his relatives in Chicago, with a change of work and environments, would prove conducive to his health, he accepted the call.

Vain such hope, however, for his illness returned in aggravated form under the cares and duties devolving upon him in his new sphere of labor. Nevertheless, he struggled on and resisted with unabated courage and fortitude the inroads of the fatal disease contracted through overwork. The end came resignedly and peacefully Sunday evening, November 15, 1868. His remains were taken to Notre Dame for interment and laid away, side by side, with those of his deceased brother, Rev. James Dillon, who had been a Civil War chaplain, in the presence of students, professors, and religious, standing with uncovered heads on the snow-covered ground of the community cemetery. Thus passed away, at the age of thirty-six, a most gifted and promising scholar, priest, and college president. His large stature and striking presence served to emphasize the manifest and unquestioned strength and resourcefulness of his mental endowments.

John Quinlan

John Quinlan, R. C. bishop, was born in Cloyne, County Cork, October 19, 1826. At the age of eighteen he came to the United States and was educated for the priesthood at Mount St. Mary's of the West, Cincinnati, Ohio, and at Emmitsburg, Md. He was ordained priest by Archbishop Purcell, in 1853, and after performing missionary duties at Piqua and Cincinnati, Ohio, he was appointed superior of the College of Mount St. Mary's of the West. On the death of Bishop Portier he was appointed to the vacant See of Mobile, and was consecrated in New Orleans by Archbishop Blanc, December 4, 1859. Taking possession of his see a few days afterwards he was installed in the Cathedral of Mobile. Upon making his first visitation, he visited Europe in 1860, and returned to his diocese with a number of ecclesiastical students.

The Civil war brought many troubles to the bishop and in a pastoral he asked the clergy and people to pray for peace. After the battle of Shiloh he ministered to the wounded soldiers of both armies. He visited the Northern states at the close of the war to raise funds for his diocese, and in 1869 attended the Vatican Council. He introduced the Sisters of St. Joseph and Sisters of Mercy into the diocese, restored many churches, and established numerous schools. He died in New Orleans, March 9, 1883.

Tobias Mullen

Tobias Mullen, R. C. bishop, was born in County Tyrone, March 4, 1818. He was educated at Castlefin school and at the College of Maynooth, where he received minor orders. He came to the United States with Bishop O'Connor of Pittsburg, in 1843, completed his theological studies, and was ordained priest September 1, 1844. He held numerous pastorates in the diocese of Pittsburg; was rector of St. Peter's Church, Allegheny, in 1854; vicar general of the diocese, 1864-68, and consecrated Bishop of Erie, Pa., August 2, 1868. Under his rule many churches were erected, and schools and academies established. In 1898, after thirty years' labor in the diocese, he was given a coadjutor. He died in Erie, Pa., April 22, 1900.

Clement Smyth

Clement Smyth, R. C. bishop, was born at Finlea, near Killaloe, County Clare, January 24, 1810. His education was received at Limerick and at Trinity College, Dublin. After completing his college course he entered a Presentation Convent at Youghal. Feeling inclined to a more retired life he subsequently entered the Trappist Monastery of Mount Melleray, in County Waterford. Here he established a school for the education of the poor children of the district, under the charge of the monastery, which he also con-

ducted. Having completed his thelogical studies
he was ordained priest in 1844. When the great
famine swept over Ireland the order at Mount
Melleray selected Father Smyth to emigrate to
this country for the purpose of establishing a part
of their community in America. He arrived in
New York in the spring of 1849, and after visiting several places in the United States and Canada, he was offered a tract of land in Dubuque
County, Iowa, by Bishop Loras. Here Father
Smyth founded the Monastery of New Melleray,
of which he became prior. A school was afterwards built and a church erected in connection
with the monastery.

He was appointed coadjutor to Bishop Loras
of Dubuque and May 3, 1857, was consecrated
in St. Louis. He was also made administrator
of the diocese of Chicago the next year. On the
death of Bishop Loras in 1858 he succeeded to
the See of Dubuque. During his short episcopate he increased the number of churches from
fifty to eighty and organized the Society of St.
Vincent de Paul throughout the diocese. He
died in Dubuque, Iowa, September 23, 1865.

Edward Barron

Edward Barron, R. C. bishop and vicar-
apostolic of Liberia, brother of Sir Henry W.
Barron of Waterford, was born in Ireland in
1801. He was a student of the College of the
Propaganda in Rome, where he was ordained
and received the degree of D. D. Returning to
Ireland, he performed missionary duties there
for some time, when he came to the United
States. After many years of service in the diocese of Philadelphia,—pastor of St. Mary's

Church, president of the Theological Seminary
of St. Charles Borromeo, and vicar-general of
the diocese,—he went to Liberia in 1841, with
Rev. John Kelly of New York, to labor among
the native Africans of that country. He was
made Bishop of Eucarpia and vicar-apostolic of
the two Guineas in 1843, but after most of his
priests had succumbed to fever, with the remaining survivors prostrated by the climate, the mission was confined to a religious order and he returned to this country.

He performed missionary duties in Philadelphia, St. Louis, and in Florida, and, when he
learned of the yellow fever pestilence in Savannah, regardless of his feeble health, he hastened
to the aid of Bishop Gartland. He contracted
the fever himself and died September 12, 1854.
In 1867 the remains of Bishops Barron, Gartland, and Barry were reinterred in the Catholic
cemetery of Savannah.

Francis Moylan

Francis Moylan, R. C. bishop, was born in
the city of Cork, September 17, 1735. He was
educated at Paris, at Montpellier, and afterwards
at the University of Toulouse, where he became
acquainted with Henry Essex Edgeworth, then
a boy. Moylan and Edgeworth became lifelong
friends. After his ordination to the priesthood,
in 1761, Father Moylan remained in Paris a
short time, when he returned to Ireland, and in
1755 was consecrated Bishop of Kerry. In 1786
he was transferred to the bishopric of Cork. Like
many Catholic clergymen who had been educated abroad, in whom the horrors of war had
taken deep root, he opposed any participation

on the part of his people in co-operating with the French fleet when it appeared off the south coast of Ireland in 1796.

At the Examining Board (composed of ten Irish bishops) convened to investigate the affairs of Maynooth College in 1799, Lord Castlereagh suggested that, providing they would admit the king's power of veto on all future ecclesiastical appointments, the government would recommend Catholic Emancipation and a state endowment for the Catholic clergy. Castlereagh's plans were repudiated and in the subsequent controversy Moylan took a leading part. He deprecated any interference whatever of the government in appointment of bishops or clergy. Bishop Moylan was a most successful administrator of his diocese and aided in establishing the Presentation Order of Nuns founded by Nano Nagle for the education of poor girls. He died February 10, 1815. He was the brother of Stephen Moylan, brigadier-general in the American army during the revolutionary war and aide-de-camp to George Washington.

John Thomas Troy

John Thomas Troy, R. C. archbishop, was born in Porterstown, near Dublin, May 10, 1739. At fifteen he left Ireland to study in Rome, where he joined the Dominican Order, in 1756, and subsequently was made rector of St. Clement's in that city. In 1776 he was consecrated Bishop of Ossory, at Louvain, by the Archbishop of Mechlin. On the death of Dr. Carpenter, in 1784, he was elevated to the See of Dublin. In 1809 Dr. Murray was appointed his coadjutor, with right of succession to the See of Dublin, but Archbishop Troy continued for many years to discharge the duties of his office. In 1815 he laid the foundation of the pro-cathedral in Dublin, though he did not live to see it completed. He died in Dublin, May 11, 1823, and his remains were the first laid within the walls of the cathedral he had built. In the administration of his archdiocese and in private life, Dr. Troy was eminently zealous, pious, and charitable. He left funds scarcely enough to meet the expenses of his burial.

From the commencement of his episcopate he discouraged all hostility against the government. Among the Irish prelates, Archbishop Troy was the most pronounced in extending his influence towards the completion of the Legislative Union and other measures favorable to British rule in Ireland. In 1798 he spoke against the rebellion, "believing that Catholic Emancipation would be forthcoming by a display of pacific methods and adherence to the Crown."

Nicholas French

Nicholas French, R. C. Bishop of Ferns, publicist, and politician, was born in Wexford in 1604. He was one of the earliest and most promising pupils of the Irish College of Louvain. After receiving orders, he returned to Wexford as a parish priest. He was consecrated Bishop of Ferns in 1643, and in 1645 was returned as burgess for Wexford to the Confederate Parliament of Kilkenny, where learning, zeal, and enthusiasm before long made him a prominent member. He was elected to the Supreme Council of the Confederates, where he was the ruling, the animating, and the guiding spirit. No period

of Irish history is more thickly studded with ex-
citing and complicated events than during those
times. Throughout this stirring epoch, Bishop
French was a constant and a prominent actor.
In 1651 he formed one of the deputation sent to
urge the Duke of Lorraine to put himself at the
head of the Irish Catholics. The negotiations
with the duke came to naught, and as Ireland
was then in the throes of the Cromwellian invasion, the bishop remained upon the continent.

He acted for a short time as coadjutor bishop
in Paris, and then traveled in different parts of
the continent, and at last found a home with the
Archbishop of Santiago, in Spain. There he
composed his Latin work, "Lucubrations of the
Bishop of Ferns in Spain." After the Restoration, a long correspondence ensued between him
and Father Walsh on behalf of Ormond, relative to his return to Ireland, which ended in
1665, with the following words: "I am resolved
. . . to go to Louvain, and there end my days
where I began my studies." From Louvain he
scattered over the continent numerous tracts relating to Irish affairs, and there he endowed a
bourse of 180 florins a year for the diocese of
Ferns. He died at Ghent, August 23, 1678, and
was interred there in the cathedral.

Among his numerous works are: "A Narrative of the Sale and Settlement of Ireland,"
Louvain, 1668; "The Bleeding Iphigenia," 1674;
and "The Unkind Deserter of Loyal Men and
True Friends," Paris, 1676. The last refers to
the Marquis of Ormond. A collected edition of
the most important of Bishop French's works
was published in two volumes at Dublin in 1846,
with a valuable "History of the Irish College of
Louvain" prefixed. A perusal of his works is

important for all students of the history of the
war of 1641-52.

James Archer

James Archer, R. C. clergyman, was born in
Kilkenny, about 1550. He entered the Society of
Jesus at Rome in 1581; was professed of the
four vows in Spain, and became the first rector
of the Irish College at Salamanca. Father Archer
was a great promoter of education, and was
greatly beloved by his countrymen, with whom
he possessed great influence. He became famous as a missionary in Ireland during the
struggle between Hugh O'Neill and Queen Elizabeth. He died in Spain, about 1620.

Florence Conroy

Florence Conroy, R. C. archbishop, was born
in Galway in 1560. At an early age he was sent
to college in the Netherlands, and afterwards
to Spain, where he entered the Franciscan order,
and distinguished himself as a student of St.
Augustine's works. His defense of the doctrine
of the Immaculate Conception enhanced his
fame, and attracted the notice of King Philip II.
of Spain. In 1588 he was appointed Provincial
of the Franciscans in Ireland, and embarked in
the Spanish Armada. We have few particulars
of his adventures in that expedition, although
he wrote a tract in reference to it, "Peregrinus
Jerichontinus." In 1593 he published a catechism in Irish (a translation of a Spanish work),
"A Christian Instruction." In 1602 he met Hugh
Roe O'Donnell, and acted as his chaplain during
the last hours of that chieftain at Simancas, fol-

lowing his remains to their resting place in the Cathedral of Valladolid.

Although he was appointed Archbishop of Tuam in 1610, the proscription of Catholicity in Ireland prevented his ever taking possession of his see. Through his exertions and his influence with Philip II., the Irish College at Louvain was founded in 1616,—an institution which afterwards became celebrated for the distinguished Irishmen connected with it, and the Irish works that issued from its press. His latter years were occupied in the publication of works on St. Augustine and his writings. He died November 18, 1629, in one of the Franciscan convents at Madrid. His remains were transferred in 1654 to the Louvain College, where they repose under a marble monument. He was the author of many works in Latin.

John Norris

Sir John Norris, admiral, was born in Ireland about the year 1674. In July, 1690, he was appointed to command the Pelican, in recognition of his gallant behavior as lieutenant at the engagement off Beachy Head. In March, 1707, he was promoted to the rank of rear-admiral of the Blue. During the same year he served under Sir Cloudesley Shovel in the Mediterranean and was actively engaged in the abortive attack upon Toulon. After having been advanced to be vice-admiral of the White, in 1708 he became vice-admiral of the Red, and a few months afterwards admiral of the Blue. His supposed ill-luck in the matter of weather procured for him the appellation of "Foul-Weather Jack." In 1717 he was envoy extraordinary to the Czar. At the time of his death he represented Rye in parliament. He was the oldest admiral in the British navy, having seen sixty years' service. He died June 13, 1749.

James Arthur

James Arthur, R. C. clergyman, born in Limerick, became a Dominican in the Abbey of St. Stephen in Salamanca. He afterwards was made professor of divinity in the university there, but lost his position in 1642 for refusing to subscribe to the doctrine of the Immaculate Conception, and retired to the Convent of St. Dominic at Lisbon, Portugal, and there, according to one account, died February 1, 1644. Ware says that he survived until 1670. In 1655 his commentary on St. Thomas Acquinas was published, and at the time of his death he was preparing a work on the latter in ten volumes.

Philip Cosby

Philip Cosby, admiral, naval officer, was born, probably at Stradbally, in 1730. He was one of the numerous descendants of Francis Cosby, who rose to high places in government employ. He entered the navy early, and from the first saw much service. General Wolfe appointed him his marine aide-de-camp, and in this capacity he served with the general until his death at Quebec in 1759. His naval services are fully set out by Ryan in his "Worthies of Ireland." In 1774 he succeeded his cousin, Baron Sidney of Leix, in the family estates. In 1788 he satisfactorily concluded a treaty with the Emperor of Morocco on behalf of Great Britain, and

in 1794, as vice-admiral of the Red, he was present at the capture of Corsica and Toulon. In
1805 he rose to be admiral of the Red. He died
at Bath, January 10, 1808, and was there buried
in the Abbey Church.

Joseph S. Coyne

Joseph Stirling Coyne was born at Birr in
1805, and received his education at Dungannon
school. He was intended for the bar, but ultimately devoted himself entirely to literature,
chiefly dramatic. His first piece, "The Phrenol-
ogist," was produced at the Theatre Royal, Dublin, in 1835. Two years later he went to London
and became a voluminous and successful dramatist, chiefly for the Haymarket and Adelphi. He
contributed to several London papers, and, with
Mark Lemon and Henry Mayhew, was one of
the projectors and original contributors to
Punch. Coyne was the author of "The Scenery
and Antiquities of Ireland," and some works of
fiction. He died July 18, 1868.

John Barrett

John Barrett, D. D., educator and author,
born in 1763, was a native of Ballyroan, where
his father held a curacy. He received his education at Trinity College, Dublin, becoming finally
vice-provost and professor of Oriental languages
in that university. He died, very wealthy, November 15, 1821, leaving most of his property
for charitable purposes. His principal works are
an edition of the gospel of St. Mathew from a
manuscript in the library of Trinity College, Dublin; "An Inquiry into the Origin of the Constel-

lations that Compose the Zodiac," 1800; and an essay on the earlier part of the life of Dean Swift, with several original pieces ascribed to him, 1808. The last work is incorporated in the collected edition of Swift's works.

During the last fifty years of his life Dr. Barrett hardly ever left the college,—occupying an attic in the Library Square, allowing himself little light and no fire, but frequently stealing down in cold weather to the college kitchen to warm himself. His singular life was spent in philosophic seclusion, devoted to his two absorbing passions,—"omnivorous reading and the most assiduous hoarding of money,"—the latter habit being probably induced by the great privations and extreme poverty of his early life. Yet he was a man of strictest honesty and it is said that he was never known to commit a dishonorable action. He was, however, accustomed to vent his strong feelings by indulging in profanity till it became an unconscious habit, but he was ever ready to do kind actions, providing he was not called on to give money, and though curiously ignorant of many of the most ordinary affairs of life, his mind was a perfect storehouse of strange, out-of-the-way knowledge, and his memory so marvelous that he could retain almost everything he had ever seen, read, or heard. Many very amusing tales are told of his eccentricities and absence of mind concerning ordinary matters.

Edward Hay

Edward Hay was born about 1761, in Ballinkeel, County Wexford, descended from an old Anglo-Norman family deprived of most of their

property for embracing the cause of James II.
He was active in the cause of the Catholics, both
before and after the Legislative Union. Although he took no active part in the insurrection of 1798, he narrowly escaped hanging,—his
successful efforts to mitigate the sufferings of
the Royalists during the occupation of Wexford
causing suspicion to center on him as a person
of influence among the insurgents.

He was for many years secretary to the
Catholics of Ireland in their efforts for emancipation. We are told that he died in poverty at
Dublin in October, 1826, and was buried in St.
James' churchyard. He was the author of a
book relating to the insurrection of 1798,—the
"History of the Rebellion in Ireland." John
Hay, his brother, once a lieutenant in the Irish
brigade in France, was executed on Wexford
bridge in 1798 for complicity in the insurrection,
while another brother, Philip, rose to be a lieutenant-general in the British service, dying at
Lambeth, August 8, 1856.

Flann Mainistrech

Flann Mainistrech was a chief professor of
the school of St. Buite, at Monasterboice, in the
11th century. He was born in Munster. "Of
Flann's private life or history, nothing remains
to us; of his public life we have on record the
fact of his having risen to the highest position
in the profession of learning, . . . and we have
evidence of his great celebrity in after ages in
the high compliment paid to him by the Four
Masters in the following entry of his death:
'A. D. 1056, Flann of the Monastery, chief professor of St. Buite's monastery, the wise master

of the Gaedhils in literature, history, philosophy, and poetry, died.' " "Flann compiled very extensive historical synchronisms, which have been much respected by some of the most able modern writers on early Irish history."

O'Curry gives a lengthened analysis of his numerous poems, and writes as follows of some of them: "They are precisely the documents that supply life and the reality of details to the blank dryness of our skeleton pedigrees. Many a name lying dead in our genealogical tracts, and which has found its way into our evidently condensed chronicles and annals, will be found in these poems, connected with the death, or associated with the brilliant deeds, of some hero whose story we would not willingly lose; while, on the other hand, many an obscure historical allusion will be illustrated, and many a historical spot as yet unknown to the topographer will be identified, when a proper investigation of these and other great historical poems preserved in the 'Book of Leinster' shall be undertaken as part of the serious study of the history and antiquities of our country."

Francis Fowke

Francis Fowke was born at Belfast in 1823. After studying in the Military College, Woolwich, he, in 1842, obtained a commission in the Engineers, and was ordered to Bermuda. He soon distinguished himself, and on his return home superintended the erection of several government buildings, the Industrial Museum, Edinburgh; the National Gallery, Dublin; the London Exhibition buildings of 1862, and others. He had just commenced the South Kensington Mu-

seum, when he died from the bursting of a blood-
vessel, December 3, 1865. The plan of the Albert Hall, London, was based upon his suggested
designs. Besides his architectural labors, he
made important improvements in fire-engines,
traveling scaffolds, and collapsing pontoons.

John Bermingham

Sir John Bermingham, Earl of Louth. He
inherited large estates from his ancestors, who
came over to Ireland with Strongbow. In 1318
he was appointed general of the Anglo-Irish
forces raised to check the advance of Edward
Bruce. The memorable battle that ensued, and
which resulted in the death of Bruce at the hands
of John de Maupas, an Anglo-Irish knight, and
the overthrow of his army, was fought at Faug-
hart, near Dundalk, October 14, 1318. Sir John
sent Bruce's head to King Edward II., and was
for his services created Earl of Louth, and
granted estates at Ardee. Next year we find him
marching into Connaught against the O'Conors
and MacKellys.

In 1321 he was appointed Lord-Justice, and
in 1322 conducted a force of 300 men-at-arms,
1,000 hobellars, and 6,000 foot into England, to
aid the king against the Scots. In 1325 he
founded a Franciscan friary at Monasteroris (so
called from his Irish name, MacFeorais). June
10, 1329, he fell, with 200 of his kindred and retainers, at Braganstown, County Louth, in a feud
with the Gernons, Verdons, and others of the
ancient Anglo-Irish families of Louth. He was
undoubtedly the ablest Anglo-Irish leader of his
day.

John Doyle

Sir John Doyle, soldier, was born in Dublin in 1756, and was educated at Trinity College. In 1775 he embarked as lieutenant with the 40th regiment for America, where he greatly distinguished himself, and was several times wounded. For some time he was captain of the "Volunters of Ireland," on the Royalist side. At the commencement of the French war in 1793, he raised a regiment, subsequently numbered as the 87th, and served under the Duke of York in the campaign of 1794, as lieutenant-colonel. He was afterwards appointed colonel of the 87th, and sent in command of a secret expedition to Holland.

Having filled the office of secretary of war in Ireland under the short vice-royalty of Lord FitzWilliam, he was continued in that position by Lord Camden. As a member of the Irish House of Commons, he sided with the National party. In the expedition to Egypt, under Abercrombie, in 1801, he showed great gallantry, leaving a sick bed and riding forty miles through the desert to defend Alexandria against General Menou. After residing for some time in Naples for the benefit of his health, in 1804 he was appointed Governor of Guernsey; in 1805 was created a baronet, and in 1819 a general. He died August 8, 1834.

Benjamin Lee Guinness

Sir Benjamin Lee Guinness, baronet, born November 1, 1798, was an opulent brewer, and M. P. for Dublin from 1865 until his death. He is best remembered as the restorer of St. Pat-

rick's Cathedral (at a cost which some have estimated at £130,000), and as the head of a business firm that has acquired a world-wide reputation. He died possessed of a large fortune, and
besides several mansions in and near Dublin, was
the owner of a beautiful estate at Cong, on the
shores of Lough Corrib. He evinced great and
practical interest in Irish archæology by his preservation of the antiquarian remains upon his
large estates. He died May 19, 1868, and was
buried at Mount Jerome, Dublin.

George Downing

Sir George Downing, baronet, lawyer, was
born in Dublin in 1624. (His father emigrated to
New England in 1638, where he represented
Salem in the General Court, 1638-43. His mother
was a sister of Governor John Winthrop.) Returning to England in 1645, the young man became a preacher among the Independents, then a
chaplain to one of Cromwell's regiments, and in
1653 was appointed commissary-general to the
army in Scotland. He was member for a Scottish borough in 1654 and in 1656, and agent in
Holland two years afterwards. Becoming a Royalist, he was knighted by Charles II., entered
parliament, and was again envoy to Holland.
There he caused the arrest, transmission to England, and consequent execution of three of his
former companions in Cromwell's government,
who had been judges of Charles I.

Through his agency principally the New
Netherlands were wrested from the Dutch and
annexed to the English possessions as New York.
In 1663 he was created a baronet. Sent in 1671
on a mission to Holland, he returned before com-

pleting his errand to the satisfaction of the king,
and was imprisoned in the Tower, but was again
received into favor. He was a man of ability and
natural aptitude for politics, and was the author
of some tracts on state affairs. Downing Street,
in London, perpetuates his name, and his grandson, Sir George, founded Downing College, Cambridge. He died at East Hatley, Cambridge-
shire, in 1684.

Charles C. Chesney

Charles Cornwallis Chesney, colonel, nephew
of General F. R. Chesney, was born at Packolet,
Ireland, in 1826. He entered the Royal Engineers as second-lieutenant, 1845; and rose to be
first-lieutenant in 1846; captain in 1854; lieutenant-colonel in 1868; and brevet-colonel in
1873. An eminent writer and critic on military
subjects, his principal works were: "Campaigns
in Virginia and Maryland," 1864-65; "Waterloo
Lectures," 1868; "Military Resources of Prussia
and France," 1870; "Essays on Modern Military
Biography," 1874, reprinted mainly from the
Edinburgh Review, to which, as well as to the
weekly and daily press, he was a large contributor. Predictions in his "Waterloo Lectures"
were singularly fulfilled in the war of 1870-71,—
as to the enervating effects upon France of a
reliance on past glories, and the lax preparation
for future wars were induced by such a state of
public feeling.

Colonel Chesney, who was for nearly ten
years professor of military history at the Royal
Military and the Staff Colleges, and at the time
of his death was commanding the Royal Engineers of the London district, died March 19, 1876,

from the effects of undue exposure to cold in the exercise of his duty. He was a man greatly beloved in private life, while, according to the Pall Mall Gazette, the United Kingdom "sustained the loss of an able, useful, and conscientiously industrious officer, whose conspicuous and peculiar merits were fully understood and appreciated by those in authority over him."

Luke Gardiner

Luke Gardiner, Viscount Mountjoy, an Irish statesman, was born February 7, 1745. He for some time represented County Dublin in parliament, was a privy-councillor, and colonel of the Dublin Militia. Both in 1778 and 1781 he introduced measures of Catholic relief, which were partially carried; while his proposals for complete equality were successfully opposed by FitzGibbon and others. In 1789 he was created Baron Mountjoy, and six years afterwards a viscount. Upon the insurrection breaking out in Wexford in 1798, he hastened thither at the head of his regiment of militia, and formed a portion of General Johnson's army that took part in the battle of New Ross on the 5th of June. According to Musgrave, Lord Mountjoy fell early in the engagement. His son, the second viscount, created Earl of Blessington, took as his second wife the well-known authoress of that name.

John Foster

John Foster, Baron Oriel, last speaker of the Irish Parliament, was born in Ireland, September 28, 1740. He was educated in Ireland, and admitted to the bar, but early devoted himself to political life. Entering parliament for Dunleer in 1768, he was appointed Chancellor of the Exchequer in 1785, and in 1786 was chosen Speaker of the House of Commons. Bitterly hostile to the measure of Union, he did all in his power as Speaker to thwart it, and was presented with addresses of thanks by the lord mayor, aldermen, and council of Dublin. He declined to surrender the mace of the House of Commons, declaring that "until the body that intrusted it to his keeping demanded it, he would preserve it for them," and it is now held by his descendants, the Massareene family.

After the Union he entered the Imperial Parliament for Louth, and accepted the post of Chancellor of the Exchequer for Ireland. In July, 1821, he was created Baron Oriel. He died at his seat at Collon, in Louth, August 23, 1828. Although not eloquent, Foster had a calm, clear, and forcible delivery. He took a somewhat prominent part in the proceedings of the Imperial Parliament. Two of his speeches in the Irish Parliament,—one against Catholic Emancipation, and the other against the Union,—were printed at the time of delivery, and enjoyed a wide circulation. His son married the Viscountess Massareene, and assumed her surname of Skeffington.

Thomas FitzMaurice

Thomas FitzMaurice, Lord of Kerry, was, according to Lodge, "born in 1502, and bred a soldier in Milan, Italy, under the Emperors of Germany." After considerable difficulty he obtained possession of the family lands and title. He was in favor with King Edward VI. and

Queen Mary, had several estates granted or confirmed to him, and he sat in several parliaments. In 1581, however, he rose in rebellion, and took Adare and Lisconnell castles. Zouche, the Governor of Cork, marched against him, and defeated him at the wood of Lisconnell, whereupon he escaped into the Galtee mountains, was reduced to great distress, and sought pardon. This was granted through the intercession of the Earl of Ormond, and he was received into favor and knighted by Sir Henry Sidney. He died at Lixnaw, December 16, 1590, and was buried in Bishop Stack's tomb in the Cathedral of Ardfert. He is said to have been handsome and athletic.

John D'Alton

John D'Alton, genealogist and antiquarian, was born at Bessville, West Meath, in 1792. He was educated at Trinity College, admitted to the bar in 1813, and appointed commissioner of the Loan Fund Board, Dublin, in 1835. He devoted himself to the study of Irish antiquities, and published "Annals of Boyle," "Lives of the Archbishops of Dublin," "History of the County of Dublin," "King James' Irish Army List," and other standard works,—valuable contributions to the study of Irish history and archæology. He was for many years a contributor to the Gentleman's Magazine. Most of his life was passed in Dublin. He died January 20, 1867.

Louisa Stuart Costello

Louisa Stuart Costello, author, was born in Ireland in 1815. She commenced her literary career at an early age by the publication of a volume of poems that attracted the attention of Moore, to whom, in 1835, she dedicated her first important work, "Specimens of the Early Poetry of France." She soon became widely known as an author of history, travel, romance, and poetry. Ainsworth speaks of her "exquisite sense of the picturesque, and vivid appreciation of local historical association, always simple and unpretending in their enunciation." Perhaps her "Memoirs of Eminent Englishwomen" (1844), and "Falls, Lakes, and Mountains of Wales" (1845) are the best known of her works. She died April 24, 1870.

Laurence Esmond

Sir Laurence Esmond, Lord Esmond, descended from an ancient Wexford family, was born probably in the second half of the sixteenth century. In 1601-02 he commanded a troop of 150 foot and horse, was knighted by Sir Henry Sidney, and served the Queen in Connaught, with Murrough O'Flaherty and Sir Theobald Burke. In 1622, being major-general of all the king's Irish forces, he was raised to the peerage as Lord Esmond. During one of his campaigns in Connaught, he fell in love with and married a beautiful Catholic lady, the sister of O'Flaherty. After the birth of their son Thomas, she carried him away to her Connaught relatives, so that he might be reared in her own faith, whereupon Lord Esmond entered into a union with Elizabeth, granddaughter of the ninth Earl of Ormond.

Lord Esmond was for many years Governor of Duncannon fort, on the Suir. In the fourth book of Carte's "Ormond" will be found full par-

ticulars of his negotiations in 1644 with the duke
regarding the custody of the fort, and of his
ultimately going over to the side of the parliament. He died March 26, 1646. From his son,
before mentioned, Sir Thomas Esmond, a general of horse in the armies of Charles I., the present Esmonds of Ballynastra, County Wexford,
are descended.

Matthew Keugh

Matthew Keugh, Governor of Wexford during its occupation by the insurgents in 1798, was
born in Ireland about 1744, entered the army,
served during the American war, and rose to
be captain-lieutenant. At the breaking out of
the insurrection he was living upon his property
in the town of Wexford. For revolutionary proclivities he had been deprived of the commission
of the peace in 1796. His appearance is thus described by Musgrave: "He was about five feet
nine inches high, and rather robust. His counte-
nance was comely, his features were large and
indicative of an active, intelligent mind. Joined
to a very happy and persuasive manner of expressing himself, he had an engaging address
and great affability of manner."

Upon the occupation of Wexford by the insurgents, May 30, 1798, he was appointed Military Governor of the town. Though his power
was much limited by the passions and prejudices
of the people, he spared no endeavors to secure
the safety of such of the Royalists as remained.
But he was not able to prevent the piking on
the bridge, June 20, of many of the Royalist prisoners, against whom charges were brought of
previous wrongs against the peasantry. When

Wexford was reoccupied by the military two days afterwards, Captain Keugh and others of the leaders remained, under the impression that their lives would be spared. He was, however, with many others immediately brought to a drumhead trial.

He made an able and manly defense, "during the whole of which," says Musgrave, "he was cool and deliberate, and so eloquent and pathetic as to excite the most tender emotions in the breasts of his auditors." Several Royalist witnesses testified that he acted on all occasions with singular humanity, and endeavored to prevent the effusion of blood, and that they owed their lives to his active interference. He was executed on the bridge on the 25th of June,—suffering with dignity and composure. His body was thrown into the river, and his head placed on the court house.

Bagenal B. Harvey

Bagenal Beauchamp Harvey, an estated gentleman in County Wexford, and a barrister, commander of the Wexford insurgents in 1798. He was born about 1762, was educated at Trinity College, Dublin, studied at the Middle Temple, and was called to the bar in 1782. Madden says that before the insurrection of 1798 he "was in tolerable practice as a barrister, and was extremely popular with all parties. He was high-spirited, kind-hearted, and good-tempered, fond of society, given to hospitality, and especially esteemed for his humane and charitable disposition towards the poor." He resided at Bargy Castle, and when the insurgents took the field, in May, 1798, in the north of the county, Harvey, with his friends Colclough and FitzGerald, was immediately imprisoned in Wexford on suspicion.

After the defeat of the Royalists at the Three Rocks, Wexford was evacuated by the small garrison that remained, and the prisoners were on the 30th of May released by the inhabitants and Harvey was appointed commander - in - chief. Nearly the whole of County Wexford was soon in the hands of the insurgents, and it was necessary that New Ross should be taken, so as to open communication with those ready to rise in other counties. Accordingly, on the 4th of June, the Wexford force, under Harvey marched out, and, having been joined by a contingent from the camp at Carrickbyrne, they concentrated at Corbet Hill for the attack on New Ross.

At first the insurgents carried all before them, drove the troops from their intrenchments, through the town, and across the bridge into County Kilkenny. Instead of following up their success, as regular troops would have done, they allowed the British soldiers to retrieve their losses, and in the ensuing battle the insurgents were defeated with a loss of 2,500 men. During the battle of Ross, Harvey and his aide-de-camp, Gray, a Protestant attorney, spent most of the day on a neighboring hill, almost inactive spectators of the fight. After these events Harvey was deposed from the supreme command, and appointed president of the council of government. The battle of Vinegar Hill was lost on the 21st of June, and the next day Wexford was reoccupied by the king's troops. Harvey and Colclough, with the wife of the latter, took refuge on one of the Saltee Islands. They were pursued, and after a long search were found concealed in a cave, disguised as peasants.

Harvey was tried by court-martial and executed on Wexford bridge on the 28th of June, with Grogan, Captain Keugh, governor of the city, and numbers of others. He met his fate reverently and bravely. His body was cast into the river and his head spiked on the court house. The body was ultimately recognized by some friends and buried at Mayglass, a few miles south of Wexford. A bill of attainder was passed against him, but his property was, in 1829, restored to his brother James.

David FitzJames De Barry

David FitzJames De Barry, Viscount Buttevant, a descendant of the same family as Robert De Barry, a Welsh-Norman knight, who came to Ireland at the time of Strongbow, and his brother, Gerald De Barry (Giraldus Cambrensis), the distinguished author who wrote a history in Latin of the Norman invasion of Ireland, was born the middle of the sixteenth century. He was one of the lords of Sir John Perrot's parliament in 1585, but afterwards took an active part with the Earl of Desmond. Eventually he gave in his submission to Lord Grey, and acknowledged a debt of £500 to the Crown,—a claim which was afterwards granted to Florence Mac-Carthy, and created much correspondence and bickering. In 1601 he was made a general by Sir George Carew, after the siege of Kinsale saw considerable service in Munster, and was granted large estates in Desmond, forfeited by the Mac-Carthys. In 1615 he was appointed one of the Council for Munster. He died at Barryscourt, near Cork, April 10, 1617.

David FitzDavid De Barry

David FitzDavid De Barry, Earl of Barrymore, grandson of preceding, a posthumous
child, was born March, 1605. At the age of
twelve he succeeded to the estates of his family,
and in 1621 married Alice, daughter of the Earl
of Cork, and through the earl's influence was
created Earl of Barrymore. When the war
broke out in 1641, he held to the English side,
and garrisoned his castle of Shandon with about
100 men; being offered the position of general in
the Irish army, he refused. On May 10, 1642, he,
with Lord Dungarvan, took the castle of Bally-
macpatrick (now Careysville), held by his grand-
aunt, a MacCarthy, rescued a large number of
English confined therein, and killed in cold blood
the whole garrison,—about fifty men. He headed
his regiment at the battle of Liscarroll in September, 1642, and died on the 29th of the same
month, probably from his wounds, or from the
fatigues of campaigning. He was buried in his
father-in-law's family vault at Youghal. He was
a Protestant. The honors of the family became
extinct upon the death of Henry Barry, eighth
Earl of Barrymore, in 1824.

Richard Prendergast

BY EDWARD F. DUNNE

Richard Prendergast, jurist, was born in Ireland, November 8, 1854. Perhaps no man of the
Irish race in America achieved so much in so
short a time in American life, and had a brighter
prospect for reaching the highest places in the
land than did Richard Prendergast at the time

of his untimely death, in the year 1899, at the early age of forty-four.

While yet engaged in his father's business, he entered St. Ignatius College and at once took first place in every class during the whole curriculum. He was admitted to the bar, at the head of his class, in the year 1876.

Possessed of a wonderful intellect, a hardy frame, and tireless energy, he immediately began to attract a large and lucrative clientele. No young man of his age at the Chicago bar was so uniformly successful before juries and courts. So extraordinary was his success that when only twenty-eight years of age he was nominated for the county bench and elected by a decisive majority. He at once raised that court from the position of a subordinate court to one of commanding influence in the city of Chicago.

Owing to the exclusive jurisdiction of that court in many matters such as insolvency, elections and special assessments, it became, under the administration of Judge Prendergast, of great and extraordinary power and influence, and when the jurisdiction of the court was assailed in superior courts, the young jurist was firm in the assertion of the exclusive powers of the court, and in many a bitterly litigated controversy its jurisdiction was successfully protected and asserted.

Decisions of the young judge were marvelously able and lucid, and were almost uniformly sustained upon appeal.

While upon the bench Judge Prendergast became much interested in the future of the great city in which he lived,—Chicago. He was among the first to discover that the sanitation of the city was wholly inadequate to its needs, and that if Chicago was ever to become the greatest city in the western hemisphere, its whole system of sanitation would have to be changed. The sewage of the city at the time was emptied into Lake Michigan, and from this clear and fresh water at the doors of the city the water supply of the city was taken. He was the first man in public life to perceive that it would be impossible for the city to grow unless it maintained its health, and that it could not maintain its health while its water supply came from the very place in which the sewage of the city was emptied. After consultation with civil and sanitary engineers, he, among the first, advocated the reversal of the flow of the Chicago River, the cutting through the watershed which separated the basin of the St. Lawrence from the basin of the Mississippi River, the drawing of the pure, clear waters of Lake Michigan through the Chicago River into the Desplaines, and thence emptying these waters with the sewage of the city through the Desplaines River into the Illinois River, the Mississippi, and the Gulf of Mexico. This daring scheme, which would entail the expenditure of at least $50,000,000, was at once advocated with characteristic boldness and audacity by the young judge.

Finding the position of a judge too narrow in its scope for the development of his abilities, and too meager a source of living, he refused a third nomination for the County Court, and retired to private practice. While practicing at the bar, his income became enormous, but even in the midst of his active practice, he found time to devote himself to public interests. He was largely instrumental in creating the Sanitary District of Chicago, which was organized by the Legislature for the purpose of cutting through the watershed, hereinbefore mentioned, and turning the waters of Lake Michigan into the Mississippi. After the Sanitary District was created as a corporation by the Legislature, Democratic and Republican parties nominated their representatives for the first Board of Trustees. By arrangement between the leaders of both parties, these nominees were selected because of their qualifications more as politicians than as practical business men. When Prendergast discovered that it was the design to administer this corporation as a political asset, he at once sounded a cry of alarm. Going from paper to paper, and from one influential citizen to another, he finally organized a great independent movement, which placed in nomination nine trustees, wholly unidentified with either of the great political parties. By common consent, Prendergast was placed at the head of the ticket, and to the astonishment and amazement of the whole community, this independent ticket, led by Richard Prendergast, was triumphantly successful. After his election as Drainage Trustee, he was elected first President of the Sanitary District of Chicago, and served with great credit to himself and to the great advantage of the community for a term of six years. Thereafter he again retired to private life and private practice of the law. This practice brought him in a princely income.

At the outbreak of the Spanish-American war, Judge Prendergast was one of the most energetic citizens in Chicago in completing the muster of the Irish-American Regiment of Chicago, known as the Seventh Infantry, and while this regiment was at the front, Judge Prendergast organized the Seventh Regiment Armory

Association, whose aim and object was to care for the wives and children of the soldiers. He was elected president of this organization, mainly through his splendid appeals to the public. The wives and children of these volunteers were provided for while their husbands were absent and while their brothers and fathers were at the front.

In the midst of one of the most successful careers of any man who practiced at the bar in Chicago, he was carried off in the prime of his manhood at the age of forty-four years, by an attack of pernicious anæmia, leaving behind him a family of six children, three boys and three girls, who were unfortunate enough to lose their young mother only seven years before.

Judge Prendergast, through all his life, was a Jeffersonian Democrat, a hearty Irish Nationalist, and a zealous Roman Catholic. Both as citizen, lawyer, judge, and public official, he earned the respect and admiration of the whole community. His untimely taking off was due in a large measure to the overstrain and overwork which his indomitable and tireless nature heaped upon him in his professional life. He died in the midst of a law suit in which he earned a fee of $80,000, which was afterward paid to his estate.

He was possessed of a commanding presence, was medium in stature, and of finely chiseled features. He had a command of language and a gift of delivery rarely equaled and never surpassed at the Chicago bar. He had, moreover, a complete command of invective and satire, and was possessed of a sunny humor, characteristic of his race. Few could equal him in the onslaught of an attack, and his defenses were marvels of ingenuity and finesse. He swayed the courts by his masterly logic and his juries by the overwhelming power of his eloquence, all of which made him one of the most remarkable men of his day.

Joseph Napier

Joseph Napier, jurist, was born in Belfast, in December, 1804, descended from the Napiers of Merchiston. He received his early education from the great dramatist, James Sheridan Knowles, and was distinguished for his progress and diligence. In 1820 he entered Trinity College, Dublin, where he soon gained considerable reputation both as a classical scholar and a mathematician, obtaining honors both in classics and science during his undergraduate course. His first intention, after graduating in 1825, was to seek for a fellowship in his college, which his learning and talent would probably have secured to him, but after taking his master's degree he was induced to abandon that intention, and applied himself to study for the bar.

In London he studied under Patteson, upon whose elevation to the bench, in 1830, Napier commenced to practice as a special pleader. In 1831 he returned to Dublin and was admitted to the Irish bar in the Easter term of that year. The following year he went to the northeastern circuit, and established for himself the reputation of a sound lawyer and an accurate pleader. In 1840 Napier, with some other legal friends, originated The Law Institute, which led to important results in the improvement of legal education in Ireland; and in this society he delivered a popular course of lectures on common law.

A point of great importance was raised by
Napier in 1843 in the case of the Queen versus
Gray,—namely, the right of persons on trial for
non-capital felonies to challenge jurors per-
emptorily. The Irish courts decided against the
right, but the House of Lords, upon appeal, reversed that decision. The argument of Napier was spoken of in very favorable terms by
high judicial persons in London, and established
his professional reputation. Upon his return to
Ireland he was called within the bar, and soon
took a high place among the leading common law
practitioners. He was now on several occasions
engaged in appeals from the Irish courts to the
House of Lords, and in the great case of Lord
Dungannon versus Smith, in June, 1845, delivered
two masterly arguments, which were eulogized
by the lord-chancellor and many of the law lords,
including Lord Brougham and Baron Parke.

Napier now turned his attention to the
House of Commons and in 1847 contested the
representation of Trinity College with Shaw.
Though on that occasion unsuccessful, he was
in the following year, upon the resignation of
Shaw, returned without opposition. Napier continued to represent his university up to 1858,
and took an active and able part in all the important discussions of the period, especially upon
the subjects of law reform, and the appointment
of a minister for the department of justice, making a high character as a statesman and an
orator.

Upon the accession of Lord Derby as prime
minister in March, 1852, Napier was appointed
attorney-general for Ireland, a post which he
held till the resignation of the Derby ministry
in January, 1853. Upon the return of Lord

Derby to power, in March, 1858, Napier was appointed Lord-Chancellor of Ireland, holding the seals till the resignation of the ministry, in June, 1859.

A volume containing the most important decisions of Lord-Chancellor Napier has been publised, which evince the industry, care, and learning which he brought to bear upon his judgments. After his retirement from professional life, Napier devoted himself to the improvement of the youth of his native land, and, as a public lecturer, eminently served the cause of education. As a lawyer, scholar, and politician, Napier is entitled to a high place among his countrymen. He died in 1882.

William Petty-FitzMaurice

William Petty-FitzMaurice, Earl of Shelburne and Marquis of Lansdowne, statesman, was born in Dublin, May 20, 1737. (His father, John FitzMaurice, assumed the name of Petty in 1751, and, on the decease of a maternal uncle inherited the large Irish estates of his grandfather, Sir William Petty, and in 1753 was created Earl of Shelburne.) His early years were spent in Munster with his grandfather, the first Earl of Kerry. At sixteen he was sent to Christ Church, Oxford. Afterwards, entering the army, he served in Germany, and gave signal proof of personal valor at the battles of Kampen and Minden.

At the accession of George III. he was appointed aide-de-camp to the king, with the rank of colonel. In 1761 he was elected member for Wycombe, a seat he held only for a few weeks, as upon his father's death, May 10 of that year, he passed to the House of Lords as Earl of Shelburne in the Irish and Baron Wycombe in the British peerage. In April, 1763, he was, though not then twenty-six years of age, appointed to the head of the Board of Trade, and sworn of the Privy-Council.

In these official positions he reported upon the organization of the government and the settlement of boundaries of the newly acquired Canadian territories. His strongly worded representations as to the danger attending the proposed plans for the taxation of the American colonies caused him to be regarded with disfavor by George III. On Grenville's modification of his cabinet, in the following September, Shelburne resigned his office and thenceforth remained closely united with Pitt, against whom, at the outset of his career, he had been strongly prejudiced. For more than a year he lived in retirement at Bowood, adding to his library and improving his estate.

In 1766 Pitt, then Earl of Chatham, formed his second administration, and the Earl of Shelburne accepted the post of Secretary of State for the Southern Department, which included the colonies. As might have been expected from his previously declared opinions, he endeavored to gain the good-will of the American colonies,— putting himself in communication with their several agents in England, and seeking full information on the points in which the colonists regarded themselves aggrieved. In these good offices he was opposed by his colleagues, and when illness obliged Lord Chatham to withdraw from an active share in the government, the influence of Grafton, Townshend and others became paramount, and Shelburne's conciliatory policy was cast to the winds. After the passage of the Import Duties Act he would probably have resigned were it not that he considered himself bound to Chatham, then too ill to see any of his coadjutors even on the most important affairs. The management of the colonies was shortly afterwards transferred to Lord Hillsborough, the other secretary, and Lord Shelburne gladly resigned office, October 19, 1768.

Lord Chatham's resignation followed, and George III. found a congenial minister in Lord North. Shortly after this Lady Shelburne died, and he paid a prolonged visit to the continent with his friend, Colonel Barre. In Paris he became acquainted with the Abbe Morellet and other eminent men, and he afterwards declared that his intimacy with Morellet was the turning point in his career; in his own words, "Morellet liberalized my ideas." Many of his French friends were afterwards induced to visit Bowood, where, in company with Franklin, Garrick, Barre, Priestly, and others, they found the equivalent of the brilliant society of Paris.

Out of office, Lord Shelburne continued the steady friend of Chatham, opposing Lord North's ministry on most leading questions, especially those relating to America. In April, 1778, Lord North resigned, and the negotiations for the return of Lord Chatham to office (put an end to by his death) were carried on almost entirely by Lord Shelburne. Next year his marriage with Lady Louisa FitzPatrick connected him more closely than before with Fox and Lord Holland. After Lord Chatham's death, Shelburne joined Lord Rockingham, consenting to waive in his favor (in case of office being offered to him) his

title to the premiership. His opposition to Lord
North increased in activity as the policy of the
latter became more and more unsuccessful, while
Shelburne himself may be said to have become
proportionately popular. The measures passed
in December, 1779, for the relief of Irish commerce had his heartiest approval.

March 20, 1782, in consequence of the surrender of Lord Cornwallis at Yorktown, Lord
North's ministry succumbed, and Lord Rockingham became his successor, with Lord Shelburne and Charles James Fox as Secretaries of
State. As Secretary of State, Shelburne, in the
House of Lords, May 17, moved those measures
which conceded parliamentary independence to
Ireland. The ministry lasted little over three
months,—Rockingham's death in July being the
immediate cause of its dissolution. Fox, with
Burke and his other friends, then insisted on
the Duke of Portland being made Premier; the
King, however, who had come to place great
confidence in Lord Shelburne, preferred him,
and entrusted him with the formation of a ministry. Fox's party, unable to dissuade him from
acceding to the King's desire, seceded in a body,
being unwilling to accept his leadership.

During Shelburne's administration of little
over seven months, Gibraltar was successfully
defended, the great victories of Howe and Rod-
ney enabled Great Britain to make honorable
terms with France, Spain, and Holland, and separate preliminaries of peace were arranged with
the United States. Shelburne resigned in February, 1783, and did not again accept office, or
take any prominent part in public affairs,—giving, however, a steady support to his younger
colleague, Pitt. He was created Marquis of

Lansdowne in 1784. His health being feeble, he felt neither strength nor inclination again to enter into the turmoil of party politics. Lord Lansdowne died May 7, 1805, and his remains were interred in the church of High Wycombe.

The Edinburgh Review says: "History has not done justice to the character of the first Marquis of Lansdowne, who only wanted the opportunity to have taken his place in the first rank. . . . During his short administration he concluded a disastrous war by a peace in which the interests and the honor of the country were duly regarded, and the domestic policy which he pursued was only in fault inasmuch as it was in advance of the knowledge and morality of the time. . . . He was an ardent champion of American independence. He hailed with enthusiasm the French Revolution. He had always firmly maintained that France ought not to be the enemy but the friend and ally of England. He was the strenuous advocate of free trade. He was for Catholic Emancipation and complete religious equality before the law."

He was twice married,—in 1765 to Lady Sophia Carteret, and, after her death, to Lady Louisa FitzPatrick, in 1779. One of his sons by the first marriage succeeded him as second Marquis of Lansdowne, and another by the second became third marquis.

Henry C. K. Petty-FitzMaurice, fifth marquis, eldest son of the fourth Marquis of Lansdowne, born in 1845, was Under-Secretary for War, 1872-74; Under-Secretary for India, 1800; Governor-General of Canada, 1883-88; Governor-General of India, 1888-93; Secretary for War, 1895-1900, and in the latter year became Foreign Secretary.

John O'Shanassy

Sir John O'Shanassy, Australian statesman,
son of Denis O'Shanassy, was born near Thurles,
County Tipperary, in 1818. He emigrated to
Australia in 1839, and finally settled at Melbourne, in 1846, where he started in business and
met with considerable success. In 1856 he was
one of the chief promoters of the colonial bank,
and for fourteen years acted as chairman of its
board of directors. Throughout life an ardent
Catholic, he was one of the founders of St. Patrick's Society, and for many years represented
his co-religionists on the denominational board
of education. But it was in politics that the
greatest part of his energies were devoted.

When the separation of Victoria from New
South Wales took place in 1851, he was returned
as one of the members for Melbourne to the first
Legislative Council, and became virtually leader
of the opposition to the official or nominee ele-
ment in that body. O'Shanassy, who had been
one of the strongest advocates for the separation
of the province of Melbourne from the colony
of New South Wales, now became a stanch supporter of responsible government. He was one
of the founders of the anti-transportation league
and strongly opposed the Australian penal settlement system.

In 1852 he and his colleagues succeeded in
defeating the official Gold Export Duty bill; and
he was appointed by Sir Charles Hotham as
member of the commission to investigate the
condition of the gold fields of Victoria. He was
also a member of the committee appointed in
1853 to report upon the best form of a constitution for the colony. In 1855 he was a member

of both the gold and crown land commissions.

In September, 1856, at the first election to the first Legislative Assembly, he was elected for Melbourne, and also for the constituency of Kilmore, and took his seat for the latter. Early in 1857, on the fall of the Haines administration, he became premier and chief secretary, and his government, formed on a democratic basis, held office only a few weeks, when it resigned in consequence of a vote of want of confidence. O'Shanassy returned to office as premier and chief secretary in March, 1858, where he remained this time until October 27, 1859. In his second term he successfully negotiated the first Victorian public loan of $8,000,000, which was floated through the agency of six Melbourne banks. He became premier and chief secretary for the third time November 14, 1861, holding office until June 27, 1863. Charles Gavan Duffy, whom he had welcomed on his arrival in Australia, was his colleague in all three administrations.

The important measures fathered by the O'Shanassy ministry during his third term were the Crown Lands act in 1862, and the Local Government act in 1863. In June, 1863, he left office, but continued to be a member of the Victorian Legislature, except in 1866-67, when he visited Europe. In recognition of his services to the cause of Catholic education he was created a Knight of the Order of St. Gregory the Great by Pope Pius IX. After his return to Victoria he was elected a member of the Legislative Council (in February, 1868), without opposition, and in 1872, re-elected for ten years, but at the end of two years resigned his seat. In 1877 he again entered the assembly as member for Belfast.

He was a supporter of free trade, a broad-

minded advocate of constitutional politics, and of
a general Australian federation. In capacity and
legislative mastery he had no superiors among
his contemporaries in the Victorian Legislature.
In 1870 he was created a C. M. G., and in 1874 a
K. C. M. G. He married in 1839, Margaret Mc-
Donnell, of Thurles. He died May 6, 1883, leaving three sons and three daughters. His wife
died in 1887.

John Egan

John Egan, Chairman of Kilmainham, County Dublin, was born about 1750, at Charleville,
County Cork. He entered Trinity College, Dublin, as a sizar, and graduated B. A. in 1773,
and LL. B. in 1776, and in 1790 the degree of
LL. D. was conferred upon him. He was admitted to the Irish bar in 1778, subsequently received a silk gown, and in 1787 was elected a
bencher of the Society of Kings Inns, Dublin.
In March, 1789, he entered the Irish parliament
as member for Ballinakill, and from 1790 to the
period of the Union of Great Britain and Ireland
sat for the borough of Tullagh, County Waterford. In 1799 he was appointed Chairman of
Kilmainham. His means at this time being reduced, the position was practically his only
source of income.

The office depended on government favor,
and it was intimated that his support of the
Legislative Union would lead to further advancement. As the final debate on the question proceeded, it was seen that he was struggling under
conflicting emotions; at length he rose, delivered
a furious speech against the Union, and sat down
exclaiming. "Ireland—Ireland for ever! and
damn Kilmainham!" He was a noted duelist and

once fought with his intimate friend John Philpot Curran, fortunately without serious consequences. In after life there were few of the old friends of Curran of whom the latter was accustomed to speak with greater affection than of Egan. He died in 1810.

David Collins

David Collins, colonial governor of Van Diemen's Land, son of General Collins of Pack, Kings County, was born March 3, 1756. When but fourteen he received an appointment as lieutenant in the Marines; fought at Bunker Hill and elsewhere in the American Revolutionary war, and on the proclamation of peace in 1782, settled in Kent, England, on half-pay with an American wife.

In May, 1787, he sailed with Governor Phillip as secretary and judge-advocate on the expedition to establish a convict settlement at Botany Bay, New South Wales, recently discovered by Captain Cook. The proposed locality was found unsuitable; Port Jackson was preferred, and there Sydney was founded. Collins remained in Australia for ten years, and after his return wrote an "Account of the English Colony in New South Wales, with some Particulars of New Zealand from Governor King's MSS," two volumes, London, 1798-1802. The work is embellished with many plates, and as the first published account of the new colony, has a permanent interest.

Shortly after the publication of this work he was commissioned to establish another convict settlement in Australia. He made an abortive attempt to found one on the southeastern shore

of Port Phillip, and then crossed to Van Diemen's Land (now Tasmania), where, on February 19, 1804, he laid the foundations of the present city of Hobart Town. Collins was the first
governor of the island, and died at his post,
March 24, 1810.

George Higinbotham

George Higinbotham, Chief-Justice of Victoria, was born in Dublin, April 19, 1826. He
was educated at the Royal School, Dungannon,
and at Trinity College, Dublin, where he graduated B. A. in 1848, and M. A. in 1853. In 1847
he went to London and while studying for the
bar became a reporter on the Morning Chronicle.
He entered Lincoln's Inn, April, 1848, and was
admitted to practice, and shortly afterwards
went to Australia.

He arrived in Melbourne early in 1854, practiced his profession, and occasionally contributed
to the Melbourne Herald. In 1856 he accepted
the editorship of the Argus, but resigned in
1859, so as to devote himself entirely to his law
practice. He now entered the political field, and
in 1861 was elected a member for Brighton to
the Legislative Assembly, as an Independent
Liberal. In 1862 he lost his seat, but the next
year was again elected from the same constituency. In June, 1863, on the defeat of the O'Shanassy Government, he became attorney-general
in the Victorian Cabinet formed under Sir James
McCulloch. In the long struggle between the
two houses over the question of finance bills and
the Darling Grant, which lasted from 1865 to
1868, Higinbotham was a leading figure, and his
attitude in the controversy won for him great

popularity. In September, 1866, he was appointed chairman of the Education Commission, and in July, 1868, when McCulloch returned to power, he declined the post of attorney-general, but remained in the Cabinet as Vice-President of the Board of Land and Works without salary. In 1869 he left the ministry altogether.

In 1871, to the astonishment of the whole colony, he lost his seat in the assembly to a local candidate, and for the next three years was engaged in a lucrative practice at the bar. In 1874 he was elected to the assembly for the East Bourke borough, but finding himself unable to support the Berry Ministry on the questions of land tax and payment of members, he resigned his seat. He now retired from active political life, and in 1880 was appointed to a seat on the Puisne Bench of the Supreme Court of Victoria. In September, 1886, on the retirement of Sir William Stawell, he became chief-justice of the colony. His great independence and his view of colonial government were shown by his refusal to accept knighthood on the ground that all rewards for local service should emanate from local sources. He had intimated to the Imperial authorities that if he were appointed acting governor of Victoria in the absence of Sir Henry Loch in 1880 (as was the custom), he would cease to refer any matters of local concern to the secretary of state.

He was for several years Vice-President of the Melbourne Benevolent Asylum, President of the Australian Health Society, and in 1877 was appointed President of the Executive Committee of the Melbourne Centennial Exhibition. In 1888 he began his second consolidation of the laws of Victoria, which resulted in a remarkably successful work, and he was publicly thanked in parliament in 1890. In the latter year Higinbotham incurred some class opprobrium through his outspoken adherence to the cause of the workers in the great general strike and by contributing to their funds until a conference was conceded.

The vehemence of his political utterances contrasted strongly with the charm and amiability of his private life—those who condemned his political views were strongly attached to him personally—and his intellectual attainments and unconventional opinions on all social questions made him one of the most popular public men of his time in Australia. His oratorical powers were of a high order. In 1854 he married Margaret Foreman, by whom he had several children. He died at his residence in Melbourne, December 31, 1892.

Richard John Griffith

Sir Richard John Griffith, baronet, geologist, was born in Dublin September 20, 1784. His father Richard Griffith, was a member of the Irish House of Commons, and was one of the promoters of the grand canals. The son, Richard, received his commission as lieutenant in the Royal Irish artillery, in 1800, but after the Legislative Union, he retired and embraced the more congenial profession of a civil engineer. In 1802 he became the pupil of William Nicholson, of London, the editor of the Philosophical Journal, and there devoted himself to the study of various sciences, including practical mining; visited the various mines of the British Isles, and made the acquaintance of Sir Humphry Davy and Sir

John St. Aubyn.   In the year 1808 he became a member of the Royal Dublin Society, for which he made a survey of the Leinster coal district, and in 1809 he received his first public appointment as one of the engineers to report upon the situation, extent and capability for culture of the bogs of Ireland.

The bog of Allan and the adjacent bog-lands fell to his lot, and he reported upon four hundred and seventy-four thousand acres of country. Besides the subject in hand he described the geological, physical and mineral aspects of the districts reported upon and showed the adaptation of the reclaimed bogs for the production of fiorin grass, remarkable for its nutritious qualities. Owing to the celebrity he then gained, the Royal Dublin Society having, in 1812, founded a professorship of geology and practical mining, Griffith received the appointment.   His next appointment was that of inspector of the royal mines in Ireland.   From this time up to the year 1822, he continued his lectures on geology and mining.

In 1822 he laid out two hundred and eighty miles of admirable road through the mountainous districts of the South.   In 1824 a general valuation and ordnance survey of Ireland having been directed by government, Griffith's recommendation of a scale of six inches to the mile was adopted, and he was appointed to carry out as a prelude a territorial or boundary survey of the country.   This work was completed in the year 1846.

From the year 1825 his career became a purely public one, and the remainder of it is but the history of his branch of the public service in Ireland with which his name is identified.   His

general valuation of Ireland, commenced in 1830,
continued in operation, and upon it the various
local and public assessments have been made.
In 1835 he was appointed by the Treasury one of
the commissioners for improving the river Shannon, and in 1836 a member of the railway commission. In 1846 he was appointed deputy-chair-
man, and in 1850 Chairman of the Board of
Public Works in Ireland.

Meantime from the year 1812, he had been
engaged in geological investigations, and though
often interrupted by other avocations, he never
lost sight of the subject. At length his labors
resulted in his great geological map of Ireland
on a scale of four miles to an inch. This work
added to his reputation, and in 1854 Professor
Forbes, on behalf of the Geological Society of
London, presented him with the Wollaston pal-
ladium medal, on which occasion the professor
termed his map "one of the most remarkable
geological maps ever produced by a single geologist." In preparing this map, he incurred the
enormous labor of visiting every parish in Ireland three times. In the year 1858, in consideration of his distinguished services, he was made a
baronet. He died in 1878.

William Dargan

William Dargan, engineer and contractor,
was born in County Carlow, February 28, 1799.
On leaving school he was placed in a surveyor's
office, where he showed great aptitude for business. Having gained some experience in England under Telford, he entered into a contract
for the construction of the road from Dublin to
Howth, in which work he was so successful that

in 1831 he contracted for the construction of the Dublin and Kingston Railway, the first in Ireland. As the railway system spread through the country, he undertook the construction of the principal lines,—Great Southern and Western, Midland Great Western, and others, in all about 1,000 miles, and accumulated a large fortune, mostly invested in Irish railway shares. His contract for the Ulster canal, between Lough Erne and Belfast, was accepted and executed most satisfactorily.

He undertook the financial risk of the Dublin Industrial Exhibition of 1853, and bore the deficit of about £10,000 resulting therefrom. On the occasion of its opening by the Queen he declined the honor of a baronetcy. To commemorate his active interest in the industrial progress of Ireland, his statue was erected in front of the National Gallery of Dublin, and from 1853 to 1865 he was among the most honored men in the country, and was supposed to be one of the wealthiest. In 1866 he was severely injured by a fall from his horse, and soon afterwards, overstrained by innumerable undertakings, became bankrupt, and died, February 7, 1867. He was buried in Glasnevin Cemetery. A small pension on the Civil List was granted to his widow.

Saint Malachy

Saint Malachy, Archbishop of Armagh, was born near Armagh about 1094. He had a brother, Gillachrist, who became bishop of Cloghen and died in 1138. His parents were of high rank and influence and his mother in particular is spoken of as an excellent woman who made it her special care to give St. Malachy a religious education. In childhood he was noted for his retiring habits and outstripped all his fellows in scholarship. Educated near his home by the Abbot Imar, the founder of the Church of SS. Peter and Paul, and gaining a high reputation for sanctity and learning, Celsus, Bishop of Armagh admitted him to orders. At the age of twenty-five he was ordained to the priesthood (according to his biographer St. Bernard five years before the canonical age), and displayed burning zeal, successfully effecting many important reforms in the diocese. St. Bernard particularly mentions that he introduced singing into the church service.

With a view of acquiring further knowledge of ecclesiastical discipline he studied under Malchus, Bishop of Lismore, for several years, whose reputation for learning was then attracting many. Cormac MacCarthy, who had recently been deposed from his sovereignty of Desmond by Turlough O'Connor, King of Connaught, was then living in retirement with Malchus. The king and St. Malachy grew to be fast friends, which lasted until the former's death.

Returning to Ulster in 1120, St. Malachy was placed in charge of the decayed abbey of Bangor in County Down, which had recently before been destroyed by pirates. Having brought ten brethren with him from Armagh he in a few days built an oratory, St. Malachy himself handling the axe, and succeeded in making it a flourishing seminary of learning and piety. In 1124 he was chosen Bishop of Connor, but at first refused to accept until compelled to do so by Celsus, though he lived at Bangor after his consecration. St. Bernard gives an account of the deplorable condition in which he found the diocese. But with characteristic energy he set to work for its reformation, laboring especially to increase conformity with the usages and discipline of the Church, and in a few years wrought a great change in the morals of his people.

Celsus, Bishop of Armagh, died in 1129 (in whose family the see had been hereditary for many years), and in his will designated St. Malachy as his successor. He accepted the dignity with reluctance, but owing to the seizure of the see by the supposed heir of Celsus, St. Malachy did not enter upon his new duties until 1134. Meanwhile the city of Connor had been destroyed by the King of Ulster, and St. Malachy fled to the South of Ireland, where, under the protection of Cormac MacCarthy, he built the monastery of Ibrach, where he took up his residence.

At the urgent request of the papal legate and bishops, however, he allowed himself to be consecrated to the primacy in 1132, with the understanding that when peace should be restored to the see he would be permitted to return to his former diocese of Connor. To avoid a conflict with the heir of Celsus he did not take up his residence in Armagh until the death of the former in 1134. On his arrival in the city another claimant appeared in the person of Nigellus, who seized the gospels and the "Staff of Jesus," which is said to have belonged to St. Patrick and regarded as the insignia of the see. In the end, however, he was forced to surrender them to St. Malachy, who, after three years resigned and retired to the bishopric of Down, which had been divided from the diocese of Connor, and here he recommenced his earnest labors among the people. In 1138 he is said to have founded a priory

of regular canons at Downpatrick and shortly
afterwards a monastery at Saul in County Down.

In 1139 he went on a mission to Rome to
solicit two palliums, one for the archbishopric
of Armagh and the other probably for the metropolitan See of Cashel.   While on his way he
visited the Abbey of Clairvaux, and thus began a
lifelong friendship with St. Bernard, his future
biographer.   St. Malachy was received by Innocent II. with great honor, and after a month's
stay in Rome, he returned to Ireland as papal
legate with instructions to summon a council
by which the palliums for the two archbishoprics
might be asked for in due form.   On his way
homeward, he revisited Clairvaux, and the following year introduced the order of Cistercians
in Ireland (who founded the Abbey of Mellifont)
by the advice of St. Bernard.

For the next eight years St. Malachy was
active in the discharge of his legatine duties, and
in 1148 he received from the bishops of Ireland
a commission to return to Rome and make new
application for the palliums.   Reaching Clairvaux in October, 1148, he was seized with fever,
and died November 2, of that year, in the arms of
St. Bernard.   He was buried at Clairvaux, but
in 1793, during the French Revolution, his remains and those of his friend St. Bernard were
removed from their sepulchres.   He was canonized in 1190, and is honored as the patron saint
of the diocese of Armagh.   His festival is the
3rd of November.

St. Malachy was the most eminent Irish
bishop of his day.   He greatly endeared himself
to the people by his humility and unselfishness.
"A brilliant lamp," the Four Masters call him,
"which illuminated territories and churches by

preaching and good work." An exhaustive memoir of St. Malachy has been written by Rev. John O'Hanlon, but all later writers have derived practically all their information from his contemporary and friend St. Bernard of Clairvaux.

Saint Laurence O'Toole

Saint Laurence O'Toole, Archbishop of Dublin, born near Castledermot in 1132, was son of Murtough O'Toole, chief of a territory south of County Kildare. His mother belonged to the kindred tribe of O'Byrne, who held the north of the county. In 1141 Dermot MacMurrough, King of Leinster, compelled Murtough to surrender his son Laurence (then twelve years old), as a hostage to him. The boy was sent to a barren district, where he was treated with such harshness that his father on learning of it, seized twelve of Dermot's followers and threatened to execute them unless his son was restored to him. As a result, the boy was sent by Dermot to the Bishop of Glendalough.

He was kindly treated at the monastery, expressed his willingness to remain, and accordingly became a member of the community, and at the age of twenty-five was appointed abbot. Glendalough was a famous and wealthy foundation of the old Irish Church, but his office was one of difficulty, owing to famine which prevailed in the district and the frequent raids made on the lands of the monastery by robber chieftains. Laurence devoted himself to the relief of the destitute and supplemented the funds of the monastery by his own private fortune.

Four years after his appointment as abbot, the death took place of the bishop, supposed by

Dr. Lanigan to have been Gilla na Naemh, who had taken part in the council of Kells in 1152. Laurence was urged to accept the bishopric, but declined, claiming that he had not reached the canonical age. In 1162, Gregory, bishop of the Danes of Dublin, having died, Gelasius the primate appointed Laurence the first Archbishop of Dublin, or Leinster, according to the Four Masters. Gregory, who was consecrated at Lambeth, had professed canonical obedience to the English primate, but the action of Gelasius now restored Dublin to the church of Ireland, and secured, as far as possible, the adhesion of the community of Glendalough by the appointment of their abbot.

In 1167 he attended "a great meeting convened by Roderic O'Conor and the chiefs of the North (both lay and ecclesiastical)" at Athboy in County Meath, where thirteen thousand horsemen assembled. The object of the assembly was to promote religion and good government. But great changes were at hand; for three years after Dermot MacMurrough, aided by Strongbow and his followers, appeared before Dublin. Laurence acted as ambassador on behalf of the citizens, and he endeavored to make terms with Dermot, but while negotiations were going on a party of the enemy scaled the walls and obtained possession of the city in 1170.

In the following year a great effort was made to drive out the invaders, the leading spirit in the project being Archbishop O'Toole. Through his exertions an army, estimated at thirty thousand, assembled before Dublin. The Anglo-Normans led by Strongbow, however, surprised the besiegers, and defeated them. He now saw that the divided Irish were unable to cope with the united invaders, and when in 1171,

King Henry II. arrived with a large force, the archbishop submitted to him. He also took part in the Council of Cashel, which was summoned by the King in 1172. It was not long before he found his hopes from Henry's beneficent mission disappointed, and he crossed to England to appeal to him on behalf of his people against injuries and oppressions of the Anglo-Norman adventurers.

Roderic, King of Ireland, had submitted to Henry, but finding it necessary to enter into a formal agreement with him, he employed Archbishop O'Toole as an ambassador, and in that capacity he attended the council of Windsor in 1175. Four years after, he received a summons from Pope Alexander III. to attend the Lateran council, and, having obtained the king's permission, he proceeded to Rome. Having acquainted the Pope with the injustice of the English governors he obtained a letter confirming the rights and jurisdiction of the archiepiscopal See of Dublin, and also the appointment of papal legate, whereupon he returned to Dublin and resumed his duties. In 1180 the archbishop once more undertook the office of ambassador from King Roderic to Henry II., and proceeded to England for the purpose, accompanied by a son of Roderic, who was to be left as a hostage. But Henry refused to listen to him, and gave orders that he was not to return to Ireland.

Some time after, the king having gone to France, Archbishop O'Toole determined to follow him, hoping that he would relent; but on his arrival at Abbeville on the Somme, he was seized with fever. From there, he hastened to Eu, where a few days after, November 14, 1180, he died. His love for his own country was the ruling passion of his life. He was buried in the church of Notre Dame at Eu, where a side-chapel bore his name. In 1226 he was canonized by **Pope Honorius III.**

Saint Adamnan

Saint Adamnan, the celebrated biographer of St. Columba, born about 624 in the south of Donegal, came of a princely family, being eighth in descent from King Niall of the Nine Hostages. In 679, when he was about 55 years of age, he was elected Abbot of Iona—the eighth after the founder, St. Columba. His life of the latter saint in three books has been edited by Dr. William Reeves. His life of St. Columba in Latin is pronounced by a celebrated Scotch writer to be "the most complete piece of such biography that all Europe can boast of, not only at so early a period, but even through the whole middle ages." He wrote the earliest account of the Holy Land extant and is the author of various other works.

In 697 a meeting of the clergy and laymen was held at Tara, where, at the instance of Adamnan, a law was adopted forbidding women to take part in war, which aimed to protect children from its barbarities and abolish the old Irish practice of women engaging in battle; this was known as the "Canon of Adamnan or Adamnan's Law." He is spoken of with great respect by his contemporaries. He is the patron saint of Raphoe in Donegal; and many churches both in Ireland and Scotland are dedicated to him. "He is popularly known in Ireland by the name Eunan, which is the Gaelic pronunciation of Adamnan." He repeatedly visited the court of King Alfred of England, who received him with great kindness. He died in 703.

Saint Caimin

Saint Caimin, or Camin, Abbot of Inish-caltra, Lough Derg, was a brother of Guaire, King of Connaught. He chose the life of an anchorite and attracted large numbers to his island retreat by his piety and learning. A commentary on the 119th Pslam in his own hand is said to have been in the Franciscan convent of Donegal in the days of Ware. His greatest desire was "that if the church were thronged with the sick and infirm, he would wish, were he able, to take all their infirmities on himself, and bear them for the love of God and his neighbor." He died about 653. His festival is March 24.

Saint Comgall

Saint Comgall, or Congal, was born in 516, of a distinguished Dalaradian family. As he grew up religious yearnings pressed on him; he traveled, and found a home with St. Fintan at Clonenagh. Repressing his dislike to the severity of the discipline, he continued there some time, and was afterwards ordained priest at Clonmacnois. After retirement on an island in Lough Erne he settled at Bangor, on the shore of Belfast Lough, in the year 559, and founded the famous monastery and rule with which his name has been ever since associated.

Numbers of monks were attracted to the institution, and even Cormac, King of Hy Kinsellagh, retired there in his old age. In the seventh year after its establishment, he, with St. Brendan and others, visited St. Columba in the Western Isles. He died at Bangor, in 601. Lanigan says: "St. Comgall has been justly reck-

oned among the fathers of the Irish Church;
whether he was the author of certain tracts attributed to him, besides his monastic rule, I leave
to others to enquire." His festival is May 10.

Saint Kilian

Saint Kilian, bishop and martyr, Apostle of
Franconia, flourished in the latter part of the
seventh century. He was of an illustrious Irish
family, and entered the monastic state early in
life. Traveling abroad, he reached Rome in 686
or 687, and was well received by the Pope, who
commissioned him to labor at Wurtzburg.
There he established himself with two friends,
Coloman and Totnan. Among others they converted the Duke of Gozbert. St. Kilian coun-
selled him to abandon his wife Geilana, because
she had been the wife of a deceased brother.

The Duke, having departed on a war-
like expedition, Geilana procured the assassination of St. Kilian and his friends. Lanigan proceeds: "Geilana was seized with an evil spirit,
which tormented her so much that she died soon
after. The remains of the holy martyrs were
found in 752 by St. Burchard, Bishop of Wurtzburg, and removed by him to a great church
which he had erected in that city." His festival
is July 8. It is said that the present eleventh century Cathedral of Wurtzburg occupies the site
of the original building erected upon the spot
where St. Kilian was martyred.

Saint Coemghin

Saint Coemghin, or Coemgin, or Kevin, was
born about 498, of a princely family, in Tir

Tuathal, comprising part of the present County Wicklow. He is described as having been a beautiful youth; he was baptized by St. Cronan and educated under "Petrocus, a holy Briton." He was specially intimate with St. Columba and St. Ciaran, and when the latter died at Clonmacnois Coemghin made a special pilgrimage there to watch by his body.

Round his cell at Glendalough a large community of disciples gathered, attracted by his learning and sanctity; and the ecclesiastical remains there are intimately associated with his name, although it is unlikely that any of them date from his lifetime. St. Coemghin is generally represented with a bird in his hand, in token of his great love of animals. The legend concerning him and Kathleen has been embodied in poetry both by Moore and Gerald Griffin. He is stated to have died in 618. His festival is June 3.

Saint Ciaran

Saint Ciaran, or Kiaran, the founder of Clonmacnois. He was of Ulster extraction, but his father, a carpenter, emigrated to Connaught, where Ciaran was born, in 515. He studied at Clonard, under St. Finen, and having completed his education there, perfected himself under the austere rule of St. Enna, on the Island of Arran and at Scattery Island. On his return to West Meath a friendly chief gave him a piece of ground and he commenced the erection of the religious establishments of Clonmacnois.

There he ministered during the remainder of his brief life, with the exception of a sojourn at Inishanghin on the Shannon.

King Diarmaid, whom the saint befriended
while in exile, was a munificent benefactor of
St. Ciaran's establishment. He died in 548, only
seven months after resuming his government of
Clonmacnois. His festival is September 9. He
is compared in the "Martyrology of Donegal"
to Christ in that his father was a carpenter, that
his life was wonderfully holy and that he died
about the same age.

Saint Ciaran

Saint Ciaran, or Kieran, of Saighir (Serkei-
ran, in Kings County), the founder of the See
of Ossory in the fifth century, is sometimes
styled the "first-born of the saints of Ireland."
He was born on Cape Clear Island, where he
afterwards founded a church. He is said to
have been one of Saint Patrick's earliest disciples, and one of Saint Finen's scholars; he established a monastic institution at Saighir. By
some he is supposed to have died in Cornwall
and to have been identical with Saint Piran,
whose little Church of Piranzabuloe was preserved intact for centuries covered with sand.
His festival is March 15.

Saint Finen

Saint Finen, or Finnian, Bishop of Clonard,
was a native of Leinster, born the end of the fifth
century. He was educated under Bishop Fort-
chern at Roscor, and when thirty years of age
traveled in Britain, and became acquainted with
British saints and missionaries. Finen ultimately returned with several ecclesiastics, and,
landing at Carn, in County Wexford, settled at

Clonard, on the Boyne, about 530, and founded
there the renowned school with which his name
has since been associated.　Among his pupils
were Ciaran and St. Columba.

We are told that "his usual food was bread
and herbs; his drink, water.　On festival days
he used to indulge himself with a little fish and
a cup of beer or whey.　He slept on the bare
ground and a stone served him as a pillow."　He
died at Clonard, in 552.　He is the patron saint
of the diocese of Meath, and his effigy is on the
seal of the clergy.　His festival is December
12.　The "Martyrology of Donegal" styles him
"a doctor of wisdom, and tutor of the saints of
Ireland in his time."

Saint Jarlath

Saint Jarlath, or Iarlath, of Tuam, the son
of Loga, was born about the beginning of the
sixth century.　He was the first bishop of Tuam,
of which he is the patron saint, and where his
memory has ever been highly venerated.　He established a school where several eminent men of
the time were educated.　He died at Tuam, in
540.　December 26 is observed as his festival.
He should not be confounded with St. Iarlath, or
Jarlath, third Archbishop of Armagh, who died
February 11, 482.

Saint Finbarr

Saint Finbarr, or Finn Barr, first Bishop of
Cork, a native of Connaught, was born in the
sixth century, his original name being Lochan.
He was educated in Leinster by MacCorb, afterwards traveled in Britain with St. Maidoc and

spent some time with St. David. In the beginning of the seventh century he founded his monastery on the banks of the Lee, on land granted to him by a chief, Aedh. The number of students who flocked there caused habitations to spring up and the foundations of the city of Cork to be laid. He was consecrated bishop of the district and died in 630, at Cloyne, after an episcopate of seventeen years. The most eminent of his disciples was St. Nessan.

One of St. Finbarr's favorite retreats was Glengariff. His festival is September 25. The island in Lough Erc (now Gougane Barra) was his hermitage. He is also patron saint of a northern diocese in Scotland. Dr. Richard Caulfield of Cork has published his life in Latin, with a collation of various MSS. The antique and picturesque hermitage of St. Finbarr occupies a small island in a lake in the west end of County Cork, within a beautiful valley, shut in by wild and precipitous mountains, made famous by the well known lines of J. J. Callanan, the poet.

Saint Feichin

Saint Feichin, or Fechin, said to have been descended from Con the Hundred Fighter, was born early in the seventh century. Having finished his studies under St. Nathy and being ordained for the priesthood, he retired to Fore, in County West Meath, where he established a community of 300 monks. He founded another establishment on the island of Inishmaan, one of the Arran Islands, off the coast of Galway. Most of his life was passed in retirement and self-mortification, and he died of a pestilence that raged over Ireland in 665. His festival is January 20. This saint is venerated in Scotland as St. Vigeon.

Saint Fachtna

Saint Fachtna was established as first bishop of Ross before 570, having been previously abbot of Molana, a monastery on an island in the River Blackwater, in County Waterford. His school at Ross (Ross Carbery, in County Cork) was one of the most celebrated in Ireland, and continued to be so considered even after his death, which took place in his forty-sixth year, towards the close of the sixth century. His festival is August 14.

Saint Senan

Saint Senan was born about 488, in Thomond. Disgusted with the wars and outrages going on around him, he placed himself under the abbot Cassidan, took the monastic habit, and about 534 founded the religious establishment of Inishscattery, on an island in the Shannon, and afterwards several of the cells and oratories on the remote. islands off Clare and Kerry. Dr. Lanigan relates how a lady of Bantry, afterwards canonized as St. Cannera, sought permission to receive the viaticum, and to be buried in Inishscattery. At first the Saint positively refused; but at length, understanding she was near death, permitted her to spend the last few days of her life on the island, and there gave her body a resting place. Senan himself died about 544.

Lanigan says: "The reputation of St. Senan has not been confined to Ireland, and his acts have been published among those of the saints of Brittany on the supposition, whether well founded or not, that he was the same as St. Sane, one of the chief patrons of the diocese of St. Pol de Leon." His festival is March 1.

Saint Ita

Saint Ita, so called "from the ita (thirst) of the love of God which she had," flourished in the sixth century. "Deirdre was her first name"; she was also known as Mide. Born in the present County Waterford about 480, she became one of the most venerated of Irish saints. O'Hanlon devotes five chapters of his great work to the particulars of her life, and gives an engraving of the ruins of her church of Killeedy, in County Limerick, where she is chiefly venerated. She died in 570; her festival is January 15.

Saint Finan

Saint Finan, born in Ireland, was in 651 appointed successor of St. Aidan as Bishop of Lindisfarne, an island off the eastern coast of Northumbria. He appears to have been educated at Iona. In his efforts for the conversion of the surrounding people, he was ably assisted by King Oswin, and he is specially noticed by the Venerable Bede as having borne an important part in the conversion of the northern Saxons. In the difference concerning the time for holding Easter, he held to the precedents of the Western Church. He died towards the close of the seventh century, and his festival is generally celebrated January 9.

Saint Canice

Saint Canice, Cainneach, or Kenny, patron of Kilkenny (with which locality the events of his life are slightly, if at all, connected), the son of Laidec, a poet, and Mella, was born at Glengiven, in Ulster, in 514. In his fourteenth year he was sent to Wales, where he studied under St. Docus. Ordained priest, he is said to have proceeded to Rome, and on his return he exerted himself to extirpate the remains of paganism in Ireland. He was intimate with SS. Comgall and Columba. "The Martyrology of Donegal" says of him: "Aghaboe, in Queen's County, was his principal church. . . . A very ancient old vellum book states that Cainneach was, in his habits and life, like unto Philip the Apostle. . . . Eighty-four years was his age when he sent his spirit to heaven, A. D. 598." His festival is October 11.

Saint Flannan

Saint Flannan, a confessor and Bishop of Killaloe, who flourished in the seventh century, was the son of Turlough, King of Thomond. Educated in the monastery founded by St. Molua, he ultimately retired to Lismore, where he was joined by his father, who resigned his throne. We are told that he spent much time in this retreat between "the soaring mountains on the north and the thick and extensive forests on the south." Archæologists have maintained that the traces of artistic taste acquired during a sojourn in Rome are evident in the churches erected at St. Flannan in Munster. He died "full of years," and was buried at Killaloe, of which he was the first bishop. His festival is December 19.

Saint Fursa

Saint Fursa, or Fursey, flourished early in
the seventh century. "Among the Irish saints,"
says Dr. Reeves, "who are but slightly commem-
orated at home, yet whose praise is in all the
churches, St. Fursa holds a conspicuous place.
With Venerable Bede as a guarantee of his extraction, piety and labors, and above a dozen different memoirs, of various ages, which were
found on the continent in Colgan's time, the history of this saint is established on the firmest
basis." He was the son of Fintan, a prince of
Munster, and Gelgis, daughter of a chief of
Brefny; he was born near Lough Corrib. When
he had grown up he placed himself under St.
Meldan, who was then abbot of a monastery in
Lough Corrib. How long he continued there is
not narrated. On leaving St. Meldan he erected
a monastery at Rathmat, on the shores of the
before-mentioned lake.

We then read of his traveling in Munster,
and during an illness witnessing some wonderful visions, which caused him to abandon the
idea of returning to his monastery and to make a
circuit of the country, relating what he had seen
and exhorting the people to repentance and
amendment of life. He thus spent fourteen
years in Ireland and then crossed over to England, where he preached the gospel with his usual
success among the East Angles. In a fort now
known as Burg Castle, in Suffolk, granted him
by King Sigbert, he founded another monastery
between the years 633 and 639. Afterwards he
gave up the charge of this place to his brother
and two priests, and then spending a year with

another brother, Ultan, passed over to France; and at Lagny, on the Marne, erected a religious establishment, where he was joined by several brethren from Ireland. In 648 he founded the monastery of Foss. His death is believed to have taken place while sojourning with his friend, Duke Haimon, in Ponthieu, on his way to visit Ireland, about 649, and his body was ultimately brought to Peronne and there interred.

A calendar of Scottish saints says: "The reputation of St. Fursa extends far beyond the limits of the Scoto-Irish church. Not only is he one of the most distinguished of those missionaries who left Erin to spread the gospel through the heathen and semi-heathenized races of mediæval Europe, bridging the gap between the old and the new civilizations, but his position in view of dogma is a most important one; for the vision of St. Fursa contributed much to define the conceptions of men with regard to that mysterious region on which every man enters after death." His festival is January 16.

Saint Fridolin

Saint Fridolin, patron of the Canton of Glarus in Switzerland, was an Irish missionary who flourished in the early part of the seventh century. The German form of his name "is to be accounted for by the common practice of translating Celtic names, or accommodating them by transformations, more or less violent, to the genius of the languages spoken in the regions where the Irish missionaries settled." All authorities refer his birth and mission to Ireland, from which country he set out as a pilgrim. He is often styled "Viator," which title is borne out

by his appearance on the seal and banner of
Glarus. He finally settled on the island of Seck-
ingen in the Rhine, above Basle, and there his remains are said to have been buried. His festival is March 6.

Saint Feargal

Saint Feargal, Fergil, or Virgilius, Bishop
of Salzburg, was a learned native of Ireland, who
arrived in France before 746. He was hospitably
received by Pepin, son of Charles Martel, remained with him two years and then proceeded
to Bavaria, where he had a dispute with St. Boni-
face relative to baptism. He was appointed
Bishop of Salzburg by Pope Stephen II., in 756.
He died in 785, and was canonized by Pope Gregory in 1233. November 27 is the date of his
festival.

Frances Ball

Frances Ball, called Mother Frances Mary
Teresa, was the daughter of a wealthy merchant
of Dublin, where she was born January 9, 1791.
At the age of twenty she joined the Institute of
the Blessed Virgin at York, England. This sis-
terhood, which had long existed at York, was
originally established on the continent in the
seventeenth century by Mary Ward, to supply
the means for a religious and secular education
for young ladies. Frances Ball introduced this
institute into Ireland in 1821, and since then it
has spread to most of the British colonies, where
the nuns are usually called Sisters of Loreto.
During her busy life this pious mother founded
thirty-seven convents in various parts of the

world. She died at Rathfarnham Abbey, Ireland, May 19, 1861.

John De Burgo

John De Burgo, Vicar-Apostolic of Killala. He left Ireland in his youth, and served as an officer in the Austrian army. He afterwards entered the church, and was appointed Abbot of Clare, from 1647 to 1650 acting as Vicar-General of Killaloe. Three years later he was arrested by Cromwell's orders, and sent into banishment. He exercised clerical functions in France and Italy until 1671, when he was appointed Vicar-Apostolic of Killala, and returned to Ireland. In 1674 he was arrested on the charge of "bringing Protestants to the Catholic faith," "preaching perverse doctrine," and "remaining in the kingdom."

After two years' imprisonment, having refused many offers of advancement if he would join the Established Church, he was sentenced to confiscation of his goods and banished to the continent. In compliance with a vow made while in confinement, he visited Palestine during his exile, and was captured by pirates and sold as a slave. He eventually found means to escape to Constantinople, and thence to Rome, where he ended his days.

James Ussher

James Ussher, Anglican Archbishop of Armagh, was born in the parish of St. Nicholas, Dublin, January 4, 1581. His father a clerk in the Court of Chancery, was said to have been descended from one Neville, who went to Ireland with King John in the capacity of usher,

and changed his name to that of his office. From
eight to thirteen years of age he attended the
school kept by Fullerton and Hamilton, private
emissaries of James VI. of Scotland, sent to keep
up his influence in Ireland, in view of the prospect of his succeeding to the throne of England
and Ireland.

Ussher's name stands second on the list of
those admitted to Trinity College, Dublin, when
first opened, January 9, 1594. There he studied
with ardor, devoting himself especially to historical and chronological inquiries. His immediate relations were divided between the reformed and the Catholic faith, and the religious
controversies of the day had thus for him an
intense and personal interest. His uncle, Richard Stanyhurst, a Jesuit, endeavored to attract
him towards Catholicity; but as he advanced in
years, Ussher became more and more confirmed
in the Protestant tenets in which he had been
brought up.

At an early age he commenced reading the
whole of the Fathers of the Church, a prodigious
labor, which he did not bring to an end for eighteen years. He took the degree of B. A. in 1597,
and, greatly against his will, was preparing to
abandon theology and commence the study of
law, when the death of his father left him at liberty to follow his own bent. He made over the
family property to his sisters, taking but a small
sum for the purchase of books and his support
in the cheapest way in college.

In 1600 he took the degree of M. A., and
was elected to a fellowship, and, although not
ordained until December, 1601, he was occasionally selected to preach in Christ Church,
Dublin, before the Irish Court. As with many,

earnest men of the time, toleration was hateful to him, and he exerted his influence to have the laws against the Catholics put rigidly in force.

In 1605 he was appointed Chancellor of St. Patrick's, Dublin, and rector of Finglas. From this time he visited England every few years for the purpose of consulting books and manuscripts at the great libraries, becoming intimate with Camden, Sir Robert Cotton, and other eminent men. These visits were generally of three months' duration,—one month each being passed in Oxford, Cambridge, and London.

In 1607 he was appointed Professor of Divinity in Dublin University; and two years afterwards he received an invitation to preach before the court in London. The provostship of Trinity College, Dublin, was pressed upon him, but he declined, fearing that its duties might interfere with his studies. In 1612 he took the degree of D. D., and next year published his first work, dedicated to James I., which drew forth an answer from his Catholic uncle, Richard Stanyhurst, then in exile on the continent.

In the beginning of 1614 he married his cousin, Phœbe, daughter of Dr. Lucas Challoner, vice-chancellor of the university. At the Irish Convocation of 1615 he probably drew up the 104 Articles then accepted, which differed considerably from the English 39 Articles. In 1614, and again in 1617, Ussher was chosen Vice-Chancellor of the University of Dublin, and during a stay in London of nearly two years (1619-21), he recommended himself to James I., and was appointed to the bishopric of Meath. He was consecrated in St. Peter's Church, Drogheda. His writings give a deplorable condition of the diocese.

He continued to pay frequent visits to London, where he was a special favorite with King James, who addressed a letter to the deputy and council, directing them to grant Ussher leave of absence for an indefinite period, and one of the king's last acts was to appoint him Archbishop of Armagh, in March, 1625. Ussher returned to Ireland in August, 1626, after a long absence, and about this period he joined with other Protestant clergymen in a protest against granting Catholics any toleration. As there was then no archiepiscopal residence at Armagh, he lived chiefly at Drogheda, while during a plague he took up his residence at Lambay Island.

His public duties did not withdraw him from the delights of literature. His mind was chiefly directed towards biblical researches, and through agents in the East he procured several copies of the Samaritan Pentateuch, and the Syrian version of the Old Testament. With the view of upholding English influence by exterminating the Irish language, he opposed Bishop Bedell's efforts for the translation and dissemination of the Bible in Irish.

He was a warm friend and adviser of Lord Wentworth, afterwards Earl of Strafford, and their intimacy terminated only when Ussher knelt beside the earl at the block when the latter was executed. In the Convocation of 1634, mainly through Strafford's influence, the English Articles were accepted to those previously drawn up by the archbishop, while a separate set of canons were agreed to.

One of the best known of Ussher's works, "Britannicarum Ecclesiarum Antiquitates," was published in August, 1639. It had been commenced at the request of King James, twenty years previously.

On the breaking out of the war of 1641, he retired to England, and was appointed by Charles I. to the see of Carlisle. In 1642 he went to Oxford, where he continued to avail himself of the treasures of the Bodleian Library. While here numbers came to hear him, and he often preached before the king. He refused to attend the assembly of Divines at Westminster in 1643, and preached against its authority. The House of Commons thereupon confiscated his valuable library, but much of it was rescued through the kindness of a friend, who bought it back for him.

When Oxford was about to be besieged, the archbishop accompanied the Prince of Wales to Bristol. He afterwards proceeded to Cardiff, where, after the battle of Naseby, he was joined by the king. Greatly perplexed as to a choice of residence, he at one time entertained serious thoughts of embarking for France or Holland, but ultimately accepted the invitation of Lady Stradling to her castle of St. Donat's in Glamorganshire. On his way there, he and his daughter were roughly handled by some bands of English soldiers, and he lost several of his most valuable manuscripts. At St. Donat's he was kindly treated, and the extensive library in the castle enabled him to turn his sojourn to good account.

In 1646 his old friend, the Countess of Peterborough, prevailed upon him to return to London,—her influence securing him from molestation by the parliament. From the roof of her house Ussher had the pain of seeing the king led forth to the scaffold. It is related that he fainted at the sight, and had to be carried to bed. He still continued to labor industriously at his books, and in 1650 published the first part of his Bible Chronology, from which the dates given in the present authorized version are taken. Five years afterwards failing health obliged him to resign his appointment of preacher to the Benchers of Lincoln's Inn.

He would have declined Cromwell's occasional invitations to conferences on religious matters and the promotion of Protestant interests at home and abroad, but that his refusal might have militated against the welfare of his brother clergy. He accepted from the Lord Protector the grant of a lease for twenty years of a portion of the primatial lands at Armagh, which, however, does not appear to have been confirmed. He received one payment at least of a quarterly allowance of £100 from parliament.

The infirmities of age were now pressing upon him, and he died in Ryegate, in Surrey, March 21, 1656. His wife died in 1654.

Cromwell honored his remains with a stately funeral at Westminster Abbey, but is said to have left his daughter to pay the greater portion of the expenses out of her scanty means.

Archbishop Ussher is described as well built and moderately tall, of an erect carriage, with brown hair and a ruddy complexion. His vigorous constitution and temperate habits enabled him to bear a life of incessant study. He was of a deeply religious cast of mind,—his narrow views being a fault common to most earnest men in that intolerant age.

A voluminous writer both in Latin and English, there are some forty of his works in the list in Harris' "Ware." Perhaps one of the most important of them was "Annales Veteris Testamenti," London, 1650. That relating to Ireland most frequently quoted is his "Religion Anciently Professed by the Irish and English," London, 1631. An edition of the "Whole Works of Archbishop Ussher," in seventeen volumes, was published at the expense of Trinity College, Dublin, between 1848 and 1864. It contains much matter for the first time printed, and Dr. Elrington is said to have devoted nearly twenty years of his life to its preparation. At his death in 1850, volume XIV. remained unfinished, which was completed by Dr. Reeves, who also compiled the indexes which form the substance of volume XVII.

Dr. Elrington says: "The works which he had published sufficiently attest the stupendous extent of his information, and the skill with which he could make use of the treasures he possessed. His name became celebrated throughout Europe, and his services to the cause of literature, more especially in the department of history and chronology, have been acknowledged by all modern writers."

Ussher had intended to bequeath his magnificent library of 10,000 volumes to Trinity College; but the shattered state of his finances compelled him to leave it as an only provision for his daughter. The King of Denmark and Cardinal Mazarin competed for its purchase. Cromwell, however, refused to let it out of the kingdom, and obliged his daughter to accept the insufficient sum of £2,200 subscribed by the army of Ireland for the library, as a donation to Trinity College, Dublin. On the receipt of the books in Dublin, they were retained at the castle, open to depredations, and it was not until the Restoration that the remnant of them were handed over to the college library, where they now remain.

Ambrose Ussher, the archbishop's brother, a fellow of Trinity College, Dublin, was a man of some eminence. According to "Ware," the library of the college was enriched with thirty-five manuscripts in his handwriting, including a complete translation of the Bible, and an "Arabic Dictionary and Grammar." His mother became a Catholic before her death. One of his descendants, James Ussher, a native of Ireland, Catholic clergyman and author, died in 1772.

Anna Maria Hall

Anna Maria Hall, novelist and miscellaneous writer, was born in Dublin, January 6, 1800. Her maiden name, Anna Maria Fielding, was not known in the literary world, her first work being published after her marriage to Samuel Carter Hall, in 1824. At fifteen she accompanied her mother to England, and it was some time before she revisited her native country; but the scenes which were familiar to her as a child had made such a vivid and lasting impression on her mind, and all her sketches showed so much freshness and vigor, that her readers might well imagine she had spent her life among the scenes she describes. To her early absence from her native country is partly at least to be traced one noteworthy characteristic of all her writings,—the absence of party feeling on politics or religion.

Mrs. Hall's first recorded contribution to periodical literature was an Irish sketch called "Master Ben," which appeared in The Spirit and Manners of the Age, in 1829. Other tales followed. Eventually they were collected in a vol-

ume entitled "Sketches of Irish Character," 1829.
The "Sketches" have much fine description and
are instinct not merely with sound and kindly
feeling, but true and delicate humor. A second
series of "Sketches of Irish Character" (1831)
was quite equal to the first; some of the satirical
presentations are depicted with great truth and
liveliness.

In 1832 Mrs. Hall ventured on a historical
romance, "The Buccaneer," the scene being laid
in England at the time of the Protectorate, and
Cromwell himself appearing among the characters. The plot is well managed, and some of
the characters,—notably that of Barbara the
Puritan,—are excellent; but the work is too
feminine, and too little of energetic passion for
the stormy times in which it is cast. Her "Tales
of Woman's Trials" (1834) are short stories in
her happiest style. "Uncle Horace" (1835) was
a novel. "Lights and Shadows of Irish Life"
(three volumes, 1838), originally published in
the New Monthly Magazine, was extraordinarily
popular; the principal story, "The Groves of
Blarney," was dramatized and played with eminent success. "Marian; or, A Young Maid's
Fortunes" (1840) makes full use again of Mrs.
Hall's knowledge of Irish character. "Stories of
the Irish Peasantry," contributed to Chamber's
Edinburgh Journal, were afterwards published
in a collected form.

In 1840 Mrs. Hall aided her husband in an
elaborately illustrated work in three volumes,
"Ireland: Its Scenery and Character," skilfully
blending topographical and statistical information with the poetical and romantic features of
the country, the legends of the peasantry, and
scenes and characters of humor or pathos. "The

Whiteboy" (1845) is usually reckoned her best novel. Other works were a fairy tale, "Midsummer Eve," 1845; "A Woman's Story," 1857; "Can Wrong Be Right?" 1862; and "The Fight of Faith," 1868-69. To her husband's Art Journal Mrs. Hall contributed many picturesque sketches, some of which were reissued as "Pilgrimages to English Shrines" and "The Book of the Thames." She also produced a volume for children, "Chronicles of a School Room," 1830.

Mrs. Hall was instrumental in founding the Hospital for Consumptives at Brompton, the Governesses' Institution, the Home for Decayed Gentlewomen, and the Nightingale Fund. Her benevolence was of the most practical nature; she worked for the temperance cause, for women's rights, and for the friendless and fallen. She died at Devon Lodge, East Moulsey, England, January 30, 1881.

Her husband, Samuel Carter Hall, who was born near Waterford in 1800, the son of an English officer, came to London in 1821, acted as parliamentary reporter in the House of Lords, wrote for various papers, edited the New Monthly Magazine, and in 1839 established and edited the Art Journal, which he conducted until 1880. The works written and edited by him and his wife, alone or often conjointly, exceed five hundred volumes; of these his "Retrospect of a Long Life" (two volumes, 1883) is a series of jottings, not a set autobiography. He died March 16, 1889, in London, England.

George Canning

George Canning, author, a native of Ireland, appears to have taken his degree of B. A. at the

University of Dublin in 1754. His father, a gentleman of property in the North of Ireland, disinherited him for marrying, in 1768, Miss Costello, a dowerless beauty. George Canning was the author of some poems, and of a translation of "Anti-Lucretius." He was admitted to the bar, but never pursued his profession with earnestness, and his sojourn in London, on an allowance from his father of £150 per annum, was a perpetual struggle against adverse circumstances. Nevertheless he and his wife were received into some of the best literary circles, and led a respected, if not a contented and happy, life. He died in the Temple, London, April 11, 1771, one year after the birth of his son, the great George Canning.

Timothy Charles Harrington

Timothy Charles Harrington, son of Denis and Eilleen O'Sullivan Harrington, was born in Castletown, Bearhaven, County Cork, in 1851. In early life he became a teacher in the National Schools of Ireland, but finally made his way into politics through the channels of journalism. In 1877 he founded the Kerry Sentinel newspaper and soon acquired a reputation as a journalist and politician of strong character and ability. In 1882, on the request of Charles Stewart Parnell, he was made secretary of the Land League, the success of which was due largely to his energy and activity. He afterwards held a similar position in the National League.

In 1883 Harrington was elected to the House of Commons for County West Meath and in the same year was sentenced to a term in Mullingar jail by the government for "intimidation" in a speech which he delivered in the latter county. Two years afterwards he was elected for the Harbor Division of the city of Dublin, and held that seat without interruption for twenty-five years. He was admitted to the Irish bar in 1887 and was engaged in many political cases, including the Mitchelstown prosecutions. He acted as one of Parnell's counsel during the sitting of the Special Commission in 1888. He was for many years one of the most devoted followers of the great statesman, and after the disunion of the National party in 1890 he became a leading member of the Parnellite minority. A determined but honest fighter, he acquired a high reputation for political consistency.

Harrington was for many years associated with municipal affairs in Dublin. He was a member of the North Dublin Union and of the Port and Docks Board. Three times Lord Mayor of Dublin,—in 1901, 1902, and 1903,—he controlled the affairs of the corporation with impartiality, and was popular among all classes. During his second term as Lord Mayor he was a member of the Round Table Conference in Dublin which laid the foundation for the Land Act of 1903. He was a director of various public companies, and in 1909 was made clerk of the committee appointed in Dublin to administer the Old-Age Pension Act. He died in Dublin, March 12, 1910, being survived by his wife and several children.

George D. Evans

Sir George De Lacy Evans, soldier, was born at Moig, County Limerick, October 7, 1787. He entered the army as ensign in 1807, and having served for about three years in India in the operations against the Pindarries, and shared in the capture of the Mauritius, he joined Wellington's army in Spain, in 1810, and was present at the battles of Vittoria, the Pyrenees, and Toulouse.

In 1814-15 he was engaged in America, and took an active part in the battle of Bladensburgh and the operations at Washington and Baltimore. He was wounded at the battle of New Orleans, in January, 1815. He returned to England early in the same year, and took part in the action at Quatre Bras and in the battle of Waterloo, and was employed on the staff of the Duke of Wellington during the occupation of Paris. From the close of the war he had no active employment until 1835, when he volunteered to undertake the command of the British legion of 10,000 men sent to Spain to aid the Spanish Queen against Don Carlos. He defeated the Carlists in several actions and returned to England early in 1837.

He had already been elected to parliament in 1831, in the liberal or radical interest, as member for Rye, and in May, 1833, was elected for Westminster, which he continued to represent (with the exception of 1841 to 1847) till 1865, when he resigned on account of ill health. He attained the rank of major-general in 1846, and on the outbreak of the Russian war in 1854 was appointed lieutenant-general and given command of the second division. He distinguished himself by his gallantry at the Alma, as well as in the attack of the Russians, October 26, and at the battle of Inkerman.

On his return to England, invalided, early in the following year, he received a vote of thanks from both Houses of Parliament. He was created K. C. B. in 1838, and G. C. B. and

honorary D. C. L. of Oxford in 1855. He became
general in 1861, and grand officer of the Legion
of Honor in 1856. He died in London, January
9, 1870. He was the author of several works,
chiefly on military subjects.

Theobald Dillon

Theobald Dillon, count, a distant relative of
the eleventh viscount, was born in Dublin about
1745. He joined the Irish brigade of the French
army as a colonel of cavalry, was made brigadier-general in 1780 and marechal-de-camp three
years afterwards. He was at the attack at
Grenada and the siege of Savannah in 1779. He
favored the popular cause in the French Revolution and was sent to Flanders in 1792, when
France declared war against Austria. While he
commanded at Lille in April, General Dumouriez
ordered him to march on Tournay with ten
squadrons of horse, six battalions of infantry,
and six pieces of artillery, to make a demonstra-
tion, but on no account provoke a conflict. In
pursuance of these orders, he advanced slowly
and with great precaution, having remarked
among his soldiers some symptoms of insubordi-
nation. At Bessieux, on a road half way between
the two towns, he perceived the enemy in superior numbers moving forward to give him battle.
It was the first time for many years that the
French and Austrians found themselves face to
face. There was hesitation on both sides. The
Austrians opened an artillery fire on the French
troops, without any effect. Dillon, true to his
orders, directed a retreat, covering it with his
cavalry. The infantry retired in good order;
but the cavalry, notably those of the Queen's

Regiment, attributing the movement to an understanding with the enemy, turned bridle and threw themselves on the infantry.

Meanwhile the Austrians, far from pursuing, returned to Tournay, while a panic seized the French, who, abandoning two of their pieces of artillery and four caissons, fled precipitately to Lille, despite all Dillon's efforts to rally them. The men declared their officers had betrayed them, and massacred all without mercy. Dillon fell by a pistol bullet, and his body, after being dragged about the streets, was burned in the market place, April 29, 1792. His murderers were afterwards executed, and by order of the Legislative Assembly the honors of the Pantheon were accorded to his memory, and a pension was granted to his children.

The regiment of Dillon had then been commanded by successive members of this distinguished family for 101 years. At the French Revolution it was, like the other French regiments, deprived of its distinctive name and numbered the 87th. His grandson, Count Theobald Dillon, died in Paris in June, 1874. He was much interested in Irish affairs and at his death was engaged upon a work on the Irish brigades. Several other members of this branch of the family, born in France or England, have also distinguished themselves. The descendants of the three children of the subject of this sketch were living in France at the close of the last century, with the title of counts.

John Gore

Sir John Gore, vice-admiral, was born at Kilkenny, February 9, 1772. He joined the Canada, under the command of William Cornwallis, in 1781, and served in her during the West India campaign of 1782. In 1789 he was promoted lieutenant, and in 1793 was appointed to the Lowestoft, in which he went to the Mediterranean. From her he was transferred to the Britannia, and afterwards into the Victory during the operations at Toulon and in Corsica. On the surrender of Bastia, in 1794, he was promoted to the command of La Fleche, a captured French vessel.

The same year he was posted in the Windsor Castle, of ninety-eight guns, and commanded her in the actions off Toulon in 1795. He was shortly afterwards appointed to the Censeur, and taken prisoner when that ship was recaptured by the French squadron off Cape St. Vincent on the 7th of October. After his return home, Gore successively commanded the Robust and in 1796 was appointed to the Triton, a thirty-two-gun frigate, which he commanded in the English channel for nearly five years. In July, 1803, he was sent to Gibraltar as senior officer in command of a small squadron to cruise in the Straits, with orders to look out for French ships of war sent to strengthen the Toulon fleet. The next year he joined the British squadron off Cadiz, where three Spanish frigates were captured carrying a valuable cargo of money.

February 21, 1805, Gore was knighted and sailed for Calcutta on the 15th of April. Returning to England in the following year, he was appointed to the Revenge, in the Bay of Biscay. Early in 1807, he joined Collingwood off Cadiz, and continued there under the command of Rear-Admiral Purvis until June, 1808, when he carried the Spanish commissioners of peace to England. From his promotion to the rank of rear-admiral in 1813, he commanded the detached squadron in the Adriatic until the peace. In January, 1815, Gore was nominated a K. C. B., and from 1818 to 1821 was commander-in-chief at the Nore.

May 27, 1825, he was advanced to the rank of vice-admiral, and from 1831 to 1835 he was commander-in-chief in the West Indies. During this time his only son, serving as his flag lieutenant, was drowned in attempting to save a seaman who had fallen overboard. The loss probably hastened his death, which took place at Datchett, August 21, 1836, where he was buried. He married, in 1808, the daughter of Admiral George Montagu, by whom, in addition to the mentioned son, he had six daughters.

Flaherty O'Neill

Flaherty O'Neill, Lord of Aileach, on the shores of Lough Swilly, was the first prominent member of the O'Neill family whose name appears in history, ruling his territories from 1004 to 1036. The Hy Neill, or the descendants of the monarch Niall of the Nine Hostages, were divided into two great branches, namely, the southern and northern.

The southern Hy Neill were kings of Meath, and many of them monarchs of Ireland. The northern Hy Neill, of which there were two great branches, namely, the race of Eogan, princess of Tyrone, and the race of Conel, princess of Tirconnell, also furnished many monarchs of Ireland; but the descendants of Eogan were the most celebrated of all Milesian clans; of them a great many were kings of Ulster, and sixteen were monarchs of Ireland. The race of Eogan took the name of O'Neill in the tenth century, from Niall Glunduff (Black Knee), who was killed in a great battle with the Danes, near Dublin, A. D. 919. The elder branch of the O'Neill took the name of O'Loughlin and MacLaughlin, from one of their ancient chiefs. The O'Neills afterwards recovered the supremacy, and made a distinguished figure in Irish history, down to the seventeenth century, as princes of Tyrone and kings of Ulster.

The O'Neills had their chief seat at Dungannon, and were inaugurated as princes of Tyrone at Tullaghoge palace in the barony of Dungannon, where a rude seat of large stones served them as a coronation chair. The "Four Masters" record fourteen plundering expeditions led by Flaherty into different parts of Ireland, both against his countrymen and the Northmen. He is sometimes called "Flaherty of the Pilgrim's Staff," from a pilgrimage he made to Rome. He was slain in 1036.

Hugh O'Neill

Hugh O'Neill, Lord of Tyrone, late in the twelfth and early in the thirteenth centuries, was one of the most determined opponents of the Anglo-Normans in the North of Ireland. In 1198 he attacked them at Larne, and for a time broke their power in the district. Next year, after a temporary success, he was defeated at Ballysadare, by the chiefs of Connaught, William De Burgh, and the Anglo-Normans of Limerick.

In 1200 he was for a time deposed from his chieftaincy, and Conor O'Loughlen elected in his stead. Eight years afterwards a battle was fought in Inishowen between him and the O'Donnells, in which many were slain on both sides. The combatants subsequently entered into an alliance against such of the Irish or Anglo-Normans as should oppose them. Hugh O'Neill was one of the princes who attended King John in 1210; but the English and Irish annalists are not agreed as to whether he gave in his submission. Next year he and O'Donnell made a descent upon the new settlers on the shores of Lough Erne. In 1212 he burned the castles of Clones, erected but a few months, and in 1213 destroyed Carrickfergus and gained a victory over the English.

His name does not appear again in the "Annals" until 1221, when, in conjunction with Hugh de Lacy the younger, he demolished the castle of Coleraine, and spoiled Meath and Leinster, being effectually opposed by a hosting of the Lords of the Pale. In 1225 he made a successful expedition against the O'Conors of Connaught.

His death, in 1230, is thus noticed: "Hugh O'Neill, Lord of Tyrone, . . . who had never rendered hostages, pledges, or tribute to English or Irish; who had gained victories over the English, and cut them off with great and frequent slaughter; . . . a man who had attempted the subjugation of all Ireland,—died a natural death, although it was never supposed that he would die in any other way than to fall by the hands of the English." His wife died in 1215.

Owen O'Neill

Owen O'Neill, Lord of Tyrone from 1432 to 1455, occupies a prominent place in the annals

of the North of Ireland during the first half of
the fifteenth century. He was engaged in constant expeditions with varying success against
the Anglo-Irish; also his neighbors, the O'Donnells and MacQuillans, and against rival branches
of the O'Neill family. In 1425 he was taken prisoner and held captive in Dublin for some time.
In 1430 and 1444 he appears to have levied contributions on the Pale; but in 1442 he is mentioned as co-operating with the Anglo-Irish
against the O'Donnells. In an expedition against
the Maguires of Fermanagh, in 1435, it is said
that the inhabitants of the district, flying from
his advance, carried their goods across the frozen
surface of Lough Erne. Owen was deposed by
his son Henry in 1455, and died in the following
year.

Henry O'Neill

Henry O'Neill, Lord of Tyrone, son of
Owen, flourished in the fifteenth century. His
wars and exploits are often referred to in the
"Four Masters." In 1431 he was taken prisoner
by Naghtan O'Donnell, but was soon liberated,
and they became for a time fast friends. In
1442 (with his father) he joined the Anglo-Irish,
and led an army against the same Naghtan,
forcing him to surrender Castlefin and the surrounding territory. For some cause his father
was banished in 1455 and he was inaugurated as
The O'Neill at Tullaghoge in presence of the
Archbishop of Armagh, the Maguires, Mac-
Mahons, and his own kinsman. Two years
afterwards he led a successful expedition against
the O'Donnells. In 1464 the king sent him a
present of a chain of gold. He died in 1489.

Con B. O'Neill

Con Bacagh O'Neill, Earl of Tyrone, was inaugurated The O'Neill upon the death of his brother in 1519, and was soon afterwards received into royal favor by Henry VIII. In 1523 he bore the sword of state before the Lord-Deputy. In 1534, however, he became involved in the rebellion of Silken Thomas FitzGerald, and in 1538, buoyed up by hopes of foreign assistance, he joined Manus O'Donnell, marched upon the English Pale, and reviewed his forces at Tara.

The next year he turned towards home, but was overtaken by Lord Grey, at Ballahoe in Monaghan, and defeated in a firece engagement. In January, 1542, King Henry VIII. desiring his presence in London, he set sail for England and presented himself at court on the 24th of September, and was created Earl of Tyrone. His son Matthew was created Baron of Dungannon (a title to be afterwards borne by the heirs apparent of Earls of Tyrone), and two of the Maguire family who accompanied him were knighted.

Of his submission to King Henry, Richey says: "Although Con O'Neill might for himself accept any title from the King of England, he, acting as chief of his tribe, had no shadow of right to take a grant of all their tribal lands to himself; but in their eyes the king's granting was simply a nullity." Before long, however, O'Neill regretted his submission, and is said to have execrated any of his posterity who should learn to speak English, "sow wheat, or build castles." In 1551, on the accusation of his son, the Baron of Dungannon, he was taken prisoner and confined in Dublin, while his younger sons waged war with the English and with the baron, in which his territories were devastated.

O'Neill died, it is said, of a broken heart in 1559, within the precincts of the Pale. His wife, by whom he had his son John, or Shane, was a daughter of the eighth Earl of Kildare. His son Matthew, Baron of Dungannon, was killed in battle two years before his father's death.

Turlough L. O'Neill

Turlough Luineach O'Neill, nephew of Con B. O'Neill, and the rival of his cousin, Hugh O'Neill, Earl of Tyrone, was, after the death of Shane in 1567, inaugurated The O'Neill. In 1570 he compassed the death of some of the principal MacSweenys, and in 1581 he attacked and humbled the O'Reillys, in retaliation for their having imprisoned some of his cousins. In the month of July of the latter year he was engaged in hostilities with the O'Donnells. The "Four Masters" say a furious and desperate battle was fought between them; and the celebrated proverb was verified on this occasion,—"Lively is each kinsman when fighting against the other."

In 1585 he went to Dublin to attend the parliament that assembled on the 26th of April, but does not appear to have taken his seat, as his name is not on the official list. It was the intention of Queen Elizabeth to create him Earl of Clan O'Neill and Baron of Clogher, but the patent was never perfected. In 1588 he defeated his cousin, the Earl of Tyrone, and a large force, at Carricklea, near Strabane. In 1592 he received an Anglo-Irish garrison into his stronghold at Strabane, and engaged in a series of operations against the earl and his allies. Next year, however, he appears to have dismissed these troops, and made peace with his cousin. He died at Strabane in 1595, and was buried at Ardstraw.

He is represented as having been a stanch friend of the bards and brehons. Professor O'Donovan says: "There are still extant several Irish poems addressed to Turlough, inciting him to shake off the English yoke and become monarch of Ireland like his ancestors. . . . But he was so old when he was made O'Neill that he seems to have then retained little military ardor to tread in the wake of his ancestors, and he was so much in dread of the sons of Shane the Proud and of Hugh (Earl of Tyrone) that he continued obedient to the queen."

Felim O'Neill

Sir Felim O'Neill, one of the most prominent actors at the opening of the war of 1641-52, fourth in descent from a younger brother of Con B. O'Neill, was born in 1604. Carte gives the following account of him: "Sir Felim O'Neill of Kinard, in County Tyrone, had a very good estate in that and the adjoining county of Armagh, and was the most considerable person of his name in Ireland. His grandfather, Sir Henry O'Neill, had deserved well of the crown; and by a patent under the Great Seal of Ireland, dated June 12, 1605, had a grant made to him of the whole and entire territory called Henry Gage's country."

In 1641 he entered warmly into plans for insurrection with Roger More, Lord Maguire, his brother, Turlough O'Neill, Sir Con Maginniss, and other persons of distinction in Ireland. His house was the headquarters for the meetings of the leaders; and he was one of the five who met in Castle Street, Dublin, in October, to concert measures for the capture of the castle. But their plans being discovered through the carelessness of a servant, the leaders were forced to withdraw. Escaping north, Sir Felim seized and garrisoned Charlemont fort, Dungannon, also the northern fortresses, and soon found himself governor of ten counties. Prendergast, in his "Cromwellian Settlement," clears him of the charge of having murdered Lord Caulfeild.

November 5, 1641, at the head of 30,000 men, he established his headquarters at Newry, pretending that he was fighting for the king. He has been accused of great and unnecessary cruelties at the opening of the war; this, however, he lamented at a later period. As a warrant for going into insurrection, he exhibited a document with the Great Seal attached, which he afterwards acknowledged was detached from a patent he found at Charlemont fort. He was twice defeated with considerable loss before the castle of Derrick in Tyrone.

He took Dundalk in November, and about January 1, 1642, invested Drogheda at the head of a large force. The place was defended by Sir Roger Tichborne, and, after a siege of about two months, O'Neill drew off his forces to Dundalk. Tichborne followed, took the town by storm, and obliged his adversary to retreat towards Armagh.

There was some jealousy between Sir Felim and Owen Roe O'Neill, as rival heads of the family. Although the former commanded in several minor conflicts, after Owen Roe's arrival from the continent, in 1642, Sir Felim did not take a leading part in military operations. He held a prominent place, however, at the council board of the Confederation. The Papal Nuncio's efforts to bring about an understanding between the O'Neills proved successful, and Sir Felim commanded with great gallantry a division of Owen Roe's army at the battle of Benburb, June 5, 1646.

In November, 1649, he married Lady Jane Gordon, a daughter of the Marquis of Huntley, and widow of Lord Strabane. He had just before relieved her castle of Strabane, attacked by Monro. Three years afterwards, in 1652, he was taken prisoner on an island in Lough Roughan, near Dungannon, and was immediately sent to Dublin. He was offered pardon if he would make a public confession that he had taken up arms by the king's command, but he refused. He was tried and convicted in October, and was executed with all the barbarities then inflicted on people convicted of high treason. His head was spiked on the bridge at Dublin.

King Conn

Conn the Hundred Fighter, commonly known as "Conn of the Hundred Battles," was King of Ireland from 175 to 195 A. D. His reign was one of almost constant warfare. He early became involved in contentions with Owen More concerning the throne of Munster. They ultimately divided the island between them, taking as boundary the chain of gravelly hills running from Tallaght west to the Shannon at Clonmacnois. Owen retained the southern, and Conn the northern part. Conn is said to have procured the assassination of his rival. In the contests between them, Owen drew many to his standard in times of scarcity by his large stores of provisions.

Conn was eventually assassinated within the precincts of Tara, by the King of Ulster and a band of fifty men attired as women.

King Dathy

Dathy, the last king of pagan Ireland, reigned twenty years, from 408 to 428. The early successes of his arms in Britain and emulation of his uncle Niall stimulated him to continental expeditions. Keating recounts the following legend of his death by lightning, while passing through the Alps: "And the manner in which Dathy was slain was this; to wit, a flashing thunderbolt, shot from heaven, smote him upon the head whilst he was making conquests in Gaul. It was near the mountains called the Alps that he fell by the vengeance of God, for he had plundered the sanctuary of a holy hermit, Parmenius, who cursed him therefore." Dathy's death has formed a favorite subject for Davis, Mangan, Aubrey De Vere, Irwin, and other poets. It is related that his body was carried home by his followers, and interred at Rathcroghan, Tulsk, in Roscommon, where a pillar of red-grit sandstone still marks the spot. He was distinguished for his activity, sprightly manners and ability in war.

King Felim

Felim, King of Munster, and for a time monarch of Ireland in the ninth century, is by some writers represented as having rivaled the worst deeds of the Danes in the devastation of his country, taking advantage of their incursions to plunder and lay waste the land. In one engage-

ment he defeated the monarch Niall and carried
off his daughter Gormlaith. O'Mahoney says:
"That he was nevertheless a brave and wise
prince, within the limits of his own principality,
may be judged from the fact that Munster was
kept comparatively free from the ravages of the
Northmen during his lifetime." O'Curry styles
him "a distinguished scholar and a scribe." He
died August 18, 845.

Finn MacCool

Finn MacCool, a distinguished chief who
flourished in the third century of our era, was
son-in-law to King Cormac, being married in succession to his daughters Grania and Ailbe. Innumerable stories are related of him,—in Irish
legends as Finn MacCool, and in Scottish as
Fingal. He was commander of the Fenian militia, a body of several thousand warriors maintained by the Irish monarchs of that age. In
peace they are said to have numbered 9,000, in
war 21,000. In winter they lived in small parties on the inhabitants of the country, while in
summer they maintained themselves by hunting
and fishing.

When Finn was on the point of being married to his first wife, Grania, she eloped with his
friend Dermat. The wanderings of the lovers
and Finn's pursuit was one of the most fruitful
themes of Fenian romance. Dermat eventually
met his death from the thrust of a wild boar on
Benbulben, in County Sligo. Finn's arrival on
the scene before his rival's death forms the subject of one of the most beautiful of Ferguson's
"Lays of the Western Gael."

In addition to his warlike accomplishments,

Finn is reported to have possessed the gifts of poetry, second sight, and healing. His principal residence was on Dun Almhain (the Hill of Allen, near Kildare),—an abode glowingly described in so many of his son Oisin's lays. The surrounding rath or fortification is still traceable, even from a distance. His other abode was Moyelly in the present Kings County. Moore says in his history: "It has been the fate of this popular Irish hero, after a long course of traditional renown in his country,—where his name still lives, not only in legends and songs, but yet in the most indelible records of scenery connected with his memory,—to have been all at once transferred, by adoption, to another country (Scotland), and start a new but false shape, in a fresh career of fame."

The Four Masters state that Finn met his death in 283, at Rath-Breagha, near the Boyne, whither he had retired in his old age to pass the remainder of his life in tranquillity. He was killed by the blow of a fishing gaff, at the hands of one Athlach, and his death was avenged by Cailte MacRonain, his faithful follower.

Peter O'Neill Crowley

Peter O'Neill Crowley, a prominent Fenian, was born May 23, 1832, at Ballymacoda, County Cork, where his father was a respectable farmer. His uncle, Rev. Peter O'Neill, was flogged at Cork in 1798 for alleged complicity in the insurrection of that year. Peter inherited his farm, and cultivated it with great industry and thrift. He was studious in his habits, and was greatly beloved by relatives and friends. He early joined the Fenian movement, became an active propa-

gandist, took the field in March, 1867, and
formed one of a party under the command of
Captain McClure in the attack on the Knocka-
doon coastguard station. Afterwards he took
refuge with a few comrades in Kilclooney Wood,
County Cork, where, on Sunday, March 31, his
small party was attacked and defeated by the
military and constabulary. He was mortally
wounded in the fight, and died a few hours afterwards at Mitchelstown, where he was conveyed,
—being treated with great kindness and consideration by his captors. One who was with him
to the last remarked: "His death was most edi-
fying. Never did I attend one who made a
greater impression upon me. He begged of me
to tell his sister not to be troubled because of
his death, which he hoped would be a happy one."
An immense concourse attended his funeral at
Ballymacoda.

John O'Mahony

John O'Mahony, organizer of the Fenians,
was born in Kilbeheny, County Limerick, in
1816, descended from one of the oldest and most
popular families in the county. His father and
uncle took part in the insurrection of 1798.
O'Mahony was sent to a classical school in
County Cork, and afterwards entered Trinity
College, Dublin, but never took a degree. He
studied Hebrew and Sanscrit, became an accomplished Gaelic, Greek and Latin scholar, and
contributed articles to French journals. In 1843
he joined the Repeal movement, but becoming
dissatisfied with O'Connell's pacific policy, he
attached himself to the Young Irelanders, and

took the field with Smith O'Brien, in 1848. After the failure at Ballingarry, he escaped to France, and lived in Paris for several years.

About 1854 he came to this country, and with John Mitchel, Michael Doheny and other Nationalists formed the Emmet Monument Association and kindred organizations in New York City. In 1857 he published in New York "The History of Ireland, by Geoffrey Keating, D. D., Translated from the Original Gaelic, and Copiously Annotated," considered by many the best translation of Keating's work. This publication brought O'Mahony no pecuniary gain, and owing to the mental strain brought to bear upon him in its preparation he was placed for a time in an asylum. The extent to which the early portion of "Keating's History" is occupied with exploits of the ancient Fenians (a celebrated military force of Pagan Ireland) probably led to the adoption of this name for the secret society organized by O'Mahony, James Stephens and others in 1857, with the object of overthrowing English rule in Ireland and establishing an independent republic.

The organization of the Fenian Brotherhood, or Irish Republican Brotherhood, was completed at conventions held at Chicago in November, 1863, at Cincinnati in January, 1865, and at Philadelphia in the following September. O'Mahony's field was America, and his task was to raise money to support the organization and obtain munitions of war and select trained military officers who were to lead the forces in battle. James Stephens was to go to Ireland and organize the society there, enlist and secretly train the men who were to do the fighting, and, as he took the post of danger, he insisted upon having supreme control of the movement at home and abroad.

At this time O'Mahony held the rank of colonel in the 69th regiment of New York militia, recruited mainly from the Fenian Brotherhood, which had also furnished a large proportion of Meagher's Brigade, Corcoran's Legion and other Irish regiments that served in the American civil war. The rapid growth of the organization demanded all of O'Mahony's attention, and resigning the colonelcy of the New York regiment, he devoted himself entirely to the object ever uppermost in his mind—the independence of his native country. The purposes of the Brotherhood were greatly favored by the close of the civil war in the spring of 1865 through the discharge of the Irish-American soldiers, who were eager for service elsewhere. At this period the greatest activity was shown and between 1860 and 1870 probably $500,000 was contributed to the Fenian fund in the United States and Canada.

Though differences occasionally arose between O'Mahony, James Stephens and others as to policy, the former continued president for some time. O'Mahony had for many years assisted in the Fenian councils, but did not take any personal part in the raids upon Canada or the attempted insurrection in Ireland. The latter years of his life were passed in literary pursuits. He contributed to various Irish-American newspapers, and in 1872 delivered a lecture on the history of Fenianism at Cooper Union in New York City.

Although thousands of dollars of public funds had passed through his hands, he showed little regard for money even for his own neces-

sities. In the shadow of penury and ill health,
O'Mahony declined the aid of friends who were
anxious to help him on learning of his condition.
He died in New York City, February 7, 1877.
His remains were removed to Ireland and attended to the grave in Glasnevin Cemetery with
the honors of a public funeral.

George Macartney

George Macartney, Earl Macartney, diplomat, was born in County Antrim, May 14, 1737.
Educated at Trinity College, Dublin, he entered
public life under the auspices of the first Lord
Holland, and was sent as a special envoy to Russia to negotiate a commercial treaty with the
Empress Catherine soon after she had ascended
the throne. After long and arduous negotiations, Macartney brought the matter to a satisfactory close. After his return, in 1767, he sat
for a time in the Irish and also in the British
parliament, and was Irish secretary from 1769
to 1772. In 1775 he was appointed governor of
the island of Grenada, which he defended
bravely but unsuccessfully against overwhelming numbers of the French under D'Estaing, in
1779, and after surrendering was sent a prisoner
to France. He was, however, soon liberated by
exchange. In 1776 he had been raised to the
Irish peerage as Baron Macartney and in 1780
was appointed governor of Madras, India.

He distinguished himself highly in the management of the war with Tippoo; and after being superseded as governor of Madras in 1785,
was offered, but declined, the governor-general-
ship of India. Six years after his return to Ireland he was appointed ambassador extraordi-

nary to China. "His mission, though not politically or commercially successful, had the important result of greatly increasing our knowledge of the Celestial empire." He had been made an Irish viscount in 1792 and an Irish earl in 1794; in the year of his return from China (1794) he was created Baron Macartney in the peerage of England, and appointed governor of the Cape of Good Hope. He returned in ill health in 1798, and lived in retirement at Chiswick until his death. A formal account of his embassy to China, the work of the secretary of the embassy, Sir George Staunton, was published in 1797. Lord Macartney's own private journal of the mission was printed, with others of his papers, in Barrow's "Life of Earl Macartney," 1807. He died childless, March 31, 1806.

Thomas Reed

Sir Thomas Reed, soldier, son of Thomas Reed, was born in Dublin, in 1796. He entered the army as cornet in the 12th Light Dragoons in 1813, and became lieutenant in 1815. He was present with his regiment at Waterloo, commanded by Colonel Ponsonby, and formed part of Vandeleur's brigade. In 1824 he was promoted captain, major in 1826, and in 1834 he became lieutenant-colonel of the 62nd Foot, a position which he held for eighteen years.

In 1842 he was assigned aide-de-camp to the Queen. Two years afterwards he was made a C. B. When the first Sikh war broke out in India his regiment formed part of the force which held Ferozepore, and at the battle of Ferozeshah, in 1845, Reed commanded a brigade in Littler's division. His troops were ordered

to attack the strongest part of the Sikh entrench-
ments, where there was a large number of heavy
guns served with grape and canister, but the attack failed, after a heavy loss among officers and
men.

The commander-in-chief, Sir Hugh Gough,
took an early opportunity to assure the brigade
that its conduct at Ferozeshah had received and
merited his most cordial approbation. Reed,
whom Littler spoke of in his report as zealous
and indefatigable, was slightly wounded. In
1852 he gave up his command, went on half-pay,
and was employed as colonel on the staff at
Birmingham. He was promoted major-general
in 1854, and the next year was sent to command
the troops in Ceylon. In 1856 he was transferred to a division of the Madras army in India,
and soon afterwards to the command of the
troops in the Punjab. He was in this position
when the mutiny broke out in 1857, and on General Anson's death he became provisional commander-in-chief, as the senior officer in the Bengal presidency, until Sir Patrick Grant arrived
at Calcutta.

He joined the Delhi field force at Alipur in
June, but he was disabled by severe sickness and
fatigue from being present at the action of Badli-
ki-Serai on that day, and the immediate command of the field force remained with Sir Henry
Barnard. In the council of war held on June 15
Reed was in favor of waiting for reinforcements
before risking an assault.

Upon the death of Sir Henry Barnard, July
5, Reed assumed command of the field force, but
owing to poor health he appointed a successor
and removed to Simla. Reed saw no further
service in the field.

He was given the colonelcy of the 44th Foot in 1858, became lieutenant-general in 1860, and general eight years later. October 1, 1877, he was placed on the retired list. Reed, who had been made K. C. B. in 1865 and G. C. B. in 1875, died at Ramsey, July 24, 1883. In 1835 he married Elizabeth Jane, daughter of John Clayton of Enfield Old Park, Middlesex.

Thomas Graves

Sir Thomas Graves, admiral, born in Ulster, about 1748, son of the Rev. John Graves of Castle Dawson, Ireland, nephew of Admiral Samuel Graves and cousin of Admiral Thomas, Lord Graves. His three brothers all served as captains in the British navy, becoming admirals on the retired list. Thomas entered the navy at an early age, and served during the Seven Years' war with his uncle Samuel on board the Scorpion, Duke, and Venus. After the peace he was appointed to the Antelope with his cousin Thomas. In 1765, while on the coast of Africa, he was promoted to be lieutenant of the Shannon.

In 1770 he was lieutenant of the Arethusa, and in 1773 was appointed to the Racehorse with Captain Phipps for the voyage of discovery in the Arctic seas. In the following year he came to America with his uncle Samuel, and was appointed by him to command the Diana, one of the small schooners employed for the prevention of smuggling. May 27, 1775, he was sent from Boston into the Charles river, and was attacked by a large force of Americans. The Diana ran aground when the colonial forces succeeded in setting her on fire, and the small crew, after a gallant defense, were compelled to abandon her. Graves was severely burnt, as well as his brother John (then a lieutenant of the Preston flagship), who had been sent to the Diana's support.

Graves continued after this employed in command of other tenders in the neighborhood of Boston and Rhode Island until, on the recall of his uncle, he rejoined the Preston and returned to England, but was again sent out to the American station in the same ship. In 1779 he was promoted to the command of the Savage sloop on the West Indian and American stations. In the temporary absence of Commodore Affleck he commanded the Bedford in the action of September 5, off the Chesapeake, and continuing afterwards in the Bedford as flag captain; was present in the engagement at St. Kitts, in January, 1782, and in the actions off Dominica in the following April.

In the autumn of the same year Graves was appointed to the frigate Magicienne, in which, January 2, 1783, he fought a severe action with the French Sybille, a frigate of superior force. Both ships were reduced to wrecks, and so parted: the Magicienne to Jamaica a fortnight later, the Sybille to be captured a few days afterwards by the Hussar. During the peace Graves spent much of his time in France, and in the early years of the French Revolution had no employment. In October, 1800, he was appointed to command the Cumberland, of seventy-four guns, in the Channel fleet.

January 1, 1801, he was promoted to be rear-admiral of the White, and in March hoisted his flag on board the Polyphemus of sixty-four guns, one of the fleet proceeding to the Baltic. Graves afterwards shifted his flag to the Defiance, and in her was second in command under Lord Nelson at the battle of Copenhagen, April 2, 1801. For his services on this occasion he received the thanks of Parliament, and was nominated by the King a Knight of the Order of the Bath.

Towards the end of July the fleet quitted the Baltic, and on its return to England, Graves, who had been in bad health during the greater part of the campaign, retired from active service. He became a vice-admiral in 1805, admiral in 1812, and died at his home near Honiton, Devon, March 29, 1814. He was twice married, but had only one daughter.

Rory O'Donnell

Rory O'Donnell, Earl of Tirconnell, younger brother of Hugh Roe O'Donnell, born in 1575, kept up a desultory warfare in the North for some months after the defeat of the Irish army at Kinsale, and the departure of his brother Hugh Roe for Spain, in 1602. In the autumn he and O'Conor Sligo were induced to submit to Lord Mountjoy at Athlone, and were thereupon permitted to settle in their own territories. Next year he was commissioned to proceed against Sir Niall Garv O'Donnell, who had gone out in opposition to the Anglo-Irish power, and assumed the title of The O'Donnell. After some skirmishes Niall submitted, and in June, 1603, he and Rory proceeded to London to have their claims to precedence settled. Rory was made Earl of Tirconnell, and confirmed in his territories, excepting the fishery at Ballyshannon and 1,000 acres contiguous.

On his return to Ireland he was duly invested in Christ Church, Dublin, the 29th of

September. He married a daughter of the twelfth Earl of Kildare. He was one of those who fled to the continent with Hugh O'Neill in 1607, and died in Rome, July 28, 1608. His remains were interred in the Church of San Pietro di Montorio. His countess remained in Ireland, and after his death married Viscount Kingsland. His brother Caffar died in September, 1608, and was buried beside him. Several descendants of both branches of the O'Donnells, born on the continent, distinguished themselves in the Spanish and Austrian services.

Hugh O'Donnell

Hugh O'Donnell, prominent in the war of 1689-91, was born in Donegal, in the middle of the seventeenth century. His boyhood was spent in Ireland. He was either a grandson of Caffar, brother of Hugh Roe O'Donnell, or a grandnephew of Niall Garv O'Donnell. After serving several years in the Spanish army, where so many of his family had risen to distinction, he rose to be a brigadier-general; in 1689 he asked leave to enter the service of King James II., and on being refused threw up his command and appeared in Ireland, where he was hailed with enthusiasm by numbers of his countrymen, who, placing faith in an ancient prophecy, believed him destined to deliver their land from its connection with England.

He was commissioned by James II. to command an irregular force of some 10,000 men, raised mainly by himself; but, in consequence of the jealousy of other Irish officers, was not permitted to take much part in the regular operations of the war.

He carried on a desultory warfare in the interest of James, and had to trust to forced requisitions for the provisioning and arming of his force. After the struggle in Ireland was virtually at an end, he went over (with about 1,000 men) to the Williamite side, on securing a pension of £500 per annum. After the capitulation of Limerick, he retired to Spain, served three years in Piedmont, and in 1695 was appointed a major-general. He was named "Balldearg" (Red-Spot) from a blood mark. Martin Haverty says: "There was no act of Balldearg O'Donnell's which was not worthy of a brave, honorable and disinterested man and a true Irishman, and all the calumnies against him may be attributed to the jealousy of Richard Talbot and the hostility of the Anglo-Irish interest." He died probably about 1703.

Arthur Forbes

Sir Arthur Forbes, first Earl of Granard, was born in 1623. His father came to Ireland in 1620 from Scotland and obtained large estates in County Longford; in 1632, while serving as an officer under Gustavus Adolphus, he was killed in a duel at Hamburg.

Sir Arthur served Prince Charles in Scotland and afterwards returned home, and was included in the Articles—not having fought against the Commonwealth in Ireland. After the Restoration he was appointed one of the commissioners of the Court of Claims, and in 1663 helped to frustrate the plot of the discontented parliamentary soldiers for seizing the castles of Dublin, Drogheda and Derry. A few years afterwards he became privy-councillor, and was made marshal of the army, with an allowance. In 1675 he was raised to the peerage as Viscount Granard, and was afterwards made an earl. He augmented the family estates.

By James II. he was continued in the post of marshal and lieutenant-general of the army in the North, and was appointed lord-justice in conjunction with the Archbishop of Armagh. Not agreeing to the plans of James II. for the reorganization of the army, he was superseded in his commands by the Earl of Tirconnell. He joined William III., and in 1691 commanded one wing of the army that reduced Sligo and other towns. He died at Castleforbes, in County Longford, in 1696.

Arthur Forbes

Sir Arthur Forbes, second Earl of Granard, son of preceding, was born about 1656. He served in the French army under Turenne. In 1686 he was made colonel of the Royal Regiment of Ireland (now the 18th Royal Irish), raised by his father. He adhered to the fortunes of James II., and was by William III. committed to the Tower. In confinement, he is said to have refused a present of £300 from William, and on his release to have declined a commission in the army; and so late as 1702, although appearing at court, he refused the government of Jamaica. Afterwards he accepted a pension of £500 a year (which appears never to have been paid), and in 1715 was made Lord-Lieutenant of County Longford. He died at his home, Simmonscourt, near Dublin, August 24, 1734, and was interred at Castleforbes.

George Forbes

Sir George Forbes, third Earl of Granard,
second son of preceding, was born October 21,
1685.   He received most of his education at
Drogheda Grammar School.   He entered the
navy in 1704, served with distinction in the
Mediterranean and elsewhere, and acted as adviser to the Emperor of Austria in naval matters.   In 1729 he was appointed Governor of the
Leeward Islands.   In 1733 he was sent as plenipotentiary to Russia, chiefly to negotiate a
treaty of commerce.   On his return, in 1734, he
was made rear-admiral of the White, then rear-
admiral of the Red, and the same year became
Earl of Granard, on his father's death.   The
latter part of his life was spent on his Irish estates, promoting the commercial interests of the
country.   He had much to do with putting the
coinage of Ireland on a more correct basis.   He
also appears to have devoted much of his time
to study and literary pursuits.   He died June 19,
1765, and was buried at Newtownforbes.

George Forbes

Sir George Forbes, sixth Earl of Granard,
great-grandson of preceding, was born June 14,
1768, and succeeded his father in April, 1780.   He
was educated at Armagh, and entered the navy
at an early age.   He commanded the Longford
Militia at Castlebar, in 1798, during the French
invasion of Connaught, and took part in the battle of Ballinamuck.   He was a steadfast adherent
of the Irish Liberal party, and as he had supported Charlemont, Grattan and Curran in early
life, so, in 1799-1800, he stood firm with his

brothers-in-law, Lords Moira, Kingston and Mountcashel, against the Legislative Union, and was one of those that signed the Peers' protest against the measure. For some years afterwards he took little part in politics, and devoted himself to his estates; but in 1806 he accepted the post of Clerk of the Crown and Hanaper, and was created a peer of Great Britain. He supported Catholic Emancipation and Reform, and declined the ribbon of St. Patrick. The latter part of his life was spent principally in France. He died in Paris, in 1837, and was buried with his ancestors at Newtownforbes. The present eighth earl, his descendant, born in 1874, succeeded to the title and estates in 1889.

Thomas Dillon

Thomas Dillon, fourth viscount, was born about 1614, and succeeded to his estates March 15, 1636. Brought up a Catholic, at fifteen he joined the Protestant church, and subsequently took his seat in parliament, and was raised to several offices of trust. Being on a mission to King Charles in February, 1642, he was, with Lord Taaffe, seized at Ware by order of the House of Commons. After some months' imprisonment, they escaped and joined the king at York. Upon Dillon's return to Ireland, he was made lieutenant-general, and was appointed joint president of Connaught with Viscount Wilmot. In 1646 he was received back into the Catholic Church by the papal nuncio, at St. Mary's, Kilkenny, in presence of a vast concourse of people.

He commanded one division of Ormond's army, which was defeated before Dublin by the parliamentary leader, General Jones, in 1649. Dillon's estates were confiscated by Cromwell, and he and his family lived in exile on the continent until the Restoration. In 1663 most of his extensive landed property was restored, and several high offices in the state were conferred upon him. He died about 1672.

Peter Dillon

Peter Dillon was born about 1785 in Ireland. He entered the navy, served as second lieutenant of H. M. S. Hunter, and gained a considerable knowledge of the South Sea Islands. He revisited them in 1826 as captain of a merchantman. On a voyage from Valparaiso to New Zealand he touched at Tikopia, one of the Queen Charlotte group, where he was led to suspect, from information received, that the ship LaPerouse, whose fate at that time was unknown, had been wrecked on a neighboring island.

Prosecuting his inquiries in the following year, under the auspices of the East India Government, which placed a vessel at his disposal for the purpose, he succeeded in obtaining from the natives not only positive evidence of the wreck of two French vessels many years before at Vanikoro, but also a number of articles belonging to them. He reached Paris in 1828, and the articles were recognized as having belonged to the ill-fated expedition. Charles X. conferred upon Captain Dillon the star of the Legion of Honor, and an annual pension of 4,000 francs. He published in 1829 a full account of his travels in two volumes, which was translated into French. Captain Dillon died February 9, 1847.

Roland Eustace

Sir Roland Eustace (or FitzEustace), Lord
Portlester, was descended from a branch of the
Geraldines to whom Henry II. had granted the
country around Naas.   In 1454 he was appointed
deputy to Richard, Duke of York, and again in
1462 he filled the same office for the Duke of Clarence.   Subsequently he was tried for plotting
with the Earl of Desmond, and acquitted. Created Lord Portlester, he married Margaret,
daughter of Janico d'Artois, by whom he had
two daughters. The elder married Gerald, eighth
Earl of Kildare. He held the office of Treasurer
of Ireland for many years, and was in 1474 appointed to the custody of the great seal, which
six years afterwards he refused to surrender
when the king granted the post to another.

This was for a time a great hindrance to public business, until the king authorized the construction of a new great seal for Ireland by
Thomas Archbold, Master of the King's Mint in
Ireland, and that in Eustace's hands was "annulled and suspended," while his acts as treasurer were also repudiated. A turbulent spirit
was at that period shown by many of those "who
should have been foremost among the king's supporters." Eustace refused to give up the seal;
his son-in-law Kildare positively declined to admit a new lord deputy, Lord Grey; James Keating, Constable of Dublin Castle, broke down the
drawbridge and defied the deputy and his three
hundred archers and men-at-arms to gain ad-
mittance; and the Mayor of Dublin proclaimed
that no subsidy should be paid the earl; while a
parliament held at Naas repudiated Lord Grey's
authority; and one summoned at Trim declared

the proceedings of Kildare's parliament at Naas null and void.

Lord Portlester died December 14, 1496, and was buried at Cotlandstown, County Kildare. Two monuments were erected to his memory— one in the new abbey, Kilcullen, which he had founded in 1460; the other in St. Audoen's Church, Dublin, where he had built a chapel to the Virgin.

James Eustace

James Eustace, third Viscount Baltinglass, a descendant of preceding, who distinguished himself in the Desmond war, was born early in the sixteenth century. Having with other lords of the Pale complained in 1576 to Elizabeth that their liberties and privileges had been annulled by the imposition of a cess, and that no tax ought to be levied upon them but by act of parliament, he was, with Lord Delvin, Howth, and Trimleston, committed prisoner to the Castle of Dublin, while their lawyers whom they sent to represent their case to the queen were committed to the Tower of London.

After a year's imprisonment they were liberated without accomplishing their desired ends. After vainly endeavoring to persuade the Earl of Kildare to rise with him, Eustace, in the middle of July 1580, threw off his allegiance, and sent letters to his friends asking them to join in defending their country and their religion from the assaults of the English. One of Lord Grey's first acts was to collect a large force and march against him and his men, entrenched in Glenmalure. The English force of 800 men were led into an ambuscade and cut off almost to a man—Sir

Peter Carew, Colonel John Moor and Francis Cosby being among the slain, and Lord Deputy Grey escaping with difficulty.

After this success Eustace appears to have hastened to join the Desmonds and their Spanish allies in Kerry, and to have taken an active part in the Desmond war. His death is supposed to have taken place in 1583. By an ex post facto law, known as the "Statute of Baltinglass," the Eustaces were deprived of their estates and titles.

Maurice Eustace

Sir Maurice Eustace, lord chancellor, descended from family of preceding, was born at his father's seat at Castlemart about 1590. He gained a fellowship at Trinity College, and was admitted to the bar, where he soon distinguished himself. A clear-headed man, he lost no opportunity of advancing his own interests in those disturbed times, and received grants of Harristown and other lands forfeited by Lord Baltinglass. As sergeant-at-law he attracted the notice of Lord Strafford, and in 1639 he was elected Speaker of the Irish House of Commons. His inauguration speech, given in Flanagan's "Chancellors," is significantly illustrative of the times.

After the Restoration, in 1660, he was appointed Lord Chancellor; but as he was one of the lord justices, Archbishop Bramhall was appointed Speaker of the Lords. He opposed some of the most unjust results of the Acts of Settlement and Explanation. He continued chancellor until failing health obliged him to resign the seals to Archbishop Boyle. He delighted in rural affairs, and his demesne at Harristown came to be regarded as the most beautiful seat in Ireland.

The ex-chancellor died in 1665, leaving his estates in Kildare, Dublin and Wicklow, besides the abbey of Cong, to his nephews, Sir John and Sir Maurice Eustace. He was interred in St. Patrick's Cathedral.

John Sheares

John Sheares, United Irishman, son of Henry Sheares (a Cork banker and member of parliament), was born in Cork in 1766. Henry Sheares died in 1776 and left his children well provided for. John being intended for the legal profession, received a liberal education at home and at Trinity College, Dublin, where he graduated B. A. in 1787. He was admitted to the bar in 1788, and in 1792 accompanied his brother Henry, who was also a lawyer, on a visit to the latter's family, then residing in France. Both brothers were possessed of ample fortunes, besides the sums they derived from their profession.

They attended political meetings, became acquainted with Roland, Brissot, and other leaders of the French Revolution, and were present at the execution of Louis XVI. Returning to England in the same vessel with Daniel O'Connell, John and Henry Sheares gloried in what they had seen, while the reign of terror had the opposite effect upon the future great statesman. John early joined the United Irishmen and often presided at public meetings. He showed his hostility to the government by attending the funeral of Rev. William Jackson in 1795, who had been convicted of high treason, but who, in entering court to receive sentence, had managed to swallow a quantity of arsenic.

When The Press newspaper was started in 1797 by Arthur O'Connor, Sheares became a frequent contributor to it, and owing to the editor's acceptance of a letter by Sheares addressed to Lord Clare as "The Author of Coercion," the paper was suppressed the day on which the article was to have appeared. The article was subsequently published in a volume entitled "The Beauties of the Press," and reprinted by Dr. R. R. Madden in "The United Irishman." On the seizure of most of the members of the Leinster Directory at the house of Oliver Bond in March, 1798, both brothers were elected to the vacancies in the directory, and John became a chief organizer of the proposed rising, which was set for May 23. Early in the same month he made the acquaintance of John W. Armstrong, a captain in the King's County militia, who worked himself into the confidence of Sheares, and betrayed his designs to the government.

The brothers were arrested May 21 in Dublin and placed in Kilmainham jail. On July 12 they were brought up for trial on the charge of high treason. The only witness against them was Armstrong. They were defended by Curran, Plunket and McNally. There was little to criminate Henry but a proclamation found in his possession, admitted to have been written by John and intended for publication when the revolt was announced. The trial had proceeded for fifteen hours when Curran, sinking with exhaustion, moved for an adjournment. The motion was opposed by the attorney general, John Toler, and at eight o'clock next morning the jury, after a retirement of a few minutes, returned a verdict of guilty against both prisoners. A painful scene followed. Henry was completely unmanned.

When they were brought up for sentence John made an earnest appeal for his brother's life.

After the trial they were removed to Newgate and none of their relatives or friends allowed to see them. The following day they were executed in front of the prison and their remains placed in the vaults of St. Michan's Church. In early life Henry served in the army for three years, but afterwards adopted the legal profession. He was married twice and had six children. Two other brothers, Christopher and Richard, died in the government service, the former as a soldier in the West Indies, the latter as lieutenant in the navy while on board the Thunderer, which was lost on the West Indian station in the great hurricane of October, 1779.